Fireside Reading.

TRAVEL AND ADVENTURE:

COMPRISING SOME OF THE

MOST STRIKING NARRATIVES ON RECORD.

EDITED

BY REV. D. W. CLARK, D. D.

Cincinnati:
PUBLISHED BY SWORMSTEDT & POE,
FOR THE METHODIST EPISCOPAL CHURCH, AT THE WESTERN BOOK
CONCERN, CORNER OF MAIN AND EIGHTH STREETS.

R. P. THOMPSON, PRINTER.
1856.

FIRESIDE READING.

General Preface.

SOME eight or ten years since, the editor of this series suggested to the then Book Agent at New York the propriety and usefulness of attempting to supply, in some measure, at least, a sort of general literature for fireside reading. His idea was that it should be "secular," as distinguished from strictly "religious," designed to interest and instruct all classes of general readers, but especially adapted to the young. The suggestion was received with favor, and the editor was urged to bear the subject in mind in his miscellaneous reading, and to prepare such a work. From that time forward, he has been making a note of such matter, as it chanced to come up before him, though not with any distinct notion of publishing. His attention having been lately directed again to the subject, and the publication seeming to be called for, he has revised and retrenched his material, and now presents the result in a series of five volumes, under the general title of "Fireside Reading." Each volume, so far as the subject-matter and mode of treatment are concerned, is entirely independent in itself; and may, therefore, be purchased by itself, or the whole series together, at the option of the purchaser.

The labor of preparing the work for publication has been considerable, much more than the editor imagined it would be or he would scarcely have undertaken it amidst the laborious duties to which he was already subject. But having undertaken it, he has spared neither labor nor pains to make it what it should be—a repository of interesting and useful knowledge.

The subjects of the volumes are "Travel and Adventure," "Historical Sketches," "Traits and Anecdotes of Animals," "Traits and Anecdotes of Birds, Fishes, and Reptiles," and "True Tales for the Spare Hour."

The sources whence the materials for the volumes have been drawn, are too numerous to be especially indicated in every instance. The more prominent of them, however, are, "Library of Entertaining Knowledge," London, 39 vols.; "Lardner's Cyclopedia," London, 131 vols.; "Naturalist's Library," Edinburgh, 31 vols.; "Chambers's Miscellany of Useful and Entertaining Tracts," Edinburgh, 10 vols.; "Chambers's Papers for the People," Edinburgh, 12 vols.; Mrs. Lee's Works on the Habits and Instincts of Animals, Birds, Fishes, etc., London, 2 vols.; "The Modern Traveler," London, 33 vols.; together with several of the juvenile publications of Nelson & Sons, of London and Edinburgh. This series will reveal to the American reader but little more than *glimpses* of the rich stores of interesting and useful knowledge contained in the above works.

We are not trenching upon the peculiar sphere of the Sunday school publishing department, whose mission is the production of a *religious* literature for the young of the Church and the nation. But outside of this sphere, we are endeavoring to supply a want largely felt by parents, who wish to cultivate in the minds of their children a taste for reading and literature.

We bespeak, then, a place by the fireside in every family, for these little volumes. They will, at the same time, be pleasant companions and useful instructors.

THE EDITOR.

TRAVEL AND ADVENTURE.

Preface.

IN this volume the editor has grouped some of the most striking narratives of excursions, exploits, adventures, shipwrecks, imprisonments, escapes, etc., on record. Some of these papers have already found a place, in one form or another, in our current literature; but they are worthy of a place more permanent, and will not merely repay a second reading, but will incite it. The editor has embodied here such narratives only as he, from the best authorities in the case, feels warranted in believing to be authentic in their essential features, if not in their minute details. Most of them are striking illustrations of the fact that "truth is stranger than fiction."

Contents.

PAGE.

1. Excursion to Oregon in 1834 9
2. Ascent of Mont Blanc 71
3. Narrative of Scenes at Norfolk Island 92
4. M. de la Tude in the Bastile 128
5. Shipwreck of the Medusa 141
6. Mutiny of the Bounty 208
7. Destruction of the Ship Ann Alexander by a Whale .. 261
8. Silvio Pellico in the Austrian Dungeons 268
9. Alexander Selkirk, the Original of Robinson Crusoe . 339
10. Escape of Count Lavalette 396

FIRESIDE READING.

I.

Excursion to Oregon

IN 1834.

THE transit from the eastern states to Oregon across the country, has now become quite a common affair. The mode of travel has, in a great measure, become systematized and regular. The peril of travel is greatly diminished, and thrilling adventures are less frequent. The route of travel is well defined, and soon we may expect to see a continuous line of railroad connecting the Atlantic with the Pacific.

As the past recedes from us, and is seen only by the dim light of history, the events of border life, and the adventures of pioneer travelers, on the broad prairies, in the vast wilderness, and in the mountain gorges, increase in the intensity of their interest. A great variety of incidents now lies within reach of the historian—much of it not only well calculated to awaken a transient interest, but also to illustrate the rapid spread of our population and the progress of civilization over the northern part of our vast continent.

Our purpose will be best accomplished by taking the incidents of a single expedition than by grouping anecdotes gleaned from the experience of border life. We shall, therefore, in this paper, trace the history of an excursion performed in 1834 by Mr. Townsend, an enthusiastic ornithologist, and his friend, Professor Nuttall, of Harvard University, an equally-zealous botanist.* Being desirous of increasing the existing stock of knowledge in the departments of science to which they were respectively attached, these gentlemen agreed to accompany a body of traders, commanded by a Captain Wyeth, to the Columbia river and adjacent parts. The traders belonged to an association called the Columbia River Fishing and Trading Company, and on this occasion they designed to fix a permanent branch-establishment in the west.

On the evening of the 24th of March, 1834, the two friends arrived in a steamboat at St. Louis. Here they furnished themselves with several pairs of leathern pantaloons, enormous

* "An Excursion to the Rocky Mountains, by J. K. Townsend."

overcoats, and white wool hats with round crowns, fitting tightly to the head, and almost hard enough to resist a musket-ball. Leaving their baggage to come on with the steamer, about three hundred miles up the Missouri, Mr. Townsend and his friend set off to amuse themselves by walking and hunting leisurely through that distance, which is composed chiefly of wide, flat prairies, with few and remotely-situated habitations of the frontier settlers.

One of the first indications of their approach to a wild country was the spectacle of a band of Indians of the Sac tribe, who were removing to new settlements. The men were fantastically painted, and the chief was distinguished by a profuse display of trinkets, and a huge necklace made of the claws of the grizzly bear. The decorations of one of the women amused the two travelers. She was an old squaw, to whom was presented a broken umbrella. The only use she made of this prize was to wrench the plated ends from the whalebones, string them on a piece of wire, take her knife from her belt, with which she deliberately cut a slit of an inch in length along the upper rim of her ear, and insert them in it. The sight was as shocking to the feelings as it was grotesque; for the cheeks of the vain being were covered with blood as she stood with fancied dignity in the midst of twenty others, who evidently envied her the possession of the worthless baubles.

While pushing forward on the borders of the wilderness, the travelers one day arrived at the house of a kind of gentleman settler, who, with his three daughters, vied in showing kindness to their visitors. "The girls," says Mr. Townsend, "were very superior to most that I had seen in Missouri, although somewhat touched with the awkward bashfulness and prudery which generally characterize the prairie maidens. They had lost their mother when young, and having no companions out of the domestic circle, and consequently no opportunity of aping the manners of the world, were perfect children of nature. Their father, however, had given them a good, plain education, and they had made some proficiency in needlework, as was evinced by numerous neatly-worked samplers hanging in wooden frames round the room." Some little curiosity and astonishment was excited in the minds of the unsophisticated girls when they were informed that their two guests were undertaking a long and difficult journey across the prairies—one of them for the purpose of shooting and stuffing birds, the other for the purpose of obtaining plants to preserve between leaves of paper; but at last they began to perceive that probably there was some hidden utility in these seemingly idle pursuits; and the last words of the eldest Miss P. to our ornithologist at parting were, "Do come again, and come in May or June, for then there are plenty of prairie-hens, and you can shoot as many as you want, and you must stay a long while with us, and we'll have nice times. Good-by; I'm so sorry you're going." Miss P., in promising an abundance of prairie-hens, evidently did not perceive in what respect an ornithologist differed from a sportsman; but her invitation was kindly meant; and Mr. Townsend promised that, if ever he visited Missouri again, he would go a good many miles out of his way to see her and her sisters. The next resting-place which our traveler describes was very different from Mr. P.'s comfortable and cheerful house. It was a *hotel*, for which a pig-sty would have been a more appropriate name. Every thing and every body were dirty, disobliging, and disagreeable; and, after staying one night, the travelers refusing the landlord's invitation to *liquorise* with him, departed without waiting for breakfast.

In the case of our travelers, however, one of the last impressions left upon them before fairly entering the wilderness, was of a more agreeable and suitable description. "In about an hour and a half," says Mr. Townsend, "we arrived at Fulton, a pretty little town, and saw the villagers in their holiday-clothes parading along to church. The bell at that moment sounded, and the peal gave rise to many reflections. It might be long ere I should hear the sound of the 'church-going bell' again. I was on my way to a far, far country, and I did not know that I should ever be permitted to revisit my own. I felt that I was leaving the scenes of my childhood—the spot which had witnessed all the happiness I ever knew, the home where all my affections were centered. I was entering a land of strangers, and would be compelled hereafter to mingle with those who might look upon me with indifference, or treat me with neglect."

The travelers, tired of their long journey on foot, waited at a small village on the Missouri till their companions and baggage should come up. The steamer arrived on the 9th of April, and the two pedestrians having gone on board, it was soon puffing up the river at the rate of seven miles an hour. In four days they reached the small town of Independence, then the outermost Anglo-American post, and disembarking, they began to prepare for their long and venturesome journey. Mr. Townsend here introduces a description of the company, about fifty in all.

There was among the men, to compose the

caravan, a great variety of dispositions. Some, who had not been accustomed to the kind of life they were to lead, looked forward to it with eager delight, and talked of stirring incidents and hairbreadth escapes. Others, who were more experienced, seemed to be as easy and unconcerned about it as a citizen would be in contemplating a drive of a few miles into the country. Some were evidently reared in the shade, and not accustomed to hardships; many were almost as rough as the grizzly bear, and not a little proud of their feats, of which they were fond of boasting; but the majority were very strong, able-bodied men. During the day, the captain kept all his men employed in arranging and packing a vast variety of goods for carriage. In addition to the necessary clothing for the company, arms, ammunition, etc., there were thousands of trinkets of various kinds, beads, paint, bells, rings, and such like trumpery, intended as presents for the Indians, as well as objects of trade with them. The bales were usually made to weigh about eighty pounds, of which a horse was to carry two. Captain Wyeth insured the good-will and obedience of the men by his affable but firm manner, and showed himself every way suitable for his very important mission. In the company there were also five missionaries, the principal of whom, Mr.

Jason Lee, was a "tall and powerful man, who looked as though he were well calculated to buffet difficulties in a wild country." Before setting out, they were joined also by Mr. Milton Sublette, a trader and trapper of several years' standing, who intended to travel a part of the way with them. Mr. Sublette brought with him about twenty trained hunters, "true as the steel of their tried blades," who had more than once gone over the very track which the caravan intended to pursue—a reinforcement which was very welcome to Captain Wyeth and his party.

On the 28th of April, at ten o'clock in the morning, all things being prepared, the caravan, consisting of seventy men and two hundred and fifty horses, began its march toward the west. All were in high spirits, and full of hope of adventure; uproarious bursts of merriment, and gay and lively songs, constantly echoed along the line of the cavalcade. The road lay over a fast rolling prairie, with occasional small spots of timber at the distance of several miles apart, and this was expected to be the complexion of the track for some weeks. For the first day and night the journey was agreeable, but on the second day a heavy rain fell, which made the ground wet and muddy, soaked the blanket bedding, and rendered camping at night any thing but pleasant.

For about a fortnight the caravan proceeded without any very remarkable incident occurring. The cook of the mess to which Mr. Townsend belonged decamped one night, having, no doubt, become tired of the expedition, and determined to go back to the settlements. The man himself was little missed; but he had taken a rifle, powder-horn, and shot-pouch along with him, and these articles were precious. In a few days after, three other men deserted, likewise carrying rifles with them. In the course of the fortnight the caravan passed through several villages of the Kaw Indians, with whom they traded a little, giving bacon and tobacco in exchange for hides. These Indians do not appear, on the whole, to have been very favorable specimens of the American aboriginals. The men had many of them fine countenances, but the women were very homely. The following is a description of one of their chiefs: "In the evening the principal Kansas chief paid us a visit in our tent. He is a young man about twenty-five years of age, straight as a poplar, and with a noble countenance and bearing, but he appeared to me to be marvelously deficient in most of the requisites which go to make the character of a *real* Indian chief, at least of such Indian chiefs as we read of in our popular books. I begin to suspect, in truth, that these lofty and dignified attributes are more apt to exist in the fertile brain of the novelist than in reality. Be this as it may, *our* chief is a very lively, laughing, and rather playful personage; perhaps he may put on his dignity, like a glove, when it suits his convenience."

On the 8th of May the party had a misfortune in the loss of Mr. Milton Sublette, who, owing to a fungus in one of his legs, was obliged to return to the settlements. On the afternoon of the next day, the party crossed a broad, Indian trail, bearing northerly, supposed to be about five days old, and to have been made by a war-party of Pawnees. Hoping to escape these formidable enemies of the white man, the party pushed on, but not without occasional mishaps; at one time the horses ran away, and had to be chased for a whole night, and even when the labor of the chase was over, three were irrecoverably lost; at another time half of the party were drenched crossing a wide creek full of black mud, which the men had to flounder through on horseback. The weather, too, was becoming intolerably warm. They had frequently been favored with fresh breezes, which made it very agreeable; but the moment these failed, they were almost suffocated with intense heat. Their rate of traveling was about twenty miles per day, which in this warm weather, and with heavily-burdened horses, was as much as could be accomplished with comfort to the travelers and their animals.

The general aspect, however, of the country through which we were traveling, was exceedingly beautiful. The little streams are fringed with a thick growth of pretty trees and bushes, and the buds are now swelling, and the leaves expanding, and the grass is starting, to "welcome back the merry spring." The birds, too, sing joyously among them—grosbeaks, thrushes, and buntings—a merry and musical band. I am particularly fond of sallying out early in the morning, and strolling around the camp. The light breeze just bends the tall tops of the grass on the boundless prairie, the birds are commencing their matin carolings, and all nature looks fresh and beautiful. The horses of the camp are lying comfortably on their sides, and seem, by the glances which they give me in passing, to know that their hour of toil is approaching, and the patient kine are ruminating in happy unconsciousness.

One morning the scouts came in with the intelligence that they had found a large trail of white men bearing north-west. Captain Wyeth concluded that this was another caravan belonging to a rival trading company, and that it had passed them noiselessly in the course of the night, in order to be beforehand with them in traffic with the Indian tribes through which they were passing. The party grumbled a little at the unfriendly conduct of the rival caravan in stealing a march upon them; but consoled themselves by making the reflection, that competition is the soul of commerce, and that, in the same circumstances, they would in all probability have acted in the same way. While discussing the affair at breakfast, three Indians, of a tribe called the Ottos, made their appearance. These visitors were suspected of being concerned in the loss of the three horses mentioned above; but as the crime could not be brought home to them by any kind of evidence, they were received in a friendly manner; and, as usual, the pipe of peace was smoked with them.

While these people were smoking the pipe of peace with us after breakfast, I observed that Richardson, our chief hunter—an experienced man in this country, of a tall and iron frame, and almost childlike simplicity of character, in fact, an exact counterpart of Hawkeye in his younger days—stood aloof, and refused to sit in the circle, in which it was always the custom of the *old hands* to join.

Feeling some curiosity to ascertain the cause of this unusual diffidence, I occasionally allowed my eyes to wander to the spot where our sturdy hunter stood looking moodily upon us, as the calumet passed from hand to hand around the circle, and I thought I perceived him now and then cast a furtive glance at one of the Indians who sat opposite to me, and sometimes his countenance would assume an expression almost demoniacal, as though the most fierce and deadly passions were raging in his bosom. I felt certain that hereby hung a tale, and I watched for a corresponding expression, or at least a look of consciousness, in the face of my opposite neighbor; but expression there was none. His large features were settled in a tranquillity which nothing could disturb, and as he puffed the smoke in huge volumes from his mouth, and the fragrant vapor wreathed and curled around his head, he seemed the embodied spirit of meekness and taciturnity.

The camp moved soon after, and I lost no time in overhauling Richardson, and asking an explanation of his singular conduct. "Why," said he, "that *Injen* that sat opposite to you is my bitterest enemy. I was once going down alone from the rendezvous with letters from St. Louis, and when I arrived on the lower part of the Platte river—just a short distance beyond us here—I fell in with about a dozen Ottos. They were known to be a friendly tribe, and I therefore felt no fear of them. I dismounted from my horse, and sat with them on the ground. It was in the depth of winter; the ground was covered with snow, and the river was frozen solid. While I was thinking of nothing but my dinner, which I was then about preparing, four or five of the cowards jumped on me, mastered my rifle, and held my arms fast, while they took from me my knife and tomahawk, my flint and steel, and all my ammunition. They then loosed me, and told me to be off. I begged them, for the love of God, to give me my rifle and a few loads of ammunition, or I should starve before I could reach the settlements. No; I should have nothing; and if I did not start off immediately, they would throw me under the ice of the river. And," continued the excited hunter, while he ground his teeth with bitter and uncontrollable rage, "that man that sat opposite to you was the chief of them. He recognized me, and knew very well why I would not smoke with him. I tell you, sir, if ever I meet that man in any other situation than that in which I saw him this morning, I'll shoot him with as little hesitation as I would shoot a deer. Several years have passed since the perpetration of this outrage, but it is still as fresh in my memory as ever; and I again declare, that if ever an opportunity offers, I will kill that man." "But,

Richardson, "did they take your horse also?" "To be sure they did, and my blankets, and every thing I had, except my clothes." "But how did you subsist till you reached the settlements? You had a long journey before you." "Why, set to trappin' prairie squirrels with little nooses made out of the hairs of my head." I should remark that his hair was so long that it fell in heavy masses on his shoulders. "But squirrels in winter, Richardson! I never heard of squirrels in winter." "Well, but there was plenty of them, though; little white ones, that lived among the snow." Such is a trait of human nature in these far western regions.

On the 18th of May the party reached the Platte river, one of the streams which pour their waters into the Missouri. Wolves and antelopes were abundant in the neighborhood of the river, and herons and long-billed curlews were stalking about in the shallows, searching for food. The prairie here is as level as a race-course, not the slightest undulation appearing throughout the whole extent of vision in a northerly and westerly direction; but to the eastward of the river, and about eight miles from it, was seen a range of high bluffs, or sand-banks, stretching away to the south-east till lost in the far distance. The travelers were not less struck with the solemn grandeur of the apparently-boundless prairie, than with the sight of its surface, which was in many places incrusted with an impure salt, seemingly a combination of the sulphate and muriate of soda: there were also seen a number of little pools, of only a few inches in depth, scattered over the plain, the water of which was so bitter and pungent, that it seemed to penetrate into the tongue, and almost to take the skin from the mouth. Next morning the party were alarmed with the appearance of two men on horseback, hovering on their path at a great distance. On looking at them with a telescope, they were discovered to be Indians, and on their approach it was found they belonged to a large band of the Grand Pawnee tribe, who were on a war excursion, and encamped at about thirty miles' distance. Having got rid of these suspicious visitors, the party moved rapidly forward in an altered direction, and did not slacken their pace till twelve o'clock at night. After a brief rest, they again went on, traveling steadily the whole day, and so got quite clear of the Grand Pawnees.

The travelers were now proceeding across one of the large central prairies of North America, and were, as they reckoned, within three days' journey of the buffalo region; that is, the region haunted by herds of buffalo. The uninitiated of the party, who for a good many days past had been listening to the spirit-stirring accounts given by the old hunters of their sport in the buffalo region, began to grow impatient for the first sight of this animal, the tenant of the prairies. At length, on the afternoon of the 20th, of May they came in sight of a large gang of the long-coveted buffalo. They were grazing on the opposite side of the Platte, as quietly as domestic cattle; but as they neared them, the foremost *winded* the travelers, and started back, and the whole herd followed in the wildest confusion, and were soon out of sight. There must have been many thousands of them. Toward evening a large band of elk came on a full gallop, and passed very near the party. The appearance of these animals produced a singular effect upon the horses, all of which became restive, and about half of the loose ones broke away, and scoured over the plain in full chase after the elk. Captain Wyeth and several of his men went immediately in pursuit of them, and returned late at night, bringing the greater number. Two had, however, been lost irrecoverably. By an observation, the latitude was found to be forty degrees, thirty-one minutes north, and the computed distance from the Missouri settlements about three hundred and sixty miles.

The day following, the party saw several small

herds of buffalo on their side of the river. Two of the hunters started out after a huge bull that had separated himself from his companions, and gave him chase on fleet horses. Away went the buffalo, and away went the men, as hard as they could dash; now the hunters gained upon him, and pressed him hard; again the enormous creature had the advantage, plunging with all his might, his terrific horns often plowing up the earth as he spurned it under him. Sometimes he would double, and rush so near the horses as almost to gore them with his horns, and in an instant would be off in a tangent, and throw his pursuers from the track. At length the poor animal came to bay, and made some unequivocal demonstrations of combat, raising and tossing his head furiously, and tearing up the ground with his feet. At this moment a shot was fired. The victim trembled like an aspen leaf, and fell on his knees, but recovering himself in an instant, started again as fast as before. Again the determined hunters dashed after him, but the poor bull was nearly exhausted: he proceeded but a short distance, and stopped again. The hunters approached, rode slowly by him, and shot two balls through his body with the most perfect coolness and precision. During the race—the whole of which occurred in full view of the party—the men seemed wild with the excitement which it occasioned; and when the animal fell, a shout rent the air which startled the antelopes by dozens from the bluffs, and sent the wolves howling from their lairs.

This is the most common mode of killing the buffalo, and is practiced very generally by the traveling hunters: many are also destroyed by approaching them on foot, when, if the bushes are sufficiently dense, or the grass high enough to afford concealment, the hunter, by keeping carefully to leeward of his game, may sometimes approach so near as almost to touch the animal. If on a plain without grass or bushes, it is necessary to be very circumspect; to approach so slowly as not to excite alarm, and when observed by the animal, to imitate dexterously the clumsy motions of a young bear, or assume the sneaking, prowling attitude of a wolf, in order to lull suspicion. The Indians resort to another stratagem, which is perhaps even more successful. The skin of a calf is properly dressed, with the head and legs left attached to it. The Indian envelops himself in this, and with his short bow and a brace of arrows ambles off into the very midst of a herd. When he has selected such animal as suits his fancy, he comes close along side of it, and, without noise, passes an arrow through its heart. One arrow is always sufficient, and it is generally delivered with such force, that at least half the shaft appears through the opposite side. The creature totters, and is about to fall, when the Indian glides around, and draws the arrow from the wound lest it should be broken. A single Indian is said to kill a great number of buffaloes in this way before any alarm is communicated to the herd.

Toward evening, on ascending a hill, the party were suddenly greeted by a sight which seemed to astonish even the oldest among them. The whole plain, as far as the eye could discern, was covered by one enormous mass of buffalo. The scene, at the very least computation, would certainly extend ten miles, and in the whole of this great space, including about eight miles in width from the bluffs to the river-bank, there was apparently no vista in the incalculable multitude. It was truly a sight that would have excited even the dullest mind to enthusiasm. The party rode up to within a few hundred yards of the edge of the herd before any alarm was communicated; then the bulls, which are always stationed around as sentinels, began pawing the ground and throwing the earth over their heads; in a few moments they started in a slow, clumsy canter, but as the hunters neared them they quickened their pace to an astonishingly-rapid gallop, and in a few minutes were entirely beyond the reach of their guns, but were still so near that their enormous horns, and long, shaggy beards were very distinctly seen. Shortly after encamping, the hunters brought in the choice parts of five that they had killed.

Of the animals belonging to those vast herds which the hunters kill, only a small portion is taken for food. Mr. Townsend and two of his associates having killed a bull buffalo, they proceeded to cut it up in the following approved manner: The animal was first raised from his side where he had lain, and supported upon his knees, with his hoofs turned under him; a longitudinal incision was then made from the nape or anterior base of the hump, and continued backward to the loins, and a large portion of the skin from each side removed; these pieces of skin were placed upon the ground, with the under surface uppermost, and the fleeces, or masses of meat taken from along the back, were laid upon them. These fleeces, from a large animal, will weigh perhaps a hundred pounds each, and comprise the whole of the hump on each side of the vertical processes—commonly called the hump-ribs—which are attached to the vertebræ. The fleeces are considered the choice parts of the buffalo, and here, where the game is so abundant, nothing else is taken, if we except the tongue and an occasional marrow-bone. This, it must be confessed, appears like a useless and unwarrantable waste of the goods of Providence; but when are men economical, unless compelled to do so by necessity? The food of the hunters consists for months of nothing but this kind of buffalo meat, roasted, and cold water—no bread of any kind. On this rude fare they enjoyed the best health, clear heads, and high spirits.

One night, shortly after their first encounter with the buffalo, Mr. Townsend, entering his tent about eleven o'clock, after having served as a supernumerary watch for several hours, was stooping to lay his gun in its usual place at the head of his couch, when he was startled by seeing a pair of eyes, wild and bright as those of a tiger, gleaming from a dark corner of the lodge, and evidently directed upon him. "My first impression," he says, "was that a wolf had been lurking around the camp, and had entered the tent in the prospect of finding meat. My gun was at my shoulder instinctively, my aim was directed between the eyes, and my finger pressed the trigger. At that moment a tall Indian sprang before me with a loud *wah!* seized the gun, and elevated the muzzle above my head; in another instant a second Indian was by my side, and I saw his keen knife glitter as it left the scabbard. I had not time for thought, and was struggling with all my might with the first savage for the recovery of my weapon, when Captain Wyeth and the other inmates of the tent were aroused, and the whole matter was explained, and set at rest in a moment. The Indians were chiefs of the tribe of Pawnee Loups, who had come with their young men to shoot buffalo; they had paid an evening visit to the captain, and, as an act of courtesy, had been invited to sleep in the tent. I had not known of their arrival, nor did I even suspect that Indians were in our neighborhood, so could not control the alarm which their sudden appearance occasioned me. These Indians," continues Mr. Townsend, "were the finest looking of any I had seen. Their persons were tall, straight, and finely formed; their noses slightly aquiline, and the whole countenance expressive of high and daring intrepidity. The face of the taller one was particularly admirable, and Gall or Spurzheim, at a single glance at his magnificent head, would have invested him with all the noblest qualities of the species. I know not what a physiognomist would have said of his eyes, but they were certainly the most wonderful I ever looked into; glittering and scintillating constantly, like the mirror-glasses in a lamp-frame, and rolling and dancing in their orbits as though possessed of abstract volition. As the party, leaving the Pawnees and the buffalo behind, began to approach the mountain district, the country altered its appearance greatly for the worse. They were now on a great sandy waste, forming a kind of upper table-land of North America—a region without a single green thing to vary and enliven the scene, and abounding in swarms of ferocious little black gnats, which assail the eyes, ears, nostrils, and mouth of the unhappy traveler. It is necessary, however, to pursue a route in this direction, in order to find accessible passes through the Rocky Mountains, which are impenetrable more to the north-west. Making the best of their way over the inhospitable desert, and fortunately escaping any roving bands of unfriendly Indians, the cavalcade struck through a range of stony mountains, called the Black Hills, and in a few days afterward came in sight of the Wind River Mountains, which form the loftiest land in the northern continent, and are at all times covered with snow of dazzling whiteness. From the great hight above the level of the sea which the party had attained, the climate was found to be cold, even although in summer; the plains were covered only by the scantiest herbage; and frequently there was great difficulty in obtaining a supply of water for the camp. The painfulness of the journey, therefore, was now extreme, both for man and beast.

Occasionally, however, a green spot did occur, where the jaded horses were allowed to halt, to roam about without their riders, and to tumble joyfully on the verdant sward; and as these *oases* always abounded in birds and plants, our two naturalists were loth to leave them. Nor was their journey through the inhospitable region of the hills devoid of incidents to vary the monotony of the way, and provoke hearty laughs from the whole party. One afternoon, one of the men had a somewhat perilous adventure with a grizzly bear. He saw the animal crouching his huge frame among some willows which skirted the river, and, approaching on horseback to within twenty yards, fired upon him. The bear was only slightly wounded by the shot, and, with a fierce growl of angry malignity, rushed from his cover, and gave chase. The horse happened to be a slow one, and for the distance of half a mile the race was severely contested—the bear frequently approaching so near the terrified animal as to snap at his heels, while the equally-terrified rider, who had lost his hat at the start, used whip and spur with the most frantic diligence, frequently looking behind, from an influence which he could not resist, at his rugged and determined foe, and shrieking in an agony of fear, "Shoot him! shoot him!" The man, who was a young hunter, happened to be about a mile behind the main body, either from the indolence of his horse or his own carelessness; but as he approached the party in his desperate flight, and his pitiable cries reached the ears of the men in front, about a dozen of them rode to his assistance, and soon succeeded in diverting the attention of his pertinacious foe. After the bear had received the contents of all the guns, he fell, and was soon dispatched. The man rode in among his fellows, pale and haggard from overwrought feelings, and was probably effectually cured of a propensity for meddling with grizzly bears.

On the 19th of June, the party arrived on the Green river, or Colorado of the west, which they forded, and encamped upon a spot which was to form a rendezvous for all the mountain companies who left the states in spring, and also the trappers who come from various parts with furs collected by them during the previous year.

Our traveler relates a misfortune which happened to him here. Having sallied forth with his gun, and wandered about for several hours shooting birds, he found, on returning to the camp, that his party had quitted the spot. In pursuing their track, he had to swim his horse across a deep and swift stream. After coming up with the party, he was congratulating himself on his escape from being drowned, when he found that he had lost his coat. "I had felt," he says, "uncomfortably warm when I mounted, and had removed the coat and attached it carelessly to the saddle; the rapidity of the current had disengaged it, and it was lost forever. The coat itself was not of much consequence after the hard service it had seen; but it contained the second volume of my journal, a pocket compass, and other articles of essential value to me. I would gladly have relinquished every thing the garment held, if I could but have recovered the book; and although I returned to the river, and searched assiduously till night, and offered large rewards to the men, it could not be found."

The loss of his journal, however, was not the only bad consequence of his river adventure. The ducking he had received brought on a fever, which confined him to his tent for several days. It was well for him that they had now arrived at the rendezvous where the caravans always make some stay before proceeding on the remainder of their journey. Still, according to Mr. Townsend's account of the encampment, it was scarcely the best hospital for an invalid.

As there were several other encampments stationed on the spot—among others that of the party of rival traders which had passed Captain Wyeth's party on the road—the encampment was constantly crowded with a heterogeneous assemblage of visitors. "The principal of these are Indians of the Nez Perce, Banneck, and Shoshone tribes, who come with the furs and peltries which they have been collecting at the risk of their lives during the past winter and spring, to trade for ammunition, trinkets, and fire-water. There is, in addition to these, a great variety of personages among us; most of them calling themselves white men, French-Canadians, half-breeds, etc., their color nearly as dark, and their manner wholly as wild, as the Indians with whom they constantly associate. These people, with their obstreperous mirth, their whooping, and howling, and quarreling, added to the mounted Indians, who are constantly dashing into and through our camp, yelling like fiends, the barking and baying of savage wolf-dogs, and the incessant cracking of rifles and carbines, render our camp a perfect bedlam. A more unpleasant situation for an invalid could scarcely be conceived. I am confined closely to the tent with illness, and am compelled all day to listen to the hiccoughing jargon of drunken traders, and the swearing and screaming of our own men, who are scarcely less savage than the rest, being heated by the detestable liquor which circulates freely among them. It is very much to be regretted that, at times like the present, there should be a positive necessity to allow the men as much rum as they can drink; but this course has been sanctioned and practiced by all the leaders of parties who have hitherto visited these regions, and reform can not be thought of now. The principal liquor in use is alcohol diluted with water. It is sold to the men at *three dollars* the pint! Tobacco, of very inferior quality, such as could be purchased in Philadelphia at about ten cents per pound, here fetches two dollars! and every thing else in proportion. There is no coin in circulation, and these articles are therefore paid for by the independent mountain-men in beaver-skins, buffalo-robes, etc.; and those who are hired to the companies, have them charged against their wages. I was somewhat amused by observing one of our newly-hired men enter the tent and order, with the air of a man who knew he would not be refused, twenty dollars' worth of rum and ten dollars' worth of sugar, to treat two of his companions who were about leaving the rendezvous."

At the rendezvous a number of men belonging to Captain Wyeth's party left it to join returning parties; but the diminution of numbers thus occasioned was made up for by the accession of about thirty Indians—Flatheads, Nez Perces, and others, with their wives, children, and dogs. These Indians joined the party in order to enjoy the benefit of its convoy through the tract of country infested by the Blackfeet Indians—a fierce and warlike race, the terror both of Indians and whites. Here also the party was joined by two English gentlemen roaming the prairies for amusement. At length, on the 2d of July, the party bade adieu to the rendezvous, packed up their movables, and journeyed along the bank of the river. The horses were much recruited by the long rest and good pasture, and, like their masters, were in excellent spirits for renewing the route across the wilderness.

They had now reached the confines of the Rocky Mountains, from which originate the upper tributaries of the Missouri on the one side, and those of the Columbia on the other. The plains in this high region are more rugged and barren than in the lower territories, and occasionally present evidences of volcanic action, being thickly covered with masses of lava and high basaltic crags. The principal vegetation on the hills consists of small cedars, while on the plains nothing flourishes but the shrubby wormwood or sage. Mr. Townsend had an opportunity, in these melancholy wastes, of becoming acquainted with a variety of animals, particularly birds. He met with flocks of a beautiful bird, called the cock of the plain—*tetrao urophasianus*—which was so very tame, or rather so little accustomed to evil treatment, as to mingle familiarly with the cavalcade, and to suffer itself to be knocked down by whips.

On the 10th of July, the party encamped near the Blackfeet river, a small, sluggish, stagnant stream, which empties itself into the Bear river. Here they had a rather stirring adventure with a grizzly bear. "As we approached our encampment," says Mr. Townsend, "near a small grove of willows on the margin of the river, a tremendous grizzly bear rushed out upon us. Our horses ran wildly in every direction, snorting with terror, and became nearly unmanageable. Several balls were instantly fired into him, but they only seemed to increase his fury. After spending a moment in rending each wound—their invariable practice—he selected the person who happened to be nearest, and darted after him; but before he proceeded far, he was sure to be stopped again by a ball from another quarter. In this way he was driven about among us for perhaps fifteen minutes, at times so near some of the horses, that he received several severe kicks from them. One of the pack-horses was fairly fastened upon by the fearful claws of the brute, and in the terrified animal's efforts to escape the dreaded gripe, the pack and saddle were broken to pieces and disengaged. One of our mules also lent him a kick in the head while pursuing it up an adjacent hill, which sent him rolling to the bottom. Here he was finally brought to a stand. The poor animal was so completely surrounded by enemies that he became bewildered; he raised himself upon his hind-feet, standing almost erect, his mouth partly open, and from his protruding tongue the blood fell fast in drops. While in this position he received about six more balls, each of which made him reel. At last, as in complete desperation, he dashed into the water and swam several yards with astonishing strength and agility, the guns cracking at him constantly. But he was not to proceed far; for just then Richardson, who had been absent, rode up, and fixing his deadly aim upon him, fired a ball into the back of his head, which killed him instantly. The strength of four men was required to drag the ferocious brute from the water, and upon examining his body, he was found completely riddled; there did not appear to be four inches of his shaggy person, from the hips upward, that had not received a ball; there must have been at least thirty shots fired at him, and probably few missed; yet such was his tenacity of life, that I have no doubt that he would have succeeded in crossing the river but for the last shot in the brain. He would probably weigh at the least six hundred pounds, and was about the hight of an ordinary steer. The spread of the foot laterally was ten inches, and the claws measured seven inches in length. This animal was remarkably lean: when in good condition he would doubtless much exceed in weight the estimate I have given. Richardson and two other hunters in company killed two in the course of the afternoon, and saw several others.

Although it was known that parties of Blackfeet were hanging in the route of the caravan, our travelers fortunately escaped being attacked by these dreaded Indians; and on the 14th, having reached the banks of the fine large Shoshone or Snake, also called Lewis river, they came to a halt for the purpose of erecting a fort, according to their instructions, and also of enjoying a rest of a fortnight or three weeks before renewing their journey. Nearly four months had now elapsed since they had commenced their expedition, and there were various evidences that they were approaching its close. The Snake river, on the banks of which they were encamped, pours its waters directly into the Columbia, and as they tried to form some idea of the great Oregon river from the size of its tributary, it became evident that they were approaching the western shore of the vast North American continent.

Food, however, was becoming scarce, the stock of dried buffalo meat being nearly exhausted; and therefore, while the majority of the party should remain to build a fort on the banks of the Snake river, it was resolved that a hunting party of twelve persons should start on the back track to shoot buffalo, and return to the fort in eight or nine days with the fruits of their diligence. To this party Mr. Townsend attached himself. The hunters were successful in procuring buffalo, on which they now entirely fed, besides bringing a quantity in a dried state to the camp. Exposed constantly to the pure air, and having abundant exercise, the appetites of the party were most ravenous. Rising in the morning with the sun, they kindled a fire and roasted their breakfast, which consisted of from one to two pounds of meat. At ten o'clock they lunched on meat; at two they dined on meat; at five they supped on meat; at eight they had a second supper of meat; and during the night, when they awoke, they took a snatch at any meat within reach. Their food was thus entirely meat, without bread or any other article except water, which was their sole beverage. On this plain and substantial fare they enjoyed robust health.

Having heard that a ball in the middle of the forehead was never known to kill a buffalo, Mr. Townsend determined to try the experiment. Accordingly one evening, seeing a large bull close at hand, he sallied forth with the utmost caution in the direction of his victim. "The unwieldy brute," he says, "was quietly and unsuspiciously cropping the herbage, and I had arrived within ten feet of him, when a sudden flashing of the eye, and an impatient motion, told me that I was observed. He raised his enormous head and looked around him, and so truly terrible and grand did he appear, that I must confess I felt awed, almost frightened, at the task I had undertaken. But I had gone too far to retreat; so, raising my gun, I took deliberate aim at the bushy center of the forehead, and fired. The monster shook his head, pawed up the earth with his hoofs, and making a sudden spring, accompanied by a terrific roar, turned to make his escape. At that instant the ball from the second barrel penetrated his vitals, and he measured his huge length upon the ground. In a few seconds he was dead. Upon examining the head, and cutting away the enormous mass of matted hair and skin which enveloped the skull, my large bullet, of twenty to the pound, was found completely flattened against the bone, having carried with it, through the interposing integument, a considerable portion of the coarse hair, but without producing the smallest fracture. I was satisfied; and taking the tongue—the hunter's perquisite—I returned to my companions."

Some of the party had seen Blackfeet Indians skulking about, and the effect was to put the hunters more on their guard. They were now certain that their worst enemies, the Blackfeet, were around them, and that they only waited for a favorable opportunity of making an attack. It was felt that these savage wanderers were not there for nothing, and that the greatest care was necessary to prevent a surprise.

The Blackfeet is a sworn and determined foe to all white men, and he has often been heard to declare that he would rather hang the scalp of a pale-face to his girdle, than kill a buffalo to prevent his starving. The hostility of this dreaded tribe is, and has for years been, proverbial. They are, perhaps, the only Indians who do not fear the power, and who refuse to acknowledge the superiority of the white man; and though so often beaten in conflicts with them, even by their own mode of warfare, and generally with numbers vastly inferior, their indomitable courage and perseverance still urges them on to renewed attempts; and if a single scalp is taken, it is considered equal to a great victory, and is hailed as a presage of future and more extensive triumphs.

It must be acknowledged, however, that this determined hostility does not originate solely in savage malignity, or an abstract thirst for the blood of white men; it is fomented and kept alive from year to year by incessant provocatives on the part of white hunters, trappers, and traders, who are at best but intruders on the rightful domain of the red man of the wilderness. "Many a night," adds our traveler, "have I sat at the camp-fire and listened to the recital of bloody and ferocious scenes, in which the narrators were the actors, and the poor Indians the victims, and I have felt my blood tingle with shame, and boil with indignation, to hear the diabolical acts applauded by those for whose amusement they were related. Many a precious villain and merciless marauder was made by these midnight tales of rapine, murder, and robbery; many a stripling, in whose tender mind the seeds of virtue and honesty had never germinated, burned for an opportunity of loading his pack-horse with the beaver skins of some solitary Blackfeet trapper, who was to be murdered and despoiled of the property he had acquired by weeks and perhaps months of toil and danger."

The proximity of the Blackfeet caused the old hunters to recollect their former adventures in the same neighborhood; and one evening, as the party sat around the camp fire, wrapped in their warm blankets, these old hunters became talkative, and related their individual adventures for the general amusement. The best story was told by Richardson, of a meeting he once had with three Blackfeet Indians. He had been out alone hunting buffalo, and toward the end of the day was returning to the camp with his meat, when he heard the clattering of hoofs in the rear, and upon looking back, observed three Indians in hot pursuit of him. To lighten his horse, he immediately threw off the meat he carried, and then urged his animal to his utmost speed, in an attempt to distance his pursuers. He soon discovered, however, that the enemy was rapidly gaining upon him, and that in a few minutes more he would be completely at their mercy, when he hit upon an expedient as singular as it was bold and courageous. Drawing his long scalping-knife from the sheath at his side, he plunged the keen weapon through his horse's neck, and severed the spine. The animal dropped instantly dead, and the determined hunter, throwing himself behind the fallen carcass, waited calmly the approach of his sanguinary pursuers. In a few moments one Indian was within range of the fatal rifle, and at its report his horse galloped riderless over the plain. The remaining two then thought to take him at advantage by approaching simultaneously on both sides of his rampart; but one of them happening to venture too near, in order to be sure of his aim, was shot to the heart by the long pistol of the white man at the very instant that the ball from the Indian's gun whistled harmlessly by. The third savage, being wearied of the dangerous game, applied the whip vigorously to the flanks of his horse, and was soon out of sight, while Richardson set about collecting the trophies of his singular victory. He caught the two Indians' horses, mounted one, and loaded the other with the meat which he had discarded, and returned to his camp with two spare rifles, and a good stock of ammunition.

Having now procured a sufficient quantity of buffalo meat, the hunting party set out on its return to the fort, and arrived there on the 25th, after nine days' absence. Their return had been anxiously expected, and "I could well perceive," says Mr. Townsend, "many a longing and eager gaze cast upon the well-filled bales of buffalo meat as our mules swung their little bodies through the camp. My companion, Mr. Nuttall, had become so exceedingly thin, that I could scarcely have known him; and upon my expressing surprise at the great change in his appearance, he heaved a sigh of inanity, and remarked that I 'would have been as thin as he, if I had lived on old bear for two weeks, and short allowance at that.' I found, in truth, that the whole camp had been subsisting during our absence on little else than two or three grizzly bears which had been killed in the neighborhood; and with a complacent glance at my own rotund and cow-fed person, I wished my poor friends better luck for the future."

Another traveling company had encamped on the banks of the Snake river, during the absence of the hunting party. It consisted of thirty men, thirteen of them Indians, Nez Perces, Chinooks, and Kayouse, the remainder French-Canadians and half-breeds. Mr. M'Kay, the leader of this company, was the son of Mr. Alexander M'Kay, one of the early adventurers across the prairies, the tragical story of whose massacre by the Indians on the north-west coast is told by Washington Irving in his "Astoria." Mr. Townsend gives an interesting description of this company and its captain. "On the evening of the 26th," he says, "Captain Wyeth,

Mr. Nuttall, and myself, supped with Mr. M'-Kay in his lodge. I am much pleased with this gentleman; he unites the free, frank, and open manners of the mountain man, with the grace and affability of the Frenchman. But above all, I admire the order, decorum, and strict subordination which exists among his men; so different from what I have been accustomed to see in parties composed of Americans. Mr. M'Kay assures me that he had considerable difficulty in bringing his men to the state in which they now are. The free and fearless Indian was particularly difficult to subdue; but steady, determined perseverance and bold measures, aided by a rigid self-example, made them as clay in his hand, and has finally reduced them to their present admirable condition. If they misbehave, a commensurate punishment is sure to follow. In extreme cases, flagellation is resorted to, but it is inflicted only by the hand of the captain; were any other appointed to perform this office on an Indian, the indignity would be deemed so great that nothing less than the blood of the individual could appease the wounded feelings of the savage. After supper was concluded, we sat down on a buffalo robe at the entrance of the lodge to see the Indians at their devotions. The whole thirteen were soon collected at the call of one whom they had chosen for their chief, and seated with sober, sedate countenances around a large fire. After remaining in perfect silence for perhaps fifteen minutes, the chief commenced a harangue in a solemn and impressive tone, reminding them of the object for which they were thus assembled—that of worshiping the 'Great Spirit who made the light and the darkness, the fire and the water,' and assured them that if they offered up their prayers to him with but 'one tongue,' they would certainly be accepted. He then rose from his squatting position to his knees, and his example was followed by all the others. In this situation he commenced a prayer, consisting of short sentences, uttered rapidly, but with great apparent fervor, his hands clasped upon his breast, and his eyes cast upward with a beseeching look toward heaven. At the conclusion of each sentence, a choral response of a few words was made, accompanied frequently by low moaning. The prayer lasted about twenty minutes.

"After its conclusion, the chief, still maintaining the same position of his body and hands, but with his head bent to his breast, commenced a kind of psalm or sacred song, in which the company presently joined. The song was a simple expression of a few sounds, no intelligible words being uttered. It resembled the words

Ho-ha-ho-ha-ho-ha-ha-a, commencing in a low tone, and gradually swelling to a full, round, and beautifully-modulated chorus. During the song the clasped hands of the worshipers were moved rapidly across the breast, and their bodies swung with great energy to the time of the music. The chief ended the song by a kind of swelling groan, which was echoed in chorus. It was then taken up by another, and the same routine was gone through. The whole ceremony occupied perhaps an hour and a half; a short silence then succeeded, after which each Indian rose from the ground, and disappeared in the darkness with a step noiseless as that of a specter. I think I never was more gratified by any exhibition in my life. The humble, subdued, and beseeching looks of the poor, untutored beings who were calling upon their heavenly Father to forgive their sins, and continue his mercies to them, and the evident and heartfelt sincerity which characterized the whole scene, was truly affecting and very impressive.

"The next day being the Sabbath, our good missionary, Mr. Jason Lee, was requested to hold a meeting, with which he obligingly complied. A convenient, shady spot was selected in the forest adjacent, and the greater part of our men, as well as the whole of Mr. M'Kay's company, including the Indians, attended. The usual forms of the Methodist service, to which Mr. Lee is attached, were gone through, and were followed by a brief but excellent and appropriate exhortation by that gentleman. The people were remarkably quiet and attentive, and the Indians sat upon the ground like statues. Although not one of them could understand a word that was said, they nevertheless maintained the most strict and decorous silence, kneeling when the preacher kneeled, and rising when he rose, evidently with a view of paying him and us a suitable respect, however much their own notions as to the proper and most acceptable forms of worship might have been opposed to ours. A meeting for worship in the Rocky Mountains is almost as unusual as the appearance of a herd of buffalo in the settlements. A sermon was perhaps never preached here before, but for myself I really enjoyed the whole scene: it possessed the charm of novelty, to say nothing of the salutary effect which I sincerely hope it may produce."

After having completed the fort, and raised the American flag upon it, the party on the 6th of August recommenced their journey westward, leaving some men in charge of the building. The company consisted now but of thirty men, several Indian women, and one hundred and sixteen horses. Having left most of the fresh buffalo meat brought in by the hunting party in the fort for the subsistence of the small garrison, they had to be contented with the old, dry meat they had carried for many weeks in their hampers, varied with the flesh of a grizzly bear, or any such animal which good fortune might send across their path. Nor was this the worst, for on the very day after leaving the fort, having traveled from sunrise over an arid plain, covered with jagged masses of lava and twisted wormwood-bushes, and where not a drop of water was to be seen, they began to suffer dreadfully from thirst. Every man kept a bullet or smooth stone in his mouth, mumbling it to provoke the saliva. At last, one of the men, a mulatto, "cast himself resolutely from his horse to the ground, and declared that he would lie there till he died; 'there was no water in this horrid country, and he might as well die here as go farther.' Some of us tried to infuse a little courage into him, but it proved of no avail, and each was too much occupied with his own particular grief to use his tongue much in persuasion; so we left him to his fate.

"Soon after nightfall, some signs of water were seen in a small valley to our left, and upon ascending it, the foremost of the party found a delightful little cold spring; but they soon exhausted it, and then commenced with axes and knives, to dig it out and enlarge it. By the time that Mr. Nuttall and myself arrived, they had excavated a large space, which was filled to overflowing with muddy water. We did not wait for it to settle, however, but throwing ourselves upon the ground, drank till we were ready to burst. The tales which I had read of suffering travelers in the Arabian deserts then recurred with some force to my recollection, and I thought I could, though in a very small measure, appreciate their sufferings by deprivation, and their unmingled delight and satisfaction in the opportunity of assuaging them.

"Poor Jim, the mulatto man, was found by one of the people who went back in search of him, lying where he had first fallen, and, either in a real or pretended swoon, still obstinate about dying, and scarcely heeding the assurances of the other that water was within a mile of him. He was, however, at length dragged and carried into camp, and soused head foremost into the mud-puddle, where he drank till his eyes seemed ready to burst from his head, and he was lifted out and laid dripping and flaccid upon the ground."

The ground over which the party was traveling was becoming more and more rugged and rocky. They entered a defile between the mountains, about five hundred yards wide, covered like the surrounding country with pines; and as they proceeded, the timber grew so closely, added to a thick undergrowth of bushes, that it appeared almost impossible to proceed with their horses. The farther they advanced the more their difficulties seemed to increase; obstacles of various kinds impeded their progress—fallen trees, their branches tangled and matted together; large rocks and deep ravines; holes in the ground, into which their animals would be precipitated without the possibility of avoiding them; and a hundred other difficulties.

After traveling for six miles through this defile, two of the party, Captain Wyeth and the experienced hunter Richardson, set out to explore the foreground, and look for a pass through the mountains. They returned next morning with the mortifying intelligence that no pass could be found. They had climbed to the very summit of the highest peaks above the snow and the reach of vegetation, and the only prospect they had was a confused mass of huge angular rocks, over which a wild goat could scarcely make his way. The Captain also had a narrow escape from being dashed to pieces during the excursion. He was walking on a ridge which sloped from the top at an angle of about forty degrees, and terminated at its lower part in a perpendicular precipice of a thousand or twelve hundred feet. He was moving along in the snow cautiously, near the lower edge, in order to attain a more level spot beyond, when his feet slipped and he fell. Before he could attempt to fix himself firmly, he slid down the declivity till within a few feet of the frightful precipice. At the instant of his fall, he had the presence of mind to plant the rifle which he held in one hand, and his knife which he drew from the scabbard with the other, into the snow, and as he almost tottered on the verge, he succeeded in checking himself, and holding his body perfectly still. He then gradually moved, first the rifle and then the knife, backward up the slanting hill behind him, and fixing them firmly, drew up his body parallel to them. In this way he moved slowly and surely till he gained his former position, when, without further difficulty, he succeeded in reaching the more level land.

Disappointed in finding a pass through the mountains at this point, the party altered the bearing of their route, and at last they came upon the remains of a recent encampment of Indians. "Following the trail of these Indians, we entered a valley similar to that which we had just explored, and terminating in a path over the mountains. The commencement of the Alpine path was, however, far better than we had expected, and we entertained the hope that the passage could be made without difficulty or much toil; but the farther we progressed, the more laborious the traveling became. Sometimes we mounted steep banks of intermingled flinty rock and friable slate, where our horses could scarcely obtain a footing, frequently sliding down several feet on the loose, broken stones. Again we passed along the extreme verge of tremendous precipices at a giddy hight, where at almost every step the stones and earth would roll from under our horses' feet, and we could hear them strike with a dull, leaden sound on the craggy rocks below. The whole journey to-day, from the time we arrived at the hights till we had crossed the mountain, has been a most fearful one. For myself, I might have diminished the danger very considerably by adopting the plan pursued by the rest of the company, that of walking and leading my horse over the most dangerous places; but I have been suffering for several days with a lame foot, and am wholly incapable of such exertion. I soon discovered that an attempt to guide my horse over the most rugged and steepest ranges was worse than useless; so I dropped the rein upon the animal's neck, and allowed him to take his own course, closing my eyes, and keeping as quiet as possible in the saddle. But I could not forbear starting occasionally when the feet of my horse would slip on a stone, and one side of him would slide rapidly toward the edge of the precipice; but I always recovered myself by a desperate effort, and it was fortunate for me that I did so."

The party continued its march for several days through this rugged and inhospitable region, coming into occasional contact with parties of the Snake Indians, and subsisting on the kamas, a kind of root resembling the potato, which is found in the prairie; on cherries, berries, and small fruit, which they found growing on bushes; and an occasional chance prize of animal food. "At about daylight on the morning of the 20th, having charge of the last guard of the night, I observed a beautiful, sleek little colt, of about four months old, trot into the camp, whinnying with great apparent pleasure, and dancing and curveting gayly among our sober and sedate band. I had no doubt that he had strayed from Indians, who were probably in the neighborhood; but as here every animal that comes near us is fair game, and as we were hungry, not having eaten any thing of consequence since yesterday morning, I thought the little stranger would make a good breakfast for us. Concluding, however, that it would be best for us to act advisedly in the matter, I put my head into Captain Wyeth's tent, and telling him the news, made the proposition which had occurred to me. The Captain's reply was encouraging enough—'Down with him, if you please, Mr. Townsend, and let us have him for breakfast.' Accordingly, in five minutes afterward, a bullet sealed the fate of the unfortunate visitor, and my men were set to work, making fires and rummaging out the long-neglected stew-pans, while I engaged myself at once and with very considerable vigor in flaying the little animal, and cutting up his body in readiness for the pots.

"When the camp was aroused, about an hour after, the savory steam of the cookery was rising and saluting the nostrils of our hungry people with its fragrance, who, rubbing their hands with delight, sat themselves down upon the ground, waiting with what patience they might for the unexpected repast which was preparing for them. It was to me almost equal to a good breakfast to witness the pleasure and satisfaction which I had been the means of diffusing through the camp. The repast was ready at length, and we did full justice to it; every man ate till he was filled, and all pronounced it one of the most delicious meals they had ever assisted in demolishing. When our breakfast was concluded, but little of the colt remained; that little was, however, carefully packed up and deposited on one of the horses, to furnish at least a portion of another meal.

"In the afternoon of the same day, after a long march, we procured three small salmon from some Indians who were fishing on the Mallade river; and these, cooked along with a grouse, a beaver, and the remains of the pony, made a very savory mess. While we were eating, we were visited by a Snake chief, a large and powerful man, of a peculiarly-dignified aspect and manner. He was naked, with the exception of a small blanket, which covered his shoulders, and descended to the middle of the back, being fastened around the neck with a silver skewer. As it was pudding time with us, our visitor was of course invited to sit down and eat; and he, nothing loth, deposited himself at once upon the ground, and made a remarkably-vigorous assault upon the mixed contents of the dish. He had not eaten long, however, before we perceived a sudden and inexplicable change in his countenance, which was instantly followed by a violent ejectment of a huge mouthful of our luxurious fare. The man rose slowly and with great dignity to his feet, and pronouncing the single word *shekum*—horse—in a tone of mingled anger and disgust, stalked rapidly out of the camp, not even wishing us a good evening. It struck me as a singular instance of accuracy and discrimination in the organs of taste. We had been eating of the multifarious compound without being able to recognize by the taste a single ingredient which it contained; a stranger came among us, who did not know, when he commenced eating, that the dish was formed of more than one item, and yet in less than five minutes he discovered one of the very least of its component parts."

The neighborhood of these Snake Indians was not very agreeable, for many reasons. Mr. Townsend paid a visit to their camp, and the description he gives of it does not lead one to conceive a high idea of savage life. "Early in the morning," he says, "I strolled into the Snake camp. It consists of about thirty lodges or wigwams, formed generally of branches of trees tied together in conic summit, and covered with buffalo, deer, or elk skins. Men and little children were lolling about the ground all around the wigwams, together with a heterogeneous assemblage of dogs, cats, some tamed prairie wolves, and other *varmints*. The dogs growled and snapped when I approached, the wolves cowered and looked cross, and the cats ran away and hid themselves in dark corners. They had not been accustomed to the face of a white man, and all the quadrupeds seemed to regard me as some monstrous production, more to be feared than loved or courted. This dislike, however, did not appear to extend to the bipeds, for many of every age and sex gathered around me, and seemed to be examining me critically in all directions. The men looked complacently at me, the women, the dear creatures, smiled upon me, and the little naked, pot-bellied children crawled around my feet, examining the fashion of my hard shoes, and playing with the long fringes of my leathern inexpressibles. But I scarcely know how to commence a description of the camp, or to frame a sentence which will give an adequate idea of the extreme filth and horrific nastiness of the whole vicinity.

"Immediately as I entered the village, my olfactories were assailed by the most vile and mephitic odors, which I found to proceed chiefly from great piles of salmon entrails and garbage, which were lying festering and rotting in the sun around the very doors of the habitations. Fish, recent and half-dried, were scattered all over the ground under the feet of the dogs, wolves, and children; and others which had been split, were hanging on rude platforms, erected within the precincts of the camp. Some of the women were making their breakfast of the great red salmon eggs, as large as peas, and using a wooden spoon to convey them to their mouths. Occasionally, also, by way of varying the repast, they would take a huge pinch of a drying fish, which was lying on the ground near them. Many of the children were similarly employed, and the little imps would also have hard contests with the dogs for a favorite morsel, the former roaring and blubbering, the latter yelping and snarling, and both rolling over and over together upon the savory soil. The whole economy of the lodges, and the inside and outside appearance, was of a piece with every thing else about them—filthy beyond description; the very skins which covered the wigwams were black and stiff with rancid salmon fat, and the dresses—if dresses they may be called—of the women were of the same color and consistence, from the same cause. These dresses are little square pieces of deer-skin, fastened with a thong around the loins, and reaching about half way to the knees; the rest of the person is entirely naked. Some of the women had little children clinging like bullfrogs to their backs, without being fastened, and in that situation extracting their lactiferous sustenance from the breast, which was thrown over the shoulders. It is almost needless to say that I did not remain long in the Snake camp; for, although I had been a considerable time estranged from the abodes of luxury, and had become somewhat accustomed to at least a partial assimilation to a state of nature, yet I was not prepared for what I saw here. I never had fancied any thing so utterly abominable, and was glad to escape to a purer and more wholesome atmosphere."

The party again toiled on, every day's march bringing them sensibly nearer the end of their journey.

"About noon of the 3d of September we struck the Walla Walla river, a pretty stream of fifty or sixty yards in width, fringed with tall willows, and containing a number of salmon, which we can see frequently leaping from the water. The pasture here being good, we allowed our horses an hour's rest to feed, and then traveled over the plain till near dark, when, on ascending a sandy hill, the noble Columbia burst upon our view. I could scarcely repress a loud exclamation of delight and pleasure as I gazed upon the magnificent river flowing silently and majestically on, and reflected that I had actually crossed the vast American continent, and now stood upon a stream that poured its waters directly into the Pacific. This then was the great Oregon, the first appearance of which gave Lewis and Clark so many emotions of joy and pleasure, and on this stream our indefatigable countrymen wintered after the toils and privations of a long and protracted journey through the wilderness. My reverie was suddenly interrupted by one of the men exclaiming from his position in advance, 'There is the fort.' We had in truth approached very near without being conscious of it. There stood the fort on the bank of the river; horses and horned cattle were roaming about the vicinity, and on the borders of the little Walla Walla we recognized the white tent of our long-lost missionaries. These we soon joined, and were met and received by them like brethren. Mr. Nuttall and myself were invited to sup with them upon a dish of stewed hares which they had just prepared, and it is almost needless to say that we did full justice to the good men's cookery. They told us that they had traveled comfortably from Fort Hall without any unusual fatigue, and like ourselves had no particularly-stirring adventures. Their route, although somewhat longer, was a much less toilsome and difficult one, and they suffered but little for want of food, being well provided with dried buffalo meat, which had been prepared near Fort Hall."

At Walla Walla the party broke up into sections, some intending to reach Fort Vancouver in one way, some in another. The missionaries had engaged a large barge to convey them from Walla Walla directly to Vancouver, down the Columbia river, and Mr. Townsend and Mr.

Nuttall were anxious to go along with them; but as the barge could not contain so many, they were obliged to travel on horseback to a point about eighty miles farther down the river, where Captain Wyeth engaged to wait for them and procure canoes to convey them to Vancouver. In the course of their land journey down the banks of the river, they passed a village of the Walla Walla Indians, a tribe so remarkable for their honesty and moral deportment, that their conduct and habits amidst great privations shine in comparison with those of Christian communities. The river in this part is described as about three-quarters of a mile wide—a clear, deep, and rapid stream.

Having reached the appointed spot on the 10th of September, the travelers found the Captain waiting with three canoes, each provided with an Indian helmsman, and on the 11th they embarked and commenced their voyage down stream. They had hardly set sail, however, when the wind "rose to a heavy gale, and the waves ran to a prodigious hight. At one moment our frail bark danced upon the crest of a wave, and at the next fell with a surge into the trough of the sea; and as we looked at the swell before us, it seemed that in an instant we must inevitably be ingulfed. At such times the canoe ahead of us was entirely hidden from view, but she was observed to rise again like the seagull, and hurry on into the same danger. The Indian in my canoe soon became completely frightened: he frequently hid his face with his hands, and sang in a low, melancholy voice a prayer which we had often heard from his people while at their evening devotions. As our dangers were every moment increasing, the man became at length absolutely childish, and with all our persuasion and threats we could not induce him to lay his paddle into the water. We were all soon compelled to put in shore, which we did without sustaining any damage; the boats were hauled up high and dry, and we concluded to remain in our quarters till next day, or till there was a cessation of the wind. In about an hour it lulled a little, and Captain Wyeth ordered the boats to be again launched, in the hope of being able to weather a point about five miles below before the gale again commenced, where we could lie by till it should be safe to proceed. The calm proved, as some of us had suspected, a treacherous one; in a very few minutes after we got under way, we were contending with the same difficulties as before, and again our cowardly helmsman laid by his paddle and began mumbling his prayer. It was too irritating to be borne. Our canoe had swung round broadside to the surge, and was shipping gallons on gallons of water at every dash.

"At this time it was absolutely necessary that every man on board should exert himself to the utmost to head up the canoe and make the shore as soon as possible. Our Indian, however, still sat with his eyes covered, the most abject and contemptible-looking thing I ever saw. We took him by the shoulders, and threatened to throw him overboard if he did not immediately lend his assistance; we might as well have spoken to a stone. He was finally aroused, however, by our presenting a loaded gun at his breast. He dashed the muzzle away, seized his paddle again, and worked with a kind of desperate and wild energy till he sank back in the canoe completely exhausted. In the mean time the boat had become half-full of water, shipping a part of every surf that struck her; and as we gained the shallows, every man sprang overboard, breast deep, and began hauling the canoe to shore. This was even a more difficult task than that of propelling her with oars; the water still broke over her, and the bottom was a deep kind of quicksand, in which we sank almost to the knees at every step, the surf at the same time dashing against us so violently as to throw us repeatedly on our faces. We at length reached the shore, and hauled the canoe up out of reach of the breakers. She was then unloaded as soon as possible, and turned bottom upward. The goods had suffered considerably by the wetting; they were all unbaled, and dried by a large fire which we built on the shore."

For two or three days they were tossed about on the river, now attempting to make way, now forced to land again, and always drenched to the skin. The missionaries and their party, too, who had set out in the barge from Walla Walla, were in no better plight. On the 14th the three canoes were again loaded, and again made the attempt to proceed; but in a short while one of them was stove, and another greatly damaged, so that they had to be unloaded and drawn out of the water. An effort was now made to procure one or two canoes with a pilot from an Indian village five miles below. This proved a hazardous and fatiguing journey; but was rewarded by getting one canoe and several Indians to assist in the navigation. With this reinforcement, and with the boats mended, the party again attempted the descent of the river. The voyage this time was more fortunate, and next day they all arrived at the fort, which was the end of their journey across the wilderness. The time occupied in this dangerous expedition had been six months and three days. Unharmed by fatigue or accident, with a constitution strengthened by healthful exercise, and a mind buoyant with the novelty of the scenes they had passed through, the travelers felt sincerely thankful to that kind and overruling Providence which had watched over and protected them.

II.

Ascent of Mont Blanc.

MONT BLANC, as is generally known, is the highest peak of the Alps, and the loftiest ground in Europe, being fifteen thousand, six hundred and sixty-six feet above the level of the sea. It is situated in the duchy of Savoy, now a part of the kingdom of Sardinia, in a range of mountains between Sardinia and Turin, and rises immediately above the narrow valley of Chamounix, from which place alone is the ascent to the summit ever made. Though Chimborazo is between six and seven thousand feet higher than Mont Blanc, it only rises eleven thousand, six hundred feet above the neighboring valley of Quito; in this respect Mont Blanc may be considered as a more remarkable mountain, as it rises twelve thousand, three hundred feet above the valley of Chamounix, the whole of which vast hight can be scanned at once from the opposite eminences. For seven thousand feet below the top Mont Blanc is perpetually covered with ice and snow. The distance from the bottom to the top, by the shortest route which can be pursued, is considered by the guides as eighteen leagues, or fifty-four miles.

Speaking with precision, Mont Blanc is only the most eminent of a range of peaks springing from a vast extent of eminent ground on the south side of the valley of Chamounix. When the traveler enters the valley on the opposite side at an eminence called the Col de Balme, this range, coming at once into view, oppresses his imagination with a vastness unexpected even in that land of Alpine grandeur. While the vale below smiles with the most luxuriant vegetation, the sides of the hills are clothed, for a considerable way up, with dark and dense forests, and higher still, with the accumulated hoariness of centuries.

To attain the summit of a mountain so lofty as Mont Blanc, was long an object of ambition, both to the native peasantry and to men of science, before any one was so fortunate as to effect it. It was first tried in 1762, again in 1775, and on four occasions down to 1786, without success. At length, in the year last mentioned—8th August—this difficult enterprise was accomplished by Dr. Paccard, a native of Chamounix, in company with a guide named Balma. The mountain was ascended in the succeeding year by M. de Saussure, who gave to the learned world a very minute account of all the phenomena which he observed in the course of the expedition. Another attempt in the same year, one in 1791, a third in 1802, were the only successful attempts down to 1812, when a Hamburg gentleman, named Rodatz, gained the summit. From that time till 1827, seven successful attempts were made, besides one of the contrary description in 1820, which was cut short by the descent of an avalanche, and the loss of three of the guides. In August, 1827, the ascent was performed by Mr. John Auldjo, of Trinity College, Cambridge, who published an account of it, illustrated by maps and drawings. In 1830 Captain Wilbraham made a successful ascent; and in 1834 another was performed by Dr. Martin Barry, who likewise gave an account of his adventures and observations to the world. This last ascent was performed on the 17th of September, a week later in the year than any preceding ascent, and considered on that account as more than usually dangerous. A few weeks still later, a French gentleman, having been informed that no countryman of his had ever made the ascent, while it had been made by eleven Englishmen, besides several natives of other countries, determined instantly to wipe away this imaginary reproach upon the fair fame of his country, and the consequence was—

success, at the expense of his feet, which were destroyed by the cold.

Those who wish to ascend Mont Blanc, have to provide themselves at Chamounix with a party of guides, six or eight in number, the necessary clothing and accouterments, and provisions for three days. The guides of Chamounix are a remarkably-intelligent, sagacious, and enterprising class of men. One named Coutet, who ascended with Dr. Barry for the ninth time, has been spoken of by various travelers as a most spirited, and, in every respect, estimable person. Immediately after a narrow escape, which he made in 1820, from an avalanche which had destroyed three of his companions, he exclaimed to the gentleman who had engaged him: 'Now, sir, for the summit!' The proposal, as may be imagined, was declined; but there could be no doubt, from the earnestness of his manner, that he would have proceeded at whatever risk. He had, on this occasion, expressed some fears as to the propriety of making the attempt at so unfavorable a period of the day, and thus excited a suspicion that he wished to secure his hire without performing the full service. Having perceived this suspicion in his employer, he wished to prove that, even after his fears had been in some degree fatally realized, he was still willing to fulfill his contract.

Most of the Chamounix guides are ambitious of the distinction to be obtained by climbing Mont Blanc; but, from a sense of the extreme danger of the enterprise, their female relatives exercise all possible influence to prevent them from undertaking the task. We have been informed by one of the gentlemen who most reverently performed the enterprise, that the expenses, in all, amounted to between £40 and £50.

When Mr. Auldjo ascended in August, 1827, he spent the whole morning in crossing the lower and vegetating portion of the mountain. On approaching the glacier at the commencement of the upper and snowy stage, he thought that it would be impossible to enter upon it, "or at all events to proceed any great distance along it, from the masses of ice which are piled on one another, and the deep and wide fissures which every moment intersect the path pointed out as that which is about to be proceeded in. Here," says Mr. Auldjo, "the skill and knowledge of the guide is shown; the quickness and ease with which he discovers a practicable part is quite extraordinary; he leads the way over places where one would believe it impossible for human foot to tread. We passed along the remains of innumerable avalanches, which had long been accumulating, and formed a most uneven and tiresome footway. An extended plain of snow now presented itself, here and there covered with masses of broken ice; sometimes a beautiful tower of that substance raised its blue form, and seemed to mock the lofty-pointed rocks above it; sometimes an immense block, its perpendicular form broken into pinnacles, now bearing a mass of snow, now supporting long and clear icicles, looked like some castle, on whose dilapidated walls the ivy, hanging its clustering beauty, or lying in rich and dark luxuriance, was, by the wand of some fairy, changed into the bright matter which now composed it."

In these lower parts of the mountain, the chief danger is from avalanches, which, however, are most apt to fall in the afternoon when the sun has operated in loosening the huge masses of superincumbent ice. On advancing a little farther, Mr. Auldjo found equal danger in threading his way along and across the numerous fissures and crevices which are constantly to be found in the vast, icy mantle of Mont Blanc, in consequence of the slipping of portions of it to the lower places along the declivity. Tied together in threes by a piece of rope, so as to diminish the chance of being precipitated into these openings, and after having sworn to be faithful to each other in all dangers, Mr. Auldjo and his guides entered upon this perilous part of their march. "We were surrounded," says he, "by ice piled up in mountains, crevices presenting themselves at every step, and masses half-sunk in some deep gulf; the remainder, raised above us, seemed to put insurmountable barriers to our proceeding; yet some part was found where steps could be cut out by the hatchet; and we passed over these bridges, often grasping the ice with one hand, while the other, bearing the pole, balanced the body, hanging over some abyss, into which the eye penetrated, and searched in vain for the extremity. Sometimes we were obliged to climb up from one crag of ice to another, sometimes to scramble along a ledge on our hands and knees, often descending into a deep chasm on one side, and scaling the slippery precipice on the other. No men could be in higher spirits than my guides, laughing, singing, and joking; but when we came to such passes, the grave, serious look which took the place of the smiling countenance was a sure indication of great danger: the moment we were safely by it, the smile returned, and every one vied in giving amusement to the other. . . . A large mass of ice now opposed our progress: we passed it by climbing up its glassy sides. It formed a bridge over a fissure of great width, which would have otherwise put an end to our expedition. After winding some time among chasms and enormous towers, we arrived at the edge of another crevice, over which we could see but one bridge, that not of ice, but of snow only, and so thin, that it was deemed impossible to trust to it. A plan was resorted to, which enabled us to pass over in safety: our batons were placed on it, and in doing so, the center gave way, and fell into the gulf; however, enough remained on each side to form supports for the ends of these poles, and nine of them made a narrow bridge, requiring great precaution and steadiness to traverse. Other crevices were passed over on bridges of snow too weak to allow walking on, or too extended to admit this application of the poles. A strong guide managed to creep over, and a rope being tied round the waist of a second, who lay on his back, he was in that position pulled across by the first. In this manner the whole party were drawn singly over the crevice."

Rather more than half-way up the mountain, two sharp pinnacles of rock, called the Grand and Petit Mulets, rise above the snow and ice. The Grand Mulet usually affords shelter to the adventurers during the first night of their journey, if not also during the second—for the ascent and descent together more frequently require three than two days. When Auldjo and his party approached the Grand Mulet, they found it nearly inaccessible, in consequence of a tremendous fissure immediately below it. In front was a solid wall of ice, of prodigious hight, to which there was only one perilous approach, by means of a promontory projecting from the side on which the party stood. Coutet cut steps in the wall with his hatchet, and thus enabled the party to climb over it. When Dr. Barry came to the same place, Coutet had to cut and climb his way for a considerable distance along the front of an equally-terrific wall, and then to climb up to the top, to which, by means of ropes, he pulled up the rest. After ascending the wall Mr. Auldjo's route lay for some distance along the top, which was very narrow, and inclined in each direction toward unfathomable gulfs. "Taking my steps," says he, "with the greatest caution, I could not prevent myself from slipping; as the space became wider, I became less cautious, and while looking over the edge into the upper crevice, my feet slid from under me: I came down on my face, and glided rapidly toward the lower one: I cried out, but the guides who held the ropes attached to me did not stop me, though they stood firm. I had got to the extent of the rope, my feet hanging over the lower crevice, one hand grasping firmly the pole, the other my hat. The guides called to me to be cool, and not afraid: a pretty time to be cool, hanging over an abyss, and in momentary expectation of falling into it! They made no attempt to pull me up for some moments, but then, desiring me to raise myself, they drew in the rope till I was close to them and in safety. The reason for this proceeding is obvious. Had they attempted, on the bad and uncertain footing in which they stood, to check me at the first gliding, they might have lost their own balance, and our destruction would have followed; but by fixing themselves firmly in the cut step, and securing themselves with their batons, they were enabled to support me with certainty when the rope had gone its length. This also gave me time to recover, that I might assist them in placing myself out of danger."

The place appropriated for the repose of the travelers during the night, is a ledge near the top of the Grand Mulet, where it is just possible, by laying the batons against the rock, to form a kind of tent sufficient to cover the party during their sleep. Dr. Barry here found the air at forty of Fahrenheit, so that there was no suffering from cold. This gentleman, awaking at midnight, drew himself forth from the tent, and beheld a scene of unexampled magnificence and impressiveness. "It was," says he, "a brilliant night. The full moon had risen over the summit of the mountain, and shone resplendent on the glazed surface of its snowy covering. The guides were sleeping. Thus, in the midnight hour, at an elevation of ten thousand feet, I stood—alone: my resting-place a pinnacle of rock, that towered darkly over the frozen wilderness above which it, isolated, rose. Below me lay, in the wildest confusion, the colossal masses of ice we had been climbing, and whose dangers we had narrowly escaped: around and above was a sea of fair but treacherous snow, whose hidden perils we had yet to encounter. The Jura Mountains, and many an unknown peak of Switzerland, seen dimly in the distance, gave me an earnest of the prospect from still more elevated regions. The vale of Chamounix was sleeping at the foot of the mountain: and, broken by the occasional thunder of an avalanche, the profoundest silence reigned. It seemed the vastest, sternest, sublimest of nature's imagery reposing—now starting as in a fitful dream—then sinking again into the stillest calm. It held me till, at the end of an hour and a half, a recollection of the coming day's fatigues rendered it prudent again to take repose."

Between the Grand Mulet and the base of the summit expressly termed Mont Blanc, the way zigzags along a vast ascending hollow, broken by three plains of ice, the last and largest of which is called the Grand Plateau. This part of the journey is also obstructed by fissures and the debris of avalanches — vast masses, as formerly, being sometimes found serving as bridges across the openings. At one place, Mr. Auldjo and his party crossed a vast chasm by a large and lofty block of ice, which had stuck in it, and the side of which had to be cut by the hatchet, to allow of places for the feet and hands; so that the party passed along as boys are sometimes observed to do on the outside of the parapet of a bridge, with nothing, in the event of their falling, to save them from destruction. At another place, they came to a chasm crossed by a hollow or pendulous bridge of snow; and on this insecure place were induced to breakfast, on account of the shelter it afforded from the piercing wind which swept over the ice. "In one moment," says the traveler, "without a chance of escape, the fall of the bridge might have precipitated them into the gulf beneath. Yet no such idea ever entered the imagination of my thoughtless but brave guides, who sat at their meal singing and laughing, either unconscious or regardless of the danger of their present situation."

A little above the Grand Plateau, the traveler

usually begins to feel intense thirst and great dryness of the skin, while the reflection of the sun's rays from the glittering snow can only be endured by the use of green spectacles, or a green vail. The ascent along the upper ridges to the top is extremely difficult, partly on account of the greater steepness, and partly owing to the phenomena arising from natural circumstances. "We had now reached an elevation where I had to verify the testimony of preceding travelers, by experiencing the exhaustion consequent on any slight exertion, in an atmosphere whose density is so exceedingly reduced. Only a few steps could now be taken at a time, and these became fewer and slower. Two or three deep inspirations appeared sufficient at each pause to enable me to proceed; but on making the attempt, I found the exhaustion returned as before. Slight faintness came on, so that I had at last to sit down for a few minutes; when, a little wine having been taken, one more effort was made, and at a quarter past two o'clock we stood on the highest summit." Such were the sensations of Dr. Barry. Mr. Auldjo seems to have been in a still more distressed condition. "I was exhausted; the weakness of my legs had become excessive; I was nearly choking from the dryness of my throat and the difficulty of breathing, and my head was almost bursting with pain. My eyes were smarting with inflammation; the reflection from the snow nearly blinding me, at the same time burning and blistering my face." This gentleman desired to proceed no farther; but his guides generously resolved to drag him up, rather than permit him to be disappointed.

"After a few minutes of rest on the summit, all the exhaustion, faintness, and indifference had ceased: the mountain-top was gained—the dangers of the descent were not for a moment considered—and it was with a thrill of exultation, never felt before, that I addressed myself to the contemplation of the prospect around and beneath. The range of sight, though limited by mountain-chains in various directions, comprehends nearly the whole of Sardinia, [Savoy and Piedmont,] the western half of Switzerland, one-third of Lombardy, and an eighth of France. This immense space is of an oval shape; its longitudinal form extending from Mont Morran, in France, on the north-west, to the neighborhood of Genoa, on the south-east; having Berne and Milan on the one hand, Lyon and Grenoble on the other. In a north-west direction lie the plains of France; in the south-east, those of Lombardy and Piedmont: a mountainous tract containing all the Pennine and part of the Rhetian Alps, with the whole chain of Jura, forming the space between. But there are directions in which the prospect is still more extended—for example, the mountains of Tuscany may be distinctly seen. . . . All this was beheld under a sky literally without a cloud." De Saussure and Dr. Barry kindled fires on the summit of Mont Blanc. The extreme rarity of the air, which rendered the breathing so difficult, also made it no easy matter to kindle and keep alive the fire, oxygen being in both cases defective. Without the unceasing application of bellows, De Saussure found the charcoal expire every minute. The boiling-point of water in this elevated situation was found by De Saussure to be 187 degrees Fahrenheit, being, as we need scarcely remark, 25 degrees below the point at which it boils on ordinary levels. The rarity of the air also diminishes the effects of sound. A pistol fired makes no greater noise than a cracker usually does. This is partly owing to the effect of the rarity diminishing the tone and force of the vibration, and partly from the absence of all echo and repercussion from solid objects on that elevated summit.

In consequence of the greater distance from the center of attraction, bodies feel sensibly lighter on the top of Mont Blanc. To quote the words of Auldjo: "The most peculiar sensation which all have felt who have gained this great hight, arises from the awful stillness which reigns, almost unbroken even by the voice of those speaking to one another, for its feeble sound can hardly be heard. Nothing I ever beheld could exceed the singular and splendid appearance which the sun and sky presented. The blue color of the one had increased to such a depth as to be almost black, while the sun's disc had become excessively small, and of a perfect and brilliant white. I also experienced the sensation of lightness of body, of which Captain Sherwill has given a description in the following words: 'It appeared as if I could have passed the blade of a knife under the sole of my shoes, or between them and the ice on which I stood.'" It is proper to mention, that Dr. Barry accounts for the blackness of the sky by the simultaneous reception by the eye of rays from the snow: having lain down upon his back, and excluded all view of the snow, the natural hue was in a great measure restored.

This last gentleman left the summit at half-past three o'clock, and spent the night on the Grand Mulet. Mr. Auldjo began the descent at noon, with the view of getting back to Chamounix that night. When this gentleman and his party had regained a particular part of the Plateau, they discovered that by a slight variation in their ascending route, they had escaped a slip of snow, which had been precipitated down the usual track at the moment when they must have been upon it, so that the whole might consider their lives as saved by a mere accident. "I can not," says he, "describe my feelings when I saw the poor guides turn pale and tremble at the sight of the danger from which they had escaped. Clasping their hands together, they returned the most heart-felt thanks for this deliverance. A deep impressive silence prevailed for some moments: the contemplation of this danger and escape was too much for even these uncultivated beings, under whose rough character are found feelings which would do honor to the most refined of their fellow-creatures. . . . . One married man vowed most solemnly that he never would be tempted to make the ascent again, whatever might be the inducement offered."

In crossing the plateaux, Mr. Auldjo and his party suffered greatly from burning heat, and also from the toilsomeness of the march, the snow being at this period of the day melted to such a degree as to take them up to the knees at every step. The precipitous intervals between the various plateaux were descended by sliding—a method not without its perils, as an individual in attempting it is liable to overshoot his point, and glide into chasms from which he might never again ascend. As they proceeded, the materials of a thunder-storm gathered in the sky, and a thick sleet began to fall. Some time after passing the Grand Mulet, perplexed by the storm, they lost their way, and soon found themselves wandering amidst numberless crevices, where progress was not less difficult than dangerous. "The storm recommenced with greater violence than before: the hail-stones, large and sharp, driven with force by the wind, inflicted great pain on the face; we were exposed to it, standing on a narrow ledge overhanging an abyss. Here we awaited for a short time the return of two guides, sent to explore the crevices and banks around us, in an endeavor to discover the route of our ascent, but with very little hope of success; indeed, it was greatly feared that we should have to remain where we were for that night. The storm, increasing every instant, compelled us to seek some place in the glacier in which we could obtain shelter; following the footmarks of the guides who had gone forward, we succeeded in finding a recess, formed by the projection of a part of the glacier over a narrow ledge in the side of the crevice. We could form no idea of the depth of the chasm, but its width appeared to be about twenty feet, and its opposite side rose considerably above us. Along this ledge we moved with great care, and had just space to stand in a bending posture, and in a row. Wet through, and suffering excruciating torture from the cold, our position was both painful and dangerous. The tempest raged with the most awful fury; the gusts of wind sweeping through the chasm with tremendous violence, the pelting showers of hail, accompanied by the most vivid lightning, and peals of thunder, alternating with a perfect calm, were enough to appall the bravest of the party.

"We waited for some time in this situation, when, in one of those moments of calm, we heard the loud halloo of one of the exploring guides, who was returning to us, and called to us to advance, for they had found the angle which we had so much difficulty in climbing up the day before. We soon joined him and his companion who had conducted us to it. Nearly deprived of the use of my limbs, from the excessive cold and wet state of my apparel, I could scarcely walk; my fingers were nearly frozen, and my hands so stiffened and senseless, that I could not hold my baton or keep myself from falling." It was in this state that Mr. Auldjo was brought to a wall of ice, which he had to descend for a certain way in order to get upon a point on the opposite side of the chasm.

"Being incapable of making any exertion, I was lowered down to the guides, who were already on the ledge, beneath the wall. At the very moment I was rocking in the air, a flash of lightning penetrated into the abyss, and showed all the horrors of my situation; while the crash of the thunder seemed to tear the glacier down upon me. I was drawn on the neck of ice, and sat down till the other guides had descended. The hearts of two or three failed, and they declared that we must all perish; the others, though conscious of our awfully-dangerous position, endeavored to raise the courage and keep up the spirits of the depressed. All suffered dreadfully from the cold, but, with a solicitude for which I shall ever feel deeply grateful, they still attended to me in the kindest manner. They desired me to stand up, and forming a circle, in the center of which I stood, closed round me. In a few minutes, the warmth of their bodies extended itself to mine, and I felt much relieved; they then took off their coats, covering me with them, and each in turn put my hands into his bosom, while another lay on my feet. In ten minutes I was in a state to proceed."

At no late hour in the evening, Mr. Auldjo returned to Chamounix, from which he had been only thirty-seven hours absent. He was met and congratulated by a great number of strangers and natives, who had felt an interest in his undertaking, and to all of whom he declared, that the magnificence of what he had seen much more than compensated for the pain of what he had felt.

In 1851, some English were successful in ascending to the top of Mont Blanc, but with risks as great as those above related, and apparently for no other purpose than the satisfying of that spirit of adventure and curiosity which is so remarkable in our countrymen.

III.

Narrative of Scenes at Norfolk Island.

FAR distant from the many other islands with which the Southern Pacific Ocean is studded, one stands alone, rich in natural beauty, and with a climate almost unrivaled. Constantly fanned by cool breezes from the sea, its green hills and deep ravines abound in graceful pines and shady fern-trees. The wild jasmin and convolvuli climb the stems, and reach from tree to tree, forming bowers and walls of exquisite beauty. The rich soil maintains a perpetually-luxuriant vegetation, and birds of brightest plumage rejoice in groves of the abundant guava, or amid the delicate blossoms of the golden lemon.

This lovely island was visited by Captain Cook in 1774, and named by him Norfolk Island; it was then uninhabited, and the party who landed were probably the first human beings who had ever set foot on it. Neither the vegetable nor the animal world had been disturbed. For about two hundred yards from the shore, the ground was covered so thickly with shrubs and plants as scarcely to be penetrable farther inland. The sea-fowl bred unmolested on the shores and cliffs. The account given by Cook led to an attempt at settlement on Norfolk Island; but this was attended with difficulty. The island is small, being only about six miles in length by four in breadth; and was, therefore, unavailable for a large or increasing population. Lying nine hundred miles from Port Jackson in Australia, it was inconveniently remote from that country; and, worst of all, its cliffy and rocky shores presented serious dangers to mariners attempting a landing. There are, indeed, only three places at which boats can effect a safe landing, and of these only with certain winds, and never in gales, which are frequent in this part of the globe. Its general unsuitableness, however, for ordinary colonization was considered to adapt it as a penal settlement, subordinate to New South Wales, and to which convicts could be sent who merited fresh punishment while in course of servitude. Thus, one of the loveliest of earthly paradises was doomed to be a receptacle for the very worst—or shall we call them the most unfortunate and most wretched—of malefactors. It might be imagined that the beauty of Norfolk Island, and the fineness of its climate, would greatly tend to soothe the depraved minds of its unhappy tenants, and reconcile them, if any thing could, to compulsory expatriation. That such effects may be produced by considerate treatment, is not improbable; but hitherto, or at least till a late period, one sentiment has overruled all others in the minds of the Norfolk Island convicts, and that has been a desire for restoration to liberty. Impatient of control, and regardless of all consequences, they eagerly seize upon every opportunity of making their escape—with what fatal consequences let the following narrative bear witness. Written by a gentleman for some time resident in Norfolk Island, and handed to us for publication, as a warning to "those who go astray," the whole may be relied upon as a true relation of facts.

"On the northern side of Norfolk Island the cliffs rise high, and are crowned by woods, in which the elegant whitewood and gigantic pine predominate. A slight indentation of the land affords a somewhat sheltered anchorage ground, and an opening in the cliffs has supplied a way to the beach by a winding road at the foot of the dividing hills. A stream of water, collected from many ravines, finds its way by a similar opening to a ledge of rock in the neighborhood, and, falling over in feathery spray, has given the name of Cascade to this part of the island.

Off this bay, on the morning of the 21st of June, 1842, the brig *Governor Philip* was sailing, having brought stores for the use of the penal establishment. It was one of those bright mornings which this hemisphere alone knows, when the air is so elastic that its buoyancy is irresistibly communicated to the spirits. At the foot of the cliff, near a group of huge fragments of rock fallen from the overhanging cliffs, a prisoner was sitting close to the sea preparing food for his companions, who had gone off to the brig the previous evening with ballast, and who were expected to return at daylight with a load of stores. The surface of the sea was smooth, and the brig slowly moved on upon its soft blue waters. Every thing was calm and still, when suddenly a sharp but distant sound as of a gun was heard. The man, who was stooping over the fire, started on his feet, and looked above and around him, unable to distinguish the quarter from whence the report came. Almost immediately he heard the sound repeated, and then distinctly perceived smoke curling from the vessel's side. His fears were at once excited. Again he listened; but all was hushed, and the brig still stood steadily in toward the shore. Nearer and nearer she approached; till, alarmed for her safety, the man ran to summon the nearest officer. By the time they returned, the vessel had wore, and was standing off from the land; but while they remained in anxious speculation as to the cause of all this, the firing was renewed on board, and it was evident that some deadly fray was going on. At length a boat was seen to put off from the brig, and upon its reaching the shore, the worst fears of the party were realized. The misguided prisoners on board had attempted to seize the vessel. They were but twelve in number, unarmed, and guarded by twelve soldiers and a crew of eighteen men; yet they had succeeded in gaining possession of the vessel, had held it for a time, but had been finally overpowered, and immediate help was required for the wounded and dying.

July 21, 1842.—My duty as a clergyman called me to the scene of blood. When I arrived on the deck of the brig, it exhibited a frightful spectacle. One man, whose head was blown to atoms, was lying near the forecastle. Close by his side a body was stretched, the face of which was covered by a cloth, as if a sight too ghastly to be looked upon; for the upper half of the head had been blown off. Not far from these, a man badly wounded was lying on the deck, with others securely handcuffed. Forward, by the companion-hatch, one of the mutineers was placed, bleeding most profusely from a wound which had shattered his thigh; yet his look was more dreadful than all—hate, passion, and disappointed rage rioted in his breast, and were deeply marked in his countenance. I turned away from the wretched man, and my eye shrunk from the sight which again met it. Lying on his back in a pool of blood, the muscular frame of a man whom I well knew was stretched, horribly mutilated. A ball had entered his mouth, and passing through his skull, had scattered his brains around. My heart sickened at the extent of carnage, and I was almost sinking with the faintness it produced, when I was roused by a groan so full of anguish and pain, that for a long time afterward its echo seemed to reach me. I found that it came from a man lying farther forward, on whose face the death-dew was standing, yet I could perceive no wound. Upon questioning him, he moved his hand from his breast, and I then perceived that a ball had pierced his chest, and could distinctly hear the air rushing from his lungs through the orifice it had left. I tore away the shirt, and endeavored to hold together the edges of the wound till it was bandaged. I spoke to him of prayer, but he soon grew insensible, and within a short time died in frightful agony. In every part of the vessel evidences of the attempt which had ended so fatally presented themselves, and the passions of the combatants were still warm. After attending those who required immediate assistance, I received the following account of the affair:

The prisoners had slept the previous night in a part of the vessel appropriated for this purpose; but it was without fastening, or other means of securing them below. Two sentries were, however, placed over the hatchway. The prisoners occasionally came on deck during the night, for their launch was towing astern, and the brig was standing off and on till the morning. Between six and seven o'clock in the morning the men were called to work. Two of them were up some time before the rest. They were struck by the air of negligence which was evident on deck, and instantly communicated the fact to one or two others. The possibility of capturing the brig had often been discussed by the prisoners, among their many other wild plans for escaping from the island, and recently had been often proposed by them. The thought was told by their looks, and soon spread from man to man. A few moments were enough; one or two were roused from sleep, and the intention was hurriedly communicated to them. It was variously received. One of them distrusted the leader, and entreated his companions to desist from so mad an attempt. It was useless; the frenzied thirst for liberty had seized them, and they were maddened by it. Within a few minutes they were all on deck; and one of the leaders rushing at the sentry nearest to him, endeavored to wrest from him his pistols, one of which had flashed in the pan as he rapidly presented it, and threw him overboard; but he was subsequently saved. The arms of the other sentry were demanded, and obtained from him without resistance. A scuffle now took place with two other soldiers who were also on the deck, but not on duty, during which one of them jumped over the vessel's side, and remained for some time in the main chains; but upon the launch being brought along side, he went down into it. The other endeavored to swim ashore—for by this time the vessel was within a gun-shot of the rocks—but, incumbered by his great-coat, he was seen, when within a few strokes of the rock, to raise his hands, and uttering a faint cry to Heaven for mercy, he instantly sunk. In the mean while, the sergeant in charge of the guard hearing the scuffling overhead, ran upon deck, and seeing some of the mutineers struggling with the sentry, shot the nearest of them dead on the spot. He had no sooner done so than he received a blow on the head, which rendered him for some time insensible. Little or no resistance was offered by the sailors; they ran into the forecastle, and the vessel was in the hands of the mutineers. All the hatches were instantly fastened down, and every available thing at hand piled upon them. But now, having secured their opponents, the mutineers were unable to work the brig; they therefore summoned two of the sailors from below, and placed one of them at the wheel, while the other was directed to assist in getting the vessel off. The cockswain, a free man in charge of the prisoners, had at the first onset taken to the rigging, and remained in the maintop with one of the men who refused to join in the attack. At this moment a soldier who had gone overboard, and endeavored to reach the shore, had turned back, and was seen swimming near the vessel. Woolfe, one of the convicts, immediately jumped into the boat along side, and saved him. While this was the state of things above, the soldiers had forced their way into the captain's cabin, and continued to fire through the gratings overhead as often as any of the mutineers passed. In this manner several of them received wounds. To prevent a continuance of this, a kettle of hot water was poured from above, and shortly afterward a proposal was made to the captain from the prisoners to leave the vessel in the launch, provided he handed up to them the necessary supplies. This he refused, and then all the sailors were ordered from below into the launch, with the intention of sending them ashore. Continuing to watch for the ringleaders, the captain caught a glimpse of one of them standing aft, and, as he supposed, out of reach. He mounted the cabin table, and almost at a venture fired through the woodwork in the direction he supposed the man to be standing. The shot was fatal; the ball struck him in the mouth, and passed through his brain. Terrified at the death of their comrades, the remainder were panic-struck, and instantly ran below. One of the leaders sprung over the tafferel, and eventually reached the launch. The sailor at the wheel, now seeing the deck almost cleared, beckoned up the captain, and, without an effort, the vessel was again in their possession. In the confusion, a soldier who had been in the boat, and was at this moment with the sailors returning on deck, was mistaken for one of the mutineers, and shot by the sergeant. The prisoners were now summoned from their place of concealment. They begged hard for mercy; and, upon condition of their quietly surrendering, it was promised to them. As the first of them, in reliance upon this assurance, was gaining the deck, by some unhappy error he received a ball in his thigh, and fell back again. The rest refused to stir; but after a few moments' hesitation, another of them ventured up, was taken aft by the captain, and secured. A third followed, and as he came up, he extended his arms, and cried, "I surrender; spare me." Either this motion was mistaken by the soldiers, or some of them were unable to restrain their passion, for at this instant the man's head was literally blown off. The captain hastened to the spot and received the others, who were secured without further injury.

When we reached the vessel, the dying, dead, and wounded were lying in every direction. In the launch astern, we saw the body of one wretched man who had leaped over the tafferel, and reached the boat badly wounded; he was seen lying in it when the deck was regained, and was then pierced through with many balls. Nothing could be more horrible than his appearance; the distortion of every feature, his clinched hands, and the limbs which had stiffened in the forms of agony into which pain had twisted them, were appalling. The countenance of every man on board bore evidence of the nature of the deadly conflict in which he had been engaged. In some, sullenness had succeeded to reckless daring, and exultation to alarm in others.

Nothing could have been more desperate than

such an attempt to seize the vessel. The most culpable neglect could alone have encouraged it; and it is difficult to conceive how it could have succeeded, if any thing like a proper stand had been made by those in charge of her when it commenced.

The wounded were immediately landed, and conveyed to the hospital, and the dead bodies were afterward brought on shore.

The burial-ground is close to the beach. A heavy surf rolls mournfully over the reef. The moon had just risen, when, in deep and solemn silence, the bodies of these misguided men were lowered into the graves prepared for them. Away from home and country, they had found a fearful termination of a miserable existence. Perhaps ties had still bound them to the world; friends whom they loved were looking for their return, and prodigals though they had been, would have blessed them, and forgiven their offenses. Perhaps even at that sad moment mothers were praying for their lost ones, whom in all their infamy they had still fondly loved. Such thoughts filled my mind; and when a few drops of rain at that moment descended, I could not help thinking that they fell as tears from heaven over the guilt and misery of its children.

On the morning following the fatal occurrence, I visited the jail in which the mutineers were confined. The cells are small, but clean and light. In the first of them I found George Beavers, Nicholas Lewis, and Henry Sears. Beavers was crouching in one corner of the cell, and looking sullen, and in despair. Lewis, who was walking the scanty space of the cell, seemed to glory in the rattle of his heavy chains; while Sears was stretched apparently asleep upon a grass mat. They were all heavily ironed, and every precaution had evidently been taken to prevent escape.

The jail is small, and by no means a secure one. It was once a public house; and notwithstanding every effort to adapt it to its present purpose, it is not a safe or proper place of confinement. It is little calculated to resist any attempt to rescue the men, whose daring conduct was the subject of high encomium among their fellow-prisoners, by whom any attempt to escape is considered a meritorious act. In the other cell I found Woolfe and Barry, the latter in much agony from an old wound in the leg, the pain of which had been aggravated by the heavy irons which galled it. All the prisoners, except Barry and Woolfe, readily acknowledged their participation in the attempt to seize the brig; but most solemnly denied any knowledge of a preconcerted plan to take her; or that they, at least, had attempted to throw the soldiers overboard. They were unwilling to be interrupted, and inveighed in the bitterest manner against some of their companions who had, they seemed to think, betrayed them, or at least had led them on, and at the moment of danger had flinched.

The names of the surviving mutineers were John Jones, Nicholas Lewis, Henry Sears, George Beavers, James Woolfe, Thomas Whelan, and Patrick Barry.

The depositions against them having been taken, all the men I have mentioned, with the exception of Jones and Whelan, who were wounded, were brought to hear them read. They listened with calm attention, but none of them appeared to be much excited. Once only during the reading, Beavers passionately denied the statements made by one of the witnesses present, and was with difficulty silenced. His countenance at that moment was terribly agitated; every bad feeling seemed to mingle in its passionate expression. They were all young, powerful, and, with one or two exceptions, not at all ill-looking men.

From the jail I proceeded to the hospital, where the wounded men were lying. They had each received severe wounds in the thigh, and were in great agony. The violence of Jones was excessive. Weakened in some degree by an immense loss of blood, the bitterness of his spirit, nevertheless, exhibited itself in passionate bursts of impatience. He was occasionally convulsed with excessive pain; for the nerves of the thigh had been much lacerated, and the bone terribly shattered. His features were distorted with pain and anger, and occasionally bitter curses broke from his lips; yet there was something about his appearance which powerfully arrested my attention—an evident marking of intellect and character, repulsive in its present development, yet in many respects remarkable. His history had been a melancholy one, and, as illustrative of many thousand others, I give it as I afterward received it from his lips.

At eleven years of age he was employed in a warehouse in Liverpool as an errand boy. While following this occupation, from which by good conduct he might have risen to something better, he was met in the street one day by the lad whom he had succeeded in this employment, and was told by him how he might obtain money by robbing the warehouse, and then go with him to the theater. He accordingly took an opportunity of stealing some articles which had been pointed out, and gave them to his companion, who, in disposing of them, was detected, and, of course, criminated Jones. After remaining some weeks in jail, Jones was tried and acquitted; but his character being now gone, he became reckless, and commenced a regular career of depredation. In attempting another warehouse robbery, he was detected, and sentenced to twelve months' imprisonment. By the time he was released from this, he was well tutored in crime, and believed that he could now adroitly perform the same robbery in which he had previously failed. He made the attempt the very night of his release from jail, and with temporary success. Subsequently, however, he was detected, and received sentence of transportation for seven years. He underwent this sentence, and an additional one in Van Diemen's Land, chiefly at Port Arthur, the most severe of the penal stations there. From this place he, with Lewis, Moss—who was shot on board the brig—and Woolfe, having seized a whaleboat, effected their escape. During three months they underwent the most extreme hardships from hunger and exposure. Once they had been without food for several days, and their last hook was over the boat's side; they were anxiously watching for a fish. A small, blue shark took the bait, and in despair one of them dashed over the boat's side to seize the fish; his leg was caught by one of the others, and they succeeded in saving both man and hook. They eventually reached Twofold Bay, on the coast of New South Wales, and were then apprehended, conveyed to Sydney, and thence sent back to Van Diemen's Land; tried, and received sentence of death; but this was subsequently commuted to transportation for life to Norfolk Island.

Jones often described to me the intense misery he had undergone during his career. He had never known what freedom was, and yet incessantly longed for it. All alike confessed the unhappiness of their career. Having made the first false step into crime, they acknowledged that their minds became polluted by the associations they formed during imprisonment. Then they were further demoralized by thinking of the *glory*—such miserable glory!—attending a trial; and the hulks and the voyage out gave them a finished criminal training. The extent of punishment many of them have undergone during the period of transportation is almost incredible. I have known men whose original sentence of seven years has been extended over three times that period, and who, in addition to other punishment, have received five thousand or six thousand lashes!

After many solemn interviews with the mutineers, I found them gradually softening. They became more communicative, and extremely anxious to receive instruction. I think I shall never forget one of the earliest of these visits to them. I first saw Sears, Beavers, and Jones. After a long and interesting conversation with them, we joined in that touching confession of sin with which the liturgy of the Church of England commences. As we kneeled together, I heard them repeat with great earnestness—"We have erred and strayed from Thy ways like lost sheep," etc. When we arose, I perceived that each of them had been shedding tears. It was the first time I had seen them betray any such emotion, and I can not tell how glad I felt; but when I proceeded afterward to read to them the first chapter of Isaiah, I had scarcely uttered that most exquisite passage in the second verse—"I have nourished and brought up children, and they have rebelled against me"—when the claims of God, and *their* violation and rejection of them; his forbearance, and *their* ingratitude, appeared to overwhelm them; they sobbed aloud, and were thoroughly overpowered.

For a considerable time we talked together of the past, the wretched years they had endured, the punishments, and the crimes which had led to them, till they seemed to feel most keenly the folly of their sad career. We passed on to contrast the manner in which their lives had been spent, with what God and society re-

required from them; their miserable perversion of God's gifts, with the design for which he gave them, till we were led on to speak of hope and of faith; of Him who "willeth not the death of a sinner, but rather that he should turn from his wickedness and live;" and then the Savior's remonstrance seemed to arrest them—"Ye will not come to me that ye might have life"—till at length the influences of the Holy Spirit were supplicated with earnestness and solemnity. These instructions, and such conversation, were daily repeated; and henceforth each time I saw them I perceived a gradual but distinct unfolding of the affections and the understanding.

August.—The wounded men are much recovered, and the whole of the mutineers are confined together in a large ward of the jail. They have long received extreme kindness from the commandant, and are literally bewildered at finding that even this last act has not diminished the exercise of his benevolence. That any body should care for them, or take such pains about them after their violent conduct, excited surprise—at first almost amounting to suspicion—but this at length gave place to the warmest gratitude. They were, in fact, subdued by it. They read very much, are extremely submissive, and carefully avoid the slightest infringement of the prison regulations. At first, all this was confined to the three men I have mentioned; but their steady consistency of conduct, and the strange transformation of character so evident in them, gradually arrested the attention of the others, and eventually led to a similar result.

They will be detained here till the case has been decided by the authorities in Sydney. They will probably be tried by a commission sent from thence to the island for the purpose. Formerly, however, prisoners charged with capital offenses here were sent up for trial; but, it is a horrible fact, this was found to lead to so much crime, that, at much inconvenience and expense, it was found absolutely necessary to send down a judicial commission on each important occasion, in order to prevent it. The mere excitement of a voyage, with the chances connected with it, nay, merely a wish to get off the island, even for a time, led many men to commit crimes of the deepest dye in order to be sent to Sydney for trial.

Two months, therefore, at least must intervene between the perpetration of the offense and their trial; and this interval is usually employed in similar cases in arranging a defense but too commonly supported by perjury. In the present instance, I found not the slightest attempt to follow such a course. They declare that they expect death, and will gladly welcome it. Of their life, which has been a course of almost constant warfare with society, ending in remorseful feelings, they are all thoroughly weary, although only one of them exceeds thirty years of age.

In addition to the ordinary services, Captain Maconochie each Sunday afternoon has read prayers to them, and has given permission to a few of their friends to be present. Singular good has resulted from it, both to the men and those who join in their devotions. At the conclusion of one of these services Sears stood up, and with his heart so full as scarcely to allow him utterance, to the surprise of every person there he addressed most impressively the men who were present. "Perhaps," said he, "the words of one of yourselves, unhappily circumstanced as I am, may have some weight with you. You all know the life I have led; it has, believe me, been a most unhappy one; and I have, I hope not too late, discovered the cause of this. I solemnly tell you that it is because I have broken God's laws. I am almost ashamed to speak, but I dare not be silent. I am going to tell you a strange thing. I never before was happy; I begin now, for the first time in my life, to *hope*. I am an ignorant man, or at least

I was so; but I thank God I begin to see things in their right light now. I have been unhappily placed from my childhood, and have endured many hardships. I do not mention this to excuse my errors; yet if I had years since received the kindness I have done here, it might have been otherwise. My poor fellows, do turn over a new leaf; try to serve God, and you, too, will be happier for it." The effect was most thrilling; there was a death-like silence; tears rolled down many cheeks, which I verily believe never before felt them; and without a word more, all slowly withdrew.

This man's story is also a common, but painful one. At fifteen years of age he was transported for life as an accomplice in an assault and alleged robbery, of which, from circumstances which have since transpired, I have little doubt he was entirely innocent. During a long imprisonment in Horsham jail, he received an initiation in crime, which was finished during the outward voyage. Upon his arrival at New South Wales, he was assigned to a settler in the interior, a notoriously hard and severe man, who gave him but a scanty supply of food and clothing, and whose aim seemed to be to take the utmost out of him at the least possible expense. Driven at length to desperation, he, with three fellow-servants, absconded; and when taken, made a complaint to the magistrate before whom they were brought almost without clothes. Their statements were found to be literally correct; but for absconding they were sent to Newcastle, one of the penal stations of New South Wales, where Sears remained nearly two years. At the expiration of that time he was again assigned, but unfortunately to a man, if possible, worse than his former employer, and again absconded. For this offense he was sent to Moreton Bay, another penal settlement, and endured three years of horrible severity, starvation, and misery of every kind. His temper was by this time much soured; and, roused by the conduct of the overseers, he became brutalized by constant punishment for resisting them. After this he was sent to Sydney, as one of the crew in the police-boat, of which he was soon made assistant cockswain. For not reporting a theft committed by one of the men under his charge, he was sentenced to a road party; and attempting to escape from it, he was apprehended, and again ordered to Moreton Bay for four years more. There he was again repeatedly flogged for disobedience and resistance of overseers, as well as attempting to escape; but having most courageously rendered assistance to a vessel wrecked off the harbor, he attracted the attention of the commandant, who afterward showed him a little favor. This was the first approach to kindness he had known since when, years before, he had left his home; and it had its usual influence. He never was again in a scrape there. His good conduct induced the commandant to recommend him for a mitigation of sentence, which he received, and he was again employed in the police-boat. The free cockswain of the boat was, however, a drunkard, and intrusted much to Sears. Oftentimes he roused the men by his violence, but Sears contrived to subdue his passion. At length, one night returning to the hut drunk, the man struck at one of the crew with his cutlass, and the rest resisted and disarmed him. But the morning came; the case was heard; their story was disbelieved; and upon the charge and evidence of the aggressor, they were sent to an ironed gang, to work on the public roads. When Sears again became eligible for assignment, a person whom he had known in Sydney applied for him. The man must be removed within a fixed period after the authority is given. In this case, application was made a day beyond the prescribed time, and churlishly refused. The disappointment roused a spirit so untutored as his, and once again he absconded; was of course apprehended, tried, and being found with a man who had committed robbery, and had a musket in his possession, was sent to Norfolk Island for life. This sentence has, however, for meritorious conduct, been reduced to fourteen years; and his ready assistance during a fire which recently broke out in the military garrison here, might possibly have helped to obtain a still further reduction. He never, during those abscondings, was absent for any long period, and never committed any act of violence. His constant attempt seems to have been to reach Sydney, in order to effect his escape from the scene of so much misery.

For some time past I have noticed his quiet and orderly conduct, and was really sorry when I found him concerned in this unhappy affair. His desire for freedom was, however, most ardent, and a chance of obtaining it was almost irresistible. He has since told me that a few words kindly spoken to himself and others by Captain Maconochie when they landed, sounded so pleasantly to him—such are his own words—that he determined from that moment he would endeavor to do well. He assures me that he was perfectly unconscious of a design to take the brig, till awoke from his sleep a few minutes before the attack commenced; that he then remonstrated with the men; but finding it useless, he considered it a point of honor not to fail them. His anxiety for instruction is intense;

he listens like a child; and his gratitude is most touching. He, together with Jones, Woolfe, and Barry, were chosen by the commandant as a police-boat's crew; and had, up to this period, acted with great steadiness and fidelity in the discharge of the duties required from them. Nor do I think they would even now, tempting as the occasion was, have thought of seizing it, had it not been currently reported that they were shortly to be placed under a system of severity such as they had already suffered so much from.

Woolfe's story of himself is most affecting. He entered upon evil courses when very young; was concerned in burglaries when only eleven years of age. Yet this was from no natural love of crime. Enticed from his home by boys older than himself, he soon wearied of the life he led, and longed to return to his home and his kind mother. Oftentimes he lingered near the street she lived in. Once he had been very unhappy, for he had seen his brother and sister that day pass near him, and it had rekindled all his love for them. They appeared happy in their innocence; he was miserable in his crime. He now determined to go home and pray to be forgiven. The evening was dark and wet, and as he entered the court in which his friends lived, his heart failed him, and he turned back;

but, unable to resist the impulse, he again returned, and stole under the window of the room. A rent in the narrow curtain enabled him to see within. His mother sat by the fire, and her countenance was so sad, that he was sure she thought of him; but the room looked so comfortable, and the whole scene was so unlike the place in which he had lately lived, that he could no longer hesitate. He approached the door; the latch was almost in his hand, when shame and fear, and a thousand other vile and foolish notions, held him back; and the boy who in another moment might have been happy—*was lost.* He turned away, and I believe has never seen them since. Going on in crime, he in due course of time was transported for robbery. His term of seven years expired in Van Diemen's Land. Released from forced servitude, he went a whaling voyage, and was free nearly two years. Unhappily, he was then charged with aiding in a robbery, and again received a sentence of transportation. He was sent to Port Arthur, there employed as one of its boat's crew, and crossing the bay one day with a commissariat officer, the boat was capsized by a sudden squall. In attempting to save the life of the officer, he was seized by his dying grasp, and almost perished with him; but extricating himself, he swam back to the boat. Seeing the drowning man exhausted, and sinking, he dashed forward again, diving after him, and happily succeeded in saving his life. For this honorable act he would have received a remission of sentence; but ere it could arrive, he and five others made their escape. He had engaged with these men in the plan to seize the boat, and although sure of the success of the application in his favor, he could not now draw back. The result I have already shown. There were two more men concerned in the mutiny, who, with those I have mentioned, and those killed on board the brig, made up the number of the boat's crew. But neither of these men came under my charge, being both Roman Catholics.

At length the brig, which had been dispatched with an account of the affair, returned, and brought the decision of the Governor of New South Wales. He had found it extremely difficult, almost impossible, to obtain fitting members for the commission, who would be willing to accept the terms proposed by the government, or trust themselves in this dreadful place, and, therefore, he had determined that the prisoners should be sent up for trial. The men were sadly disappointed at this arrangement. They wished much to end their days here, and they dreaded both the voyage and the distracting effect of new scenes. They cling, too, with grateful attachment to the commandant's family, and the persons who, during their long imprisonment, had taken so strong an interest in their welfare. I determined to accompany them, and watch for their perseverance in well-doing, that I might counsel and strengthen them under the fearful ordeal I could not doubt they would have to pass.

The same steady consistency marked the conduct of these men to the moment of their embarkation. There was a total absence of all excitement; one deep, serious feeling appeared to possess them, and its solemnity was communicated to all of us. They spoke and acted as men standing on the confines of the unseen world, and who not only thought of its wonders, but, better still, who seemed to have caught something of its spirit and purity.

November.—The voyage up was a weary, and, to the prisoners, a very trying one. In a prison, on the lower deck of a brig of one hundred and eighty-two tuns, fifty-two men were confined. The place itself was about twenty feet square, of course low, and badly ventilated. The men were all ironed, and fastened to a heavy chain rove through iron rings let into the deck, so that they were unable, for any purpose, to move from the spot they occupied—scarcely, indeed, to lie down. The weather was also unfavorable.

The vessel tossed and pitched most fearfully during a succession of violent squalls, accompanied by thunder and lightning. I can not describe the wretchedness of these unhappy convicts—sick, and surrounded by filth, they were huddled together in the most disgusting manner. The heat was at times unbearable. There were men of sixty—quiet and inoffensive old men—placed with others who were as accomplished villains as the world could produce. These were either proceeding to Sydney, their sentences on the island having expired, or as witnesses in another case—a bold and wicked murder—sent there also for trial. The sailors on board the brig were for the most part the cowardly fellows who had so disgracefully allowed the brig to be taken from them; and they, as well as the soldiers on guard—some of them formed a part of the former one—had no very kindly feeling toward the mutineers. It may be imagined, therefore, that such feelings occasioned no alleviation of their condition. In truth, although there was no actual cruelty exhibited, they suffered many oppressive annoyances; yet I never saw more patient endurance. It was hard to bear, but their better principles prevailed. Upon the arrival of the vessel in Sydney, we learned that the case had excited an unusual interest. Crowds assembled to catch a glimpse of the men as they landed; and while some applauded their daring, the great majority very loudly expressed their horror at the crime of which they stood accused.

I do not think it necessary to describe the trial, which took place in a few days after landing. All were arraigned except Barry. The prisoners' counsel addressed the jurors with powerful eloquence; but it was in vain; the crime was substantiated; and the jury returned a verdict of guilty against all the prisoners, recommending Woolfe to mercy.

During the whole trial, the prisoners' conduct was admirable; so much so, indeed, as to excite the astonishment of the immense crowd collected by curiosity to see men who had made so mad an attempt for liberty. They scarcely spoke, except once to request that the wounded man, who yet suffered much pain, might be allowed to sit down. Judgment was deferred till the following day. When they were then placed at the bar, the judge, in the usual manner, asked whether they had any reason to urge why sentence should not be pronounced upon them? It was a moment of deep solemnity; every breath was held; and the eyes of the whole court were directed toward the dock. Jones spoke in a deep, clear voice, and in a deliberate harangue pointed out some defects in the evidence, though without the slightest hope, he said, of mitigating the sentence now to be pronounced on himself and fellows. Three of the others also spoke. Whelan said "that he was not one of the men properly belonging to the boat's crew, but had been called upon to fill the place of another man, and had no knowledge of any intention to take the vessel, and the part he took on board was forced upon him. He was compelled to act as he had done; he had used no violence, nor was he in any way a participator in any that had been committed." At the conclusion of the address to them, Jones, amidst the deep silence of the court, pronounced a most emphatic prayer for mercy on his own soul and those of his fellow-prisoners, for the judge and jury, and finally for the witnesses. Sentence of death was then solemnly pronounced upon them all; but the judge informed Woolfe that he might hold out to him expectations that his life would be spared. They were then removed from the bar, and sent back to the condemned cells.

I can not say how much I dreaded my interview with them that day; for, although I had all along endeavored to prepare their minds for the worst result, and they had themselves never for a moment appeared to expect any other than this, I feared that the realization of their sad expectation would break them down. Hitherto there might have been some secret hope sustaining them. The convulsive clinging to life, so common to all of us, would now, perhaps, be more palpably exhibited.

Entering their cells, I found them, as I feared, stunned by the blow which had now fallen on them, and almost overpowered by mental and bodily exhaustion. A few remarks about the trial were at length made by them; and from that moment I never heard them refer to it again. There was no bitterness of spirit against the witnesses, no expression of hostility toward the soldiers, no equivocation in any explanation they gave. They solemnly denied many of the statements made against them; but nevertheless the broad fact remained, that they were guilty of an attempt to violently seize the vessel, and it was useless debating on minor considerations.

In the mean time, without their knowledge, petitions were prepared and forwarded to the judges, the governor, and executive council. In them were stated various mitigatory facts in their favor; and the meliorated character of the criminal code at home was also strongly urged. Every attention was paid to these addresses, following each other to the last moment. But all was in vain. The council sat, and determined that five of the men should be hanged on the following Tuesday. Whelan, who could have no previous knowledge of a plan to seize the vessel, together with Woolfe, was spared. The remaining four were to suffer. The painful office of communicating this final intelligence to these men was intrusted to me, and they listened to the announcement not without deep feeling, but still with composure.

It would be very painful for me to dwell on the closing scene. The unhappy and guilty men were attended by the zealous chaplain of the jail, whose earnest exhortations and instructions they most gratefully received. The light of truth shone clearly on the past, and they felt that their manifold lapses from the path of virtue had been the original cause of the complicated misery they had endured. They entreated forgiveness of all against whom they had offended, and in the last words to their friends were uttered grateful remembrances to Captain Maconochie, his family, and others. At the place of execution, they behaved with fortitude and a composure befitting the solemnity of the occasion. Having retired from attendance upon them in their last moments, I was startled from the painful stupor which succeeded in my own mind, by the loud and heavy bound of the drop as it fell, and told me that their spirits had gone to God who gave them.

Our main object in laying the foregoing narrative before the world in its present shape, is to impress those who may be tottering on the verge of crime with the danger of their situation—to show them that a course of error is a course of misery, ending in consequences the most afflicting.

It may be seen from the history of the unhappy men before us, that transportation is at the best equivalent to going into slavery—that the convict loses, for the time, his civil rights. Torn from his family, his home, and his country, he is placed at the disposal of the crown and its functionaries; can be put to any kind of labor, however repugnant to his feelings; dressed in the most degrading apparel; chained like a wild beast if refractory; and on the commission of any new offense while in this state of servitude, he is liable to fresh punishment by transportation to such penal settlements as Norfolk Island. It might almost be said that no man in his senses would voluntarily commit crimes which would expose him to the risk of so terrible an infliction as that of transportation even for the limited period of seven years. But, alas! men who have entered on a course of error, forgetful of every duty which they owe to themselves and society, can scarcely be said to be in possession of a sound mind; and they go on floundering from one degree of vice to another, till brought into the condition of transported and personally-enslaved convicts. Should the present narrative fall accidentally into the hands of individuals who are in danger of falling into a course of vice, we would hope that it will help to restrain them. The unfortunate men whose death has been recorded were once as they are; they went over the golden line of honor and duty—and behold the consequences; a short life of hardship, misery, and a violent and ignominious death.

IV.

M. de la Tude in the Bastile.

OF the numerous tales related of the incarceration of real or pretended criminals in the Bastile and other state-prisons of France during the principal part of last century, none are so remarkable or so affecting, none so much calculated to rouse feelings of indignation in the bosom of the philanthropist, as that told by M. de la Tude, in the published memoirs of his life. It appears that this gentleman, while no more than twenty-three years of age, and when residing and pursuing his studies in Paris, fell under the displeasure of Madame de Pompadour, a potent court favorite during the reign of Louis XV, and by her orders, enforced probably through the medium of a *lettre de cachet*, was seized, and, without form of trial or accusation, committed to the Bastile. This event took place on the 1st of May, 1749; and from that date commences the history of the sufferings and attempts to escape of this unfortunate and enterprising individual, whose memoirs are only paralleled by those of the equally unhappy Baron Trenck.

From the 1st of May till the beginning of September, De la Tude remained confined in the Bastile, when he was removed, for some unexplained reason, to the Castle of Vincennes. He had not been long in this gloomy fortress, till he put in execution a project for accomplishing his escape. Being indulged by the lieutenant-governor with the privilege of walking two hours a day in the garden of the castle, he bethought himself of taking advantage of this circumstance for his purpose. Two turnkeys usually attended him, one of whom waited in the garden and the other conducted him down stairs from his room. Having formed his project, he for several days together descended a little faster than the turnkey, who, as he always found him by the side of his companion in the garden, took no notice of this maneuver. Observing this, and taking a favorable opportunity, he tripped as fast as possible down the flight of steps, and shutting the bottom door of the staircase, advanced boldly to the garden-gate, where a sentinel was posted by way of security.

The vigilance of this man, as well as that of several others who were placed on the opposite side of the draw-bridge, he eluded, by pretending to inquire for a person who had just gone that way; but after having obtained his liberty in this artful manner, he was imprudent enough, through the advice of a friend, to surrender himself up again to the King, trusting that the artless confidence of an innocent man would not be abused. He was, nevertheless, reconducted to the Bastile, where he was closely confined for eighteen months in one of the most dismal dungeons of that prison. At the expiration of that term, he was taken from this horrid situation, and put into another room, with a prisoner named D'Alegre, who was likewise detained by Madame de Pompadour.

Both he and his companion had been long taught to expect with patience the disgrace of the marchioness; but with the unfortunate, days are as tedious as years, and it is no wonder that they should turn their thoughts toward regaining their liberty. This, however, appeared a romantic idea; for, besides the high walls of the Bastile, which were six feet thick, and four iron grates at each window, the prison was continually guarded by a number of sentinels, and the trenches which surrounded it were most commonly full of water. How, then, could two prisoners, confined in a narrow cell, and destitute of all human assistance, effect their escape?

M. de la Tude, who was fruitful in expedients, first informed himself, by means of an artful trick which he played while they were conducted back to the room after hearing mass, that the apartment in which they were confined had a double ceiling; and after mentioning what he had observed to his friend, told him that he had formed a plan for their enlargement, which could not fail of success. From his confidence upon this occasion, D'Alegre thought him disordered in his mind, and asked him, with a sneer, where they were to get the ropes and other implements necessary to such an undertaking.

"As for the ropes," said De la Tude, "give yourself no manner of trouble: in that trunk there are twelve dozen shirts, six dozen pair of silk stockings, twelve dozen pair of under-stockings, five dozen drawers, and as many dozen of napkins; now, by unraveling these, we shall have more than enough to make one thousand feet of rope."

"True," said the other: "but how shall we remove the iron bars from the window? for without instruments it is impossible to do any thing."

De la Tude told him that the hand was the instrument of all instruments, and that men, whose heads are capable of working, are never at a loss for resources; what though neither scissors, knives, nor any edged tools, are allowed us, have not we the iron hinges of our folding-table, which, with patience and skill, we can make answer the same purpose?

From this discourse D'Alegre began to entertain some hopes, and they now employed all their time and talents in the execution of this curious project. The first evening, by means of one of the hinges, they took up a tile from the floor, and after digging for six hours, found it was a double partition, as De la Tude had conjectured. They then carefully replaced the tile, and began to unravel some of the shirts, drawing them out thread by thread, and twisting them together, till they had formed a rope fifty-five feet long; this they made into a ladder, consisting of twenty-five rounds, made of the wood which was brought them for firing.

The next thing to be done was to remove the iron bars from the chimney, by which outlet they had resolved to escape; they accomplished it in about two months, and then returned them to their places, leaving them ready to be removed when they should be wanted. This appears to have been an exceedingly-troublesome operation, as they never descended from the work without bloody hands, and their bodies were so bruised in the chimney, that they could not renew their labor for an hour or two afterward. This toil over, they now set about making a wooden ladder of twenty feet long, which, as fast as it was finished, was hid with the other things between the two floors.

As the officers and turnkeys often entered the apartment in the day-time, without any previous notice, they were obliged not only to secrete their tools, but the smallest chips and rubbish that were made, the least appearance of which would have betrayed them. To answer this purpose the more effectually, they gave each of them a private name, and when any body was coming in, he who was next the door gave the cant term to the other, that he might conceal them as expeditiously as possible. When their ropes were all ready, their measure was four hundred feet; they had still to make two hundred steps for their ladders, which, when accomplished, they covered with the lining of their bed-gowns and under-waistcoats, to prevent their rustling against the walls as they descended.

These preparations cost them eighteen months' work, night and day, and they now waited for a dark, stormy night to favor their escape. At length, after a great number of difficulties, and many narrow escapes from being detected by the officers, the happy moment they had been so long expecting arrived, and De la Tude was the first to mount the chimney. Here he was almost smothered with the soot, and the blood streamed from his hands, elbows, and knees, down to his legs. After some time, however, he got to the top, and, by means of a string, drew up his companion, and all their implements, to the top of the building, from which they lowered their baggage, by fastening a rope to the chimney; and in this way they descended, both at once on the platform, serving as a counterpoise to each other.

Here they fastened their rope-ladder to a piece of cannon, and let themselves and their baggage down into the trench, an operation which was attended with the utmost difficulty; for out of 1,000 spectators who should have seen them by daylight, vibrating backward and forward in the air, not one of them, says M. de la Tude, but would have given us over for lost. They arrived, however, at length, safely in the trench, and felicitated themselves upon the success of this part of their enterprise; having been extremely apprehensive of detection, as the sentinel was all the time walking on the corridor, at not more than thirty feet distance.

From this place they proceeded to the wall which parted the trench of the Bastile from that of St. Anthony's Gate, where there was a ditch six feet wide, and deep enough to wet them to the armpits. When they had crossed this, they had yet to work their way through the stone-wall of the governor's garden, which was more than four feet thick: and all the time they were employed in this business, the major's round passed them with a great lantern every half hour, at about ten or twelve feet over their heads; during which times they were always obliged to retreat into the ditch, and to stand up to their chins in water, in order to avoid being seen.

Before midnight, by means of the iron bars which had been taken out of the chimney, they had displaced two or three wheelbarrows of stones, and in a few hours more a breach was made in the wall sufficiently large for them to get through it. They were now in the trench of St. Anthony's Gate, and thought themselves entirely out of danger, when they both suddenly fell into an aqueduct, with at least six feet of water over their heads. In this dangerous situation, De la Tude caught hold of the bank, and plunging his arm into the water, drew his companion to him by the hair of his head, and thus happily escaped the danger which threatened them.

"Here," says M. de la Tude, "ended the horrors of that dreadful night; and here we embraced each other, and fell upon our knees to thank God for the great mercy he had bestowed upon us, in thus restoring us to liberty." They now mounted the slope of the ditch as it struck four o'clock, and after calling upon a friend who was not at home, flew for refuge to the abbey of St. Germain-des-prez.

Soon after this almost miraculous escape, they both set out, by different routes, for Brussels, agreeing to meet at the same inn; but when De la Tude, who had to encounter with a number of perils on his journey, arrived at the place appointed, he found that his friend had been discovered, and conducted back to prison. Shocked at this intelligence, he set out immediately for Amsterdam, where he had not been long before he was demanded of the states by the French embassador, in the name of the king, and carried back to his old quarters in the Bastile, fettered hands and feet, and only allowed a bed of straw, without covering, to repose on.

In this wretched situation he remained forty months, and during this confinement was one day indulged with the barbarous privilege of being permitted to see his friend D'Alegre, whom he found raving mad in the hospital for lunatics at Charenton. The poor creature had no remembrance of him, and made him no other answer, when he reminded him of their escape from the Bastile, than by telling him that he was God.

Some time after this shocking interview, in the year 1764, and when he had been fifteen years in confinement, he observed from the tower of the Bastile a large piece of paper at the window of a chamber, in St. Anthony's street, on which was written these words: "Yesterday died the Marchioness of Pompadour." This had been placed there by some young ladies, who were acquainted with his story, and he was now persuaded that he should be released from his confinement; but M. de Sartine had expressly forbidden all the officers of the Bastile to inform the prisoners of her decease. When De la Tude, therefore, wrote to him, entreating his deliverance, he came to the prison, and insisted upon knowing his author.

His behavior upon this occasion proving offensive to M. de Sartine, he was removed from prison to the governor's house, loaded with chains from head to foot, and afterward sent to the Castle of Vincennes, to be confined in the black-hole. Here, however, the lieutenant-governor, being a humane man, suffered him to walk two hours a day in the fosse, guarded by two fusileers and a sergeant, who stood at the gate with another sentinel. While he was walking here one evening, it happened to be a prodigious thick fog, which he thought was a circumstance by no means to be neglected; he therefore struck down the two sentinels with his elbows, and pushing boldly past the others, flew as fast as his legs would carry him. A great cry of "Stop thief!" ensued, in which he joined, and by that means made his escape to Paris.

Although the author of De la Tude's misfortunes was now no more, although her death was little regretted by the king, and rejoiced over by the nation, still, strange to say, the persecution of our hero was not remitted. His escape was no sooner made known than a number of spies and setters were sent out upon the search after him, and 1000 crowns were offered as a reward for discovering him. Finding, therefore, that it would be impossible to elude the vigilance of scouts and informers, he wrote a letter to the minister of the war department, acquainting him that he would not fail to be with him on such a day, and begging he would have the goodness to suspend the orders for arresting him till he had been indulged with a moment's audience. Going, according to his promise, to the apartment of the minister, he was immediately secured, without being permitted to utter a syllable, and put into one of the most gloomy dungeons of the Castle of Vincennes.

All hope of relief now died within the bosom

of this victim of a cruel and arbitrary government. He sank into despair. He looked forward to death as the only event calculated to bring a termination of his sufferings. Yet death came not, and a gleam of hope now and then cheered him to sustain the mortal coil. Thus, for an additional period of twenty years, did he endure the horrors of confinement in the vaults of Vincennes and the Bicetre. At length, Cardinal de Rohan, a minister of Louis XVI, discovered him in the bottom of a dungeon in the last-mentioned Parisian prison, and being moved with his extreme wretchedness, promised him his liberty, provided he could give proper security for his good behavior. The last kind office was undertaken by a charitable lady of the name of Le Gros, who, on being accidentally informed of his misfortunes, resolved to dedicate her whole time and attention toward procuring his enlargement. The difficulties she had to encounter, together with the narrowness of her own circumstances, rendered the accomplishment of this project almost impossible; but, by incessant and persevering diligence, she at last obtained the object of her wishes; and, after having set him free from all restraints, helped to support him by the small earnings of her own and her husband's industry.

His joyful liberation took place in 1784, having altogether been confined for about thirty-five years. He entered prison a gay, light-hearted young man of three-and-twenty; and when restored to the world, it was at the mature age of fifty-eight; but the sufferings he had endured had broken his constitution and blighted his prospects, and he now had all the appearance of a man in the extreme of old age and decrepitude. Such is the story of the unfortunate M. de la Tude, which forms another testimony of that terrific species of oppression which has been for ages perpetrated by the continental powers of Europe, and an exemption from which is one of the proudest boasts of this land of liberty and intelligence.

V.

Shipwreck of the Medusa.

THE colony of Senegal, on the western coast of Africa, was captured from the French by the English in the year 1809, but was ceded to its former masters at the peace of 1815. As soon after this event as the state of affairs would admit, the French Government fitted out an expedition, consisting of the newly-appointed governor, M. Schmaltz, and other functionaries, civil and military, to take possession of and colonize the restored settlement. The squadron fitted out on this occasion consisted of four vessels—the Medusa, a frigate of forty-four guns, the Loire store-ship, and the Argus brig, and the Echo corvette—the whole carrying upward of six hundred individuals, of whom two hundred and fifty were soldiers. On board the Medusa, the chief vessel in the squadron, commanded by Captain Lachaumareys, were the governor and other principal functionaries, along with a considerable number of the soldiers, and a number of women and children: the entire number of individuals on board being four hundred.

Among this large body on board the Medusa, was a family to whom we shall have to advert more particularly in the sequel. It consisted of M. Picard, his wife, two grown-up daughters by a previous marriage, both accomplished young women, and several younger children, with a girl, their cousin—the whole nine in number, the youngest of whom was an infant at the breast. M. Picard was by profession an attorney; he had been resident in Senegal previous to 1809, and now, on the resumption of French authority, he was returning, for the purpose of occupying a situation connected with the government of the colony. Provided with a small cabin on the main-deck of the Medusa, and with some valuable goods on board, the family formed a happy group, full of bright anticipations of the future, and having every reason to expect a prosperous voyage to the shores of Africa.

Setting out from the port of Rochefort, in the west of France, all the vessels of the expedition were under sail on the 17th of June, 1816, and remained for several days together; at length, from the changeableness of the wind, they were separated, each pursuing its course alone, and the Echo only keeping in sight of the Medusa, as if to guide it on its route. Some fine weather which ensued served to confirm hopes of happiness in the Picards, and on the 28th of June they felt interested in contemplating the lofty peak of Teneriffe, which rose on the horizon. The satisfaction which the passengers now generally felt and expressed, was doomed to be of no long duration. Captain Lachaumareys was apparently so unfit for the trust reposed in him, not only from his ignorance of seamanship and general management, but as regards temper and humanity, that it is impossible to understand how he should have obtained the command of the vessel. One day, when the frigate was going before a fine breeze, at the rate of nine knots an hour, a sailor-boy fell overboard. Several persons were at the moment standing on the poop, witnessing the gambols of seals, but no effective measures were taken to save the poor boy's life. For some time the unfortunate lad kept hold of a rope which he had caught in his fall, but the vessel was making such way, that he soon lost his hold. A sailor now seized him by the arm, but for the same reason he was forced to let go. To communicate this accident to the Echo, a gun was ordered to be fired, but not a single piece was found charged; it required also a long time to lower the sails, when the more simple method would have been to put the helm about. It was at last thought of letting down a six-oared boat, into which, in the confusion and hurry, only three men entered. Every effort was unavailing; the boat returned, after rowing a short distance, without having even found the cork buoy which had been thrown overboard when the accident was first announced. The same want of foresight, promptitude, and regularity on the part of the captain and lieutenants, afterward led to greater disasters.

On the first of July the Medusa entered the tropics, the seamen on the occasion performing the ceremonies which ordinarily take place in crossing the equinoctial line. In the midst of this fatal merriment the vessel was surrounded by dangers, of which those in command were insensible. For some days the captain had abandoned the entire guidance of the frigate to a person named Richfort, who pretended to a great knowledge of this part of the Atlantic. In vain the passengers remonstrated on this imprudent confidence in a stranger; the commander obstinately persisted in allowing him to steer the vessel in whatever direction he thought proper. Richfort appears to have been a fool as well as an impostor, for, while risking the lives of others, he also risked his own; and in the face of multiplying dangers, he continued his perilous course. In thus abandoning the ship to Richfort's direction, the captain transgressed the written instructions, which enjoined him to steer due west for sixty-six miles after making Cape Blanco, in order to clear the sand-bank of Arguin; instead of which, after proceeding about half that distance, the vessel's head was set to the southward. During the night which followed, the Echo hung out lanterns to warn her consort of her danger; but they were unavailing; the Medusa was kept on her course, and in the morning the Echo was out of sight.

On the morning of this memorable day, July 2d, the sea assumed a sandy color, and the more reflective passengers and naval officers became seriously alarmed; strong representations of the danger the frigate was in were again made to the captain, but with no better success than formerly. Such was his infatuation, that the vessel was at the time actually standing directly for the low, sandy shore which it was his duty to avoid. At noon, the officer of the watch asserted that the vessel was getting near the edge of the bank; but no change was permitted in her course. This obstinacy caused a mournful presentiment among the passengers. A species of stupor, approaching to despair, overspread all their spirits. M. Picard, seated in the midst of his family, gave all up for lost; yet he durst not remonstrate; for already one of the officers had been put under arrest for daring to condemn the fallacy of Richfort's proceedings. In the mean while, the wind, blowing with violence, impelled the vessel nearer the danger which menaced it. Between two and three o'clock in the afternoon, the lead showed that the frigate was in eighteen fathoms water. This startling intelligence for the first time roused the captain. He gave orders to change the ship's course, by coming closer to the wind. It was too late. The lead was again cast, and showed only six fathoms. The captain, now thoroughly terrified, gave orders to haul the wind as close as possible. It was useless. The frigate had touched the sandy bottom, and almost immediately struck with a strong concussion. This disastrous event took place at a quarter past three o'clock, afternoon, in 19 degrees 30 minutes north latitude, and 19 degrees 45 minutes west longitude. The vessel now lay at the mercy of the winds and waves, in less than four fathoms, and this was during high water; when the tide ebbed, the depth would become less.

When the concussion of striking was felt through the vessel, terror and consternation were immediately depicted on every countenance. The crew stood motionless; the passengers gave themselves up to despair. In the midst of this general panic, cries of vengeance were heard against the principal author of the misfortune, the greater number wishing to throw him overboard; but some, more generously disposed, endeavored to calm the excitement, and pointed out how much more fitting it would be to adopt means of safety, than spend time in vengeful and useless criminations. To ease the pressure on the ship, the sails were hastily lowered, the top-gallant mast and topmast taken down, and some other means tried to get her off the bank. They were all, however, only half measures; they did little good; and when night came on, the efforts were suspended.

At dawn of day, July 3, new attempts were made to move the vessel. Anchors were carried, with vast trouble, in boats, to a distance, and being dropped into the sea, cables from them were pulled at the capstan; but the anchors presented no sufficient resistance, and the effort proved fruitless. Masts, yards, and booms were now thrown overboard, and a number of casks of water emptied; still the frigate continued fixed. Many wished the cannon also to be tossed overboard; but this the captain refused to do, on the plea that they belonged to the king! There was a large stock of provisions in barrels, which the frigate was carrying to Senegal; and these barrels the governor, with equal pertinacity, would not allow to be thrown overboard, on the ground that the colony was in want of provisions.

What was now to be done? All was clamor and confusion; in the midst of which the poor Picards shrunk into their little cabin, consumed with grief and apprehensions of a miserable death on the wreck. The superior officers felt the necessity for providing means of escape, in case all attempts to get off the ship should prove unavailing. A council was called. The lives of four hundred persons were to be saved; and there were only six boats, into which it would have been impossible to stow so many. In this dilemma M. Schmaltz, the governor, proposed to save a large portion of the passengers on a raft, of which he exhibited a plan. The raft was to be capable of carrying two hundred men, with provisions for all. The boats were to tow the raft, to which their crews were to come at meal times for their rations. The whole crew were to land in a body on the sandy shore of the desert, and provided with arms and ammunition, which were to be taken from the vessel, were to form a caravan, and proceed to the town of Saint Louis in Senegal. All this, as events afterward proved, was practicable; for the land, though not visible from the frigate, was only about forty-five miles distant; yet the plan, in the manner proposed, was not carried into execution.

Next day, the 4th, there was a glimpse of hope. At the hour of high water, the frigate, being considerably lightened, was found nearly afloat; and it is believed that if the guns had now been thrown overboard, the Medusa would have been saved. Even a tow-line would have brought her round; but it was not thought of. When the tide ebbed, the unfortunate vessel again sank firmly into the sand, and the hope of getting her off was abandoned.

A raft was now begun to be constructed by means of masts, spars, planks, and cordage, which were thrown into the sea for the purpose: the whole being lashed together, formed a kind of platform, of about a foot and a half in thickness, buoyed up by empty barrels placed beneath the corners. Its length was sixty-five feet; its breadth about twenty. Each end terminated in a point; and these ends were very fragile. The only safe part was in the center; but even that was sometimes under water.

Night came on while the raft was constructing, and the work ceased till next day. It was a night productive of dire anticipations. The sky became cloudy, the wind blew strong, and came from the sea, causing a great swell of the waves. The vessel now began to heel with violence, and it was every moment expected to see her planks start. This catastrophe at length, to a certain extent, ensued. The lower timbers bulged; the keel broke in two; the rudder was also unshipped, but still holding to the stern by the chains, and it was dashed by the waves against the vessel. From this cause the captain's cabin was beat in, and the water entered in an alarming manner. In this emergency the captain could preserve neither order nor discipline; and indeed his incompetency and inhumanity rendered disobedience a duty. The general feeling throughout the ship was, every man for himself—a scramble for life. Toward midnight a large part of the crew and more active passengers were preparing to leave the vessel secretly in the boats. This selfish and perfidious conduct was, however, checked by the soldiers, who firmly declared they would fire upon whosoever attempted to quit the frigate clandestinely. The threats of these brave men alarmed the governor, who had already formed a scheme for himself. He therefore judged it proper to assemble a council, at which he endeavored to allay the general distrust. He solemnly swore that, according to the plan which would be adopted, the boats would not abandon the raft, but would tow it to the shore of the desert, where all would travel in a body to Senegal.

It was agreed that the embarkation should take place at six o'clock in the morning.

The treacherous promises of the governor, supported by Captain Lachaumareys, served to allay the apprehensions of the more timid passengers, including the unfortunate Picards. A number began to secure their more valuable articles about their persons, while part of the crew and soldiers broke into the cabins and store-rooms, appropriating the articles which struck their fancy, and drinking the wine and spirits, till they fell exhausted and insensible. Amidst an uproar of singing, shouting, groans, and imprecations, day broke, and all prepared to depart. A list had been made out, assigning each his proper place in the boats and raft; but this arrangement was now disregarded, and every one pursued the plan he deemed best for his own preservation. Few were inclined to go upon the raft, which heaved uneasily on the turbid waves. To compel obedience, an officer, armed with two pistols, stood by the bulwarks, and, with furious language, threatened to fire on whoever would not go upon it; and thus a miscellaneous crowd of persons were forced to place themselves on this floating tomb. To accommodate so large a number, and keep the raft from sinking, several barrels of provisions which had been placed on it the day before, were thrown into the sea. The only provisions left for the support of the large number on it, consisted of a bag of twenty-five pounds of soaked biscuit, which, having been tossed from the vessel, fell into the sea, and was with difficulty recovered. There were also several casks of wine and water. On the raft there were no charts, sails, oars, nor compass, every thing proper being forgot in the confusion. In all, there were upon the raft one hundred and fifty persons, twenty-nine of whom were sailors; there was one woman, and all the remainder were soldiers. These latter were not allowed to take their muskets; but they retained their swords; besides which the officers saved their fowling-pieces and pistols.

The command of the raft had been assigned to M. Coudin, midshipman. This was not the least of the cruelties perpetrated by Lachaumareys. Coudin had received a severe bruise on his leg before the expedition had sailed from Rochefort, and he was now suffering so severely, that he was incapable of moving. Determined, however, not to flinch from a post which had been assigned to him on the ground of his being the senior midshipman in the vessel, he refused to allow one of his companions to take his place, and accordingly proceeded to the raft. The exertion, however, was almost too much for him:

the pain of his wound, aggravated by the heaving of the raft, and the salt water which dashed upon him, rendered him nearly insensible. Information of his condition being communicated to the captain, a promise was made that he should be relieved, and taken into one of the boats; but this, like all other promises, was not fulfilled. The unfortunate Coudin was left on the raft.

The boats were in the mean while receiving their lading. The barge, which was commanded by a lieutenant, took the governor, with his wife, daughters, and friends, making in all thirty-five persons; it also received several trunks, and a stock of choice provisions and liquors. The captain's boat received twenty-eight persons, most of whom were sailors, good rowers. The shallop, commanded by M. Espiau, ensign of the frigate, took forty-two passengers; the long-boat, eighty-three; the pinnace, thirty; and the yawl, the smallest of all the boats, fifteen. Such was the final arrangement; but before it was effected, there was much struggling and fighting, some gaining a place only by threatening the lives of the commanders. The boats were, to all appearance, filled, and putting to sea without any one casting a thought on the Picards, who, less able to enforce attention than others, were about to be abandoned on the wreck. A place had been promised them in the pinnace; but that boat had put off, and its commander would not return to take the helpless family. Roused by the horrors of his situation, M. Picard lifted a musket from the deck, and hailing the yawl, which was near at hand, declared that he would shoot every one on board, if they would not carry himself and family to the pinnace. The sailors, murmuring, assented, and, by this means, the Picards reached the pinnace, on which they were, with affected politeness, taken on board.

When all had left the vessel who would go, there remained seventeen persons, some of whom were intoxicated, and incapable of providing for their safety.

For some time after quitting the wreck, five of the boats united in a line, towing the raft behind them by a rope; and, as the wind was fortunately favorable, there can be no reasonable doubt that, had they continued to pull, the whole fleet would have reached the shore in from thirty to forty hours. To the everlasting disgrace of the French navy, the commanders of the boats changed altogether the plan to which they had engaged themselves to adhere, and, one and all dropping the tow-line, left their brethren on the raft to their fate. The immediate cause of this most dishonest and inhuman procedure, was an appeal made to them by M. Espiau in the yawl. This gentleman, the only officer who seemed to pity the unfortunates on the Medusa, was the last to quit the wreck, and, in compassion for those left behind, had taken more on board than his boat could well contain. Hastening after the boats in advance, he earnestly besought their commanders to relieve him of part of his crew; but all refused to assist him. In the desperation to which they were put, some of the crew in the yawl proposed swimming after the boats, and, if possible, working on the compassion of their commanders. One sailor put this proposal in practice. Plunging into the sea, he swam toward one of the leading and least-burdened boats; but on reaching, and endeavoring to climb into it, the officer in command pushed him back, and, drawing his sword, threatened to cut off his hands, if he did not let go. The poor wretch, being thus compelled to desist from the attempt, next tried the pinnace; but here he met with no better success. Some of the party on board entreated the officer, M. Laperere, to receive him; but he refused the request, and the man was left to his fate. M. Laperere, it appears, got rid of the unhappy applicant for admission not only by refusing to take him in, but by hastening away from him. To put the boat beyond his reach, he caused the tug-line to be dropped, and so made off with all speed from the spot. The commanders of the other boats imitated this execrable example. Wishing to get beyond the reach of the unfortunate being who was floundering amid the waves, and of the yawl from which he had precipitated himself, all dropped the towing rope, and each boat made off precipitately from the dismal scene.

The raft was thus abandoned by all who had sworn to assist in towing it to land. A hundred and fifty fellow-creatures were unscrupulously left in the midst of the ocean—to perish. We question if the whole annals of shipwreck present a case of greater iniquity than this; it must forever stand unparalleled for heartless inhumanity. At first, when the unfortunate individuals on the raft saw the boats break loose from the line they had been pursuing, they imagined that the towing-rope had snapped, and they raised their voices to make their companions aware of the fact. "The rope is broke—the rope is broke!" burst from them with increasing intensity of agony. To their surprise, no attention was paid to their cries, and for a moment they imagined that some new tactics advantageous to all were to be practiced. The French, with characteristic vivacity, raised the national flag on the raft, and united in the cry of *Vive le Roi;* trusting, perhaps, to awaken a sympathizing feeling in the bosoms of their retreating companions, and so bring them back to a sense of humanity and duty. If such were their meaning it signally failed. The commanders of the boats bombastically returned the cry; and Captain Lachaumareys, assuming a martial attitude, politely waved his hat in the air, as a parting testimony of regard. The wretched crew of the raft now too surely saw what was to be their doom. They perceived that, after being treacherously decoyed upon their floating prison, they were left with indifference to die of hunger, or to be drowned in the sea. Wild cries forthwith rent the air—cries of heart-rending despair—cries for justice and compassion—cries also of vengeance and contempt. All were alike unheeded. The boats hastened on their course.

From the narrative of Mademoiselle Picard, we learn that the cries on this melancholy occasion would have melted any but the most obdurate of hearts. "Alas! why do you leave us—why do you leave us?" was wafted to their ears. "I felt," says she, "my heart bursting with emotion. I believed that the waves would speedily overwhelm all these forlorn wretches, and I could not suppress the tears which burst from my eyes. My father, exasperated to excess, and bursting with indignation at seeing so much cowardice and inhumanity among the officers of the boats, began to express his regret for not having allowed himself to be placed on the raft along with the sufferers. 'At least,' he observed, 'we would have died with the brave, or we would have returned to the wreck of the Medusa, and been spared the disgrace of having saved ourselves with cowards.'"

Such is the account given by an eye-witness of this scene of disaster and disgrace. The history of the shipwreck now divides itself into three parts—the account of the boats and their crews, of the raft, and of the wreck of the Medusa. In the first place, we shall follow the account of

THE BOATS AND THEIR CREWS.

Among the six boats which left the Medusa, two only had a sufficient stock of provisions, and these made off with all dispatch from their companions in misfortune. It had been arranged that they all should make for the nearest land; but these two boats taking the lead, proceeded, by orders of the governor, in the direction of Senegal. This unforeseen change of course surprised and alarmed the crews of the other boats; for none of them had provisions for more than one or two days; and to encounter a voyage of longer duration, was altogether hopeless. Undecided, however, they continued to move on in the wake of the boats which were in advance. The provisions on board the pinnace consisted of a barrel of biscuit and a tierce of water; but the biscuit had been soaked in the sea, and was little better than salted paste. A small portion of this nauseous biscuit, with a glass of water, formed the daily portion of each on board. The other boats were in some degree better provided, for they had a little wine.

During the night of the 5th, the day on which the raft had been abandoned, the boats lay to; and on the morning of the 6th, they were again under weigh. The pinnace, according to the account of Mademoiselle Picard, which we shall principally follow, now began to leak fearfully, and the holes in it were stuffed with oakum, which an old sailor had had the precaution to provide. At noon the heat was intense; hot winds blew from the desert, and many thought their last moments were come. In the afternoon a distribution of a little water and biscuit was made; and hope revived of reaching Senegal on the morrow. As evening came on, the sky changed, and then a tempest of wind, thunder, and lightning, which threatened to overwhelm the boat. Again the leaks broke out, and there were stuffed into them old clothes, sleeves of shirts, shawls, any thing that came to hand; and for six hours, every one momentarily anticipated death. Toward midnight the atmosphere tranquilized, and once more a gleam of hope passed through the minds of the forlorn crew.

In the morning of the 7th, the shores of the desert were again seen, and a number of the sailors murmuring, and wishing to land, the boat was directed toward the coast. On approaching the land the hearts of the most courageous failed, on seeing the breakers which it would be necessary to pass through to the shore. Again the pinnace put to sea, and another day was spent under a burning sun, and in a state of intolerable thirst. The freshness of the night-wind revived the spirits of all on board; but all were becoming excessively weak for want of nourishment; and on the morrow it was determined to attempt a landing. Early in the morning of the 8th, accordingly, after a scanty meal of a mouthful of biscuit and a few drops of water, the boats once more put in-shore, and being cheered with observing a group of persons from two of the boats already landed, they pushed toward a landing-place. It was a desperate struggle. The breakers overwhelmed the boat, and only after weltering in the waves, and being all thoroughly drenched, they got to dry land.

The crews of all the boats were here united, except those on board the governor's and captain's boats, both of which pursued their way to Senegal, which they reached next day, the 9th; that is, four days after quitting the wreck. As soon as they arrived a council was held, to concert measures necessary to be taken on the occasion. It will scarcely be credited that, notwithstanding this apparent activity, nothing was done for some days. At length a vessel, the Argus, was dispatched in quest of the boats and of the raft, and what it achieved will appear in the sequel.

Returning, in the mean while, to the large party who had effected a landing from the boats—numbering about a hundred and seventy persons—we find them in a dismal plight, on the shore of a barren desert, without food or water, and many nearly naked. All, it appears, had got ashore without material injury, except one person, who had his legs broken, while landing, by a concussion from one of the boats. He was laid on the shore of the desert, and left to his fate, which would most likely be destruction by wild animals on the ensuing night. In this incident alone is seen an inhumanity for which there is no valid excuse.

Leaving the poor wretch on the sands, the party proceeded to consult on measures for proceeding to Senegal; but that involved a march of several days, and great fatigues and dangers, not to be contemplated without dismay. As remaining on the spot, however, would have been worse than madness, all prepared to set out. What ensued will be best told in the unaffected words of Mademoiselle Picard:

"Shortly after landing, or about seven in the morning, a party was formed to penetrate into the interior, for the purpose of finding some fresh water. Some accordingly was found at a little distance from the sea, by digging among the sand. Every one instantly flocked round the little wells, which furnished enough to quench our thirst. This water was found to be delicious, although it had a sulphurous taste; its color was that of whey. As all our clothes were wet, and in tatters, and as we had nothing to change them, some generous officers offered theirs. My step-mother, my cousin, and my sister, were dressed in them; for myself, I preferred keeping my own. We remained nearly an hour beside our beneficent fountain, then took the route for Senegal; that is, a southerly direction, for we did not know exactly where that country lay. It was agreed that the females and children should walk before the caravan, as the general body was called, that they might not be left behind. The sailors voluntarily carried the youngest on their shoulders, and every one took the route along the coast. Notwithstanding it was nearly seven o'clock, the sand was quite burning, and we suffered severely, walking without shoes, having lost them while landing. As soon as we arrived on the shore, we went to walk on the wet sand, to cool us a little. Thus we traveled during the night, without encountering any thing but shells, which wounded our feet.

"Early on the morning of the 9th we saw an antelope on a little hill; it instantly disappeared, before any of the party had time to shoot it. The desert seemed to our view one immense plain of sand, on which not a blade of verdure was seen. However, we still found water by digging in the sand. In the forenoon, two officers of marine complained that our family incommoded the progress of the general body. It is true that the females and the children could not walk so quickly as the men. We walked as fast as it was possible for us; nevertheless, we often fell behind, which obliged them to halt till we came up. These officers, joined with other individuals, considered among themselves whether they would wait for us, or abandon us in the desert. I will be bold to say, however, that but few were of the latter opinion. My father being informed of what was plotting against us, stepped up to the chiefs of the conspiracy, and reproached them in the bitterest terms for their selfishness and cruelty. The dispute waxed warm. Those who were desirous of leaving us drew their swords, and my father put his hand upon a poniard, with which he had provided himself on quitting the frigate. At this scene we threw ourselves between them, conjuring him rather to remain in the desert with his family, than to seek the assistance of those who were perhaps less humane than the Moors themselves. Several people took our part, particularly M. Begnere, captain of infantry, who allayed the dispute by saying to his soldiers, 'My friends, you are Frenchmen, and I have the honor to be your commander; let us never abandon an unfortunate family in the desert, so long as we are able to be of use to them.' This brief but energetic speech caused those to blush who wished to quit us. All then joined with the old captain, saying they would not leave us, on condition that we would walk a little quicker. M. Begnere and his soldiers replied, they did not wish to impose conditions on those to whom they were desirous of doing a favor; and the unfortunate family of Picard were again on the road with the whole caravan.

"About noon, hunger was felt so powerfully among us, that it was agreed upon to go to the small hills of sand which were near the coast, to see if any herbs could be found fit for eating: nothing, however, was procured but poisonous plants, among which were various kinds of euphorbium. Convolvuli of a bright green carpeted the downs; but, on tasting their leaves, we found them as bitter as gall. The party rested in this place, while several officers went farther into the interior. They returned in about an hour, loaded with wild purslain, which they distributed to each of us. Every one instantly devoured his bunch of herbage, without leaving the smallest branch; but as our hunger was far from being satisfied with this small allowance, the soldiers and sailors betook themselves to look for more. They soon brought a sufficient quantity, which was equally distributed, and devoured upon the spot, so delicious had hunger made that food to us. For myself, I declare I never ate any thing with so much appetite in all my life. Water was also found in this place, but it was of a nauseous taste. After this truly frugal repast we continued our route. The heat was insupportable in the last degree. The sands on which we trod were burning; nevertheless, several of us walked on these scorching coals without shoes; and the females had nothing but their hair for a cap. When we reached the sea-shore, we all ran and lay down among the surf. After remaining there some time, we took our route along the wet beach. On our journey we met with several large crabs, which were of considerable service to us. Every now and then we endeavored to slake our thirst by sucking their crooked claws. About nine at night we halted between two pretty high sand-hills. After a short talk concerning our misfortunes, all seemed desirous of passing the night in this place, notwithstanding we heard on every side the roaring of leopards. Our situation had been thus perilous during the night; nevertheless, at break of day, we had the satisfaction of finding none missing."

At sunrise next morning the party resumed its march, holding a little toward the east, in the hope of finding water. In this they were disappointed; but were gratified in observing that the country was less arid, and possessed a species of vegetation. Some of the travelers having pushed forward to make observations, "they returned and told us they had seen two Arab tents upon a slightly-rising ground. We instantly directed our steps thither. We had to pass great downs of sand, very slippery, and arrived in a large plain, streaked here and there with verdure; but the turf was so hard and piercing, that we could scarcely walk over it without wounding our feet. Our presence in these frightful solitudes put to flight three or four Moorish shepherds, who herded a small flock of sheep and goats in an oasis. At last we arrived at the tents after which we were searching, and found in them three Mooresses and two little children, who did not seem in the least frightened by our visit. A negro servant, belonging to one of the officers, interpreted between us and the women, who, when they had heard of our misfortunes, offered us millet and water for payment. We bought a little of that grain at the rate of three francs a handful: the water was got for three francs a glass; it was very good, and none grudged the money it cost. As a glass of water, with a handful of millet, was but a poor dinner for famished people, my father bought two kids, for which twenty piasters were charged. We immediately killed them, and the Moorish women boiled them for us in a large kettle."

Resuming their march, their party fell in with several friendly Moors or Arabs, who conducted them to their encampment. "We found a Moor in the camp who had previously known my father in Senegal, and who spoke a little French. We were all struck with astonishment at the unexpected meeting. My father recollected having employed long ago a young goldsmith at Senegal, and discovering the Moor Amet to be the same person, shook him by the hand. After that good fellow had been made acquainted with our shipwreck, and to what extremities our unfortunate family had been reduced, he could not refrain from tears. Amet was not satisfied with deploring our hard fate; he was desirous of proving that he was generous and humane, and instantly distributed among us a large quantity of milk and water, free of any charge. He also raised for our family a large tent of the skins of camels, cattle, and sheep; because his religion would not allow him to lodge under the same roof with Christians."

Next day the band of wayfarers, assisted by asses which they had hired from the Moors, regained the sea-shore, still pursuing the route for Senegal; and they had the satisfaction of perceiving a ship out at sea, to which they made signals. "The vessel having approached sufficiently near to the coast, the Moors who were with us threw themselves into the sea, and swam to it. In about half an hour we saw these friendly assistants returning, pushing before them three small barrels. Arrived on shore, one of them gave a letter to the leader of our party from the commander of the ship, which was the Argus, a vessel sent to seek after the raft, and to give us provisions. This letter announced a small barrel of biscuit, a tierce of wine, a half tierce of brandy, and a cheese. O, fortunate circumstance! We were very desirous of testifying our gratitude to the generous commander of the brig, but he instantly set out and left us. We staved the barrels which held our small stock of provisions, and made a distribution. Each of us had a biscuit, about a glass of wine, a half glass of brandy, and a small morsel of cheese. To describe our joy while taking this repast would be impossible. Exposed to the fierce rays of a vertical sun, exhausted by a long train of suffering, deprived for a long time of the use of any kind of spiritous liquors, when our portions of water, wine, and brandy mingled in our stomachs, we became like insane people. Life, which had lately been a great burden, now became precious to us. Foreheads, lowering and sulky, began to unwrinkle; enemies became most brotherly; the avaricious endeavored to forget their selfishness and cupidity; the children smiled for the first time since our shipwreck; in a word, every one seemed to revive from a state of melancholy and dejection.

"About six in the evening, my father finding himself extremely fatigued, wished to rest himself. We allowed the caravan to move on, while my step-mother and myself remained near him, and the rest of the family followed with their asses. We all three soon fell asleep. When we awoke, we were astonished at not seeing our companions. The sun was sinking in the west. We saw several Moors approaching us, mounted on camels; and my father reproached himself for having slept so long. Their appearance gave us great uneasiness, and we wished much to escape from them, but my step-mother and myself fell quite exhausted. The Moors, with long beards, having come quite close to us, one of them alighted, and addressed us in the following words: 'Be comforted, ladies; under the costume of an Arab, you see an Englishman who is desirous of serving you. Having heard at Senegal that Frenchmen were thrown ashore on these deserts, I thought my presence might be of some service to them, as I was acquainted with several of the princes of this arid country.' These noble words from the mouth of a man we had at first taken to be a Moor, instantly calmed our fears. Recovering from our fright, we rose and expressed to the philanthropic Englishman the gratitude we felt. Mr. Carnet, the name of the generous Briton, told us that our caravan, which he had met, waited for us at about the distance of two leagues. He then gave us some biscuit, which we ate; and we then set off together to join our companions. Mr. Carnet wished us to mount his camels, but my step-mother and myself, being unable to persuade ourselves we could sit securely on their hairy haunches, continued to walk on the moist sand; while my father, Mr. Carnet, and the Moors who accompanied him, proceeded on the camels. We soon reached a little river, of which we wished to drink, but found it as bitter as the sea. Mr. Carnet desired us to have patience, and we should find some at the place where our caravan waited. We forded that river knee-deep. At last, having walked about an hour, we rejoined our companions, who had found several wells of fresh water. It was resolved to pass the night in this place, which seemed less arid than any we saw near us. The soldiers being requested to go and seek wood to light a fire, for the purpose of frightening the ferocious beasts which were heard roaring around us, refused; but Mr. Carnet assured us that the Moors who were with him knew well how to keep all such intruders from our camp."

The succeeding night passed over without any unpleasant event, and the party were again on the march along the shore at four in the morning. All were hungry, and Mr. Carnet left them to procure some provisions. "At noon, the sun's heat became so violent, that even the

Moors themselves endured it with difficulty. We then determined on finding some shade behind the high mounds of sand which appeared in the interior; but how were we to reach them? The sands could not be hotter. We had been obliged to leave our asses on the shore; for they would neither advance nor recede. The greater part of us had neither shoes nor hats; notwithstanding, we were obliged to go forward almost a long league to find a little shade. Whether from want of air, or the heat of the ground on which we seated ourselves, we were nearly suffocated. I thought my last moments were come. Already my eyes saw nothing but a dark cloud, when a person of the name of Borner, who was to have been a smith at Senegal, gave me a boot containing some muddy water, which he had had the precaution to keep. I seized the elastic vase, and hastened to swallow the liquid in large draughts. One of my companions, equally tormented with thirst, envious of the pleasure I seemed to feel, and which I felt effectually, drew the foot from the boot, and seized it in his turn; but it availed him nothing. The water which remained was so disgusting that he could not drink it, and spilt it on the ground. Captain Begnere, who was present, judging, by the water that fell, how loathsome that must have been which I had drank, offered me some crumbs of biscuit, which he had kept most carefully in his pocket. I chewed that mixture of bread, dust, and tobacco; but I could not swallow it, and gave it all masticated to one of my younger brothers, who had fallen from inanition.

"We were on the point of quitting this furnace, when we saw our English friend approaching, who brought us provisions. At this sight I felt my strength revive, and ceased to desire death, which I had before called on to release me from my sufferings. Several Moors accompanied Mr. Carnet, and every one was loaded. On their arrival we had water, with rice and dried fish in abundance. Every one drank his allowance of water; but had not ability to eat, although the rice was excellent. We were all anxious to return to the sea, that we might bathe ourselves, and the caravan put itself on the road to the breakers of Sahara. After an hour's march of great suffering we regained the shore, as well as our asses, which were lying in the water. We rushed among the waves, and, after a bath of half an hour, reposed ourselves upon the beach."

There was still another day's painful traveling before reaching the banks of the river Senegal, where boats were expected to be ready to convey the party to the town of St. Louis, the place of their destination. "During the day we quickened our march; and for the first time since our shipwreck, a smiling picture presented itself to our view. The trees, always green, with which that noble river is shaded, the humming-birds, the red-birds, the paroquets, the promerops, and others, which flitted among their long, yielding branches, caused in us emotions difficult to express. We could not satiate our eyes with gazing on the beauties of this place, verdure being so enchanting to the sight, especially after having traveled through the desert. Before reaching the river, we had to descend a little hill covered with thorny bushes. It was four o'clock in the afternoon before the boats of the government arrived, and we all embarked. Biscuit and wine were found in each of them, and all were refreshed. After sailing for an hour down the stream, we came in sight of St. Louis, a town miserable in appearance, but delightful to our vision after so much suffering. At six in the evening we arrived at the fort, where the late English governor and others, including our generous friend Mr. Carnet, were met to receive us. My father presented us to the governor, who had alighted; he appeared to be sensibly affected with our misfortunes, the females and children chiefly exciting his commiseration; and the native inhabitants and Europeans tenderly shook the hands of the unfortunate people; the negro slaves even seemed to deplore our disastrous fate. Every thing was done to relieve our necessities, and render us comfortable after our dangers and fatigues."

We now turn to the account of the raft, and the unfortunates who had been treacherously deserted on it.

THE RAFT.

Ruthlessly abandoned in the midst of the ocean, and at the distance of five or six miles from the wreck of the Medusa, the crew of the raft, numbering altogether a hundred and fifty individuals, gave themselves up to all the horrors of despair. This feeling, however, was less manifested by the officers than by their companions, who were principally soldiers and sailors. M. Coudin, the nominal commander, was unfit, from illness, to issue orders or exert his influence, and the duty of attending to the general wants and safety appears to have been assumed by M. Correard and M. Savigny, with one or two other officers. These gentlemen, by putting on a countenance of greater fortitude than they really possessed, endeavored to soothe the general apprehensions, and held out hopes of succor, of which they had but a feeble expectation.

When tranquillity was restored, and attention could be given to the more immediate cóndition of affairs, the first idea that occurred to the officers in command, was that of steering the raft by the aid of sails and compass. A search was now made for the chart, compass, and anchor, which, on quitting the wreck, were understood to have been placed on the raft; but they were no where to be found, and had never been embarked. In this emergency, M. Correard recollected that he had seen one of the sailors with a small pocket compass in his hands, and on inquiry, it was still fortunately in his possession. This was a piece of joyful intelligence. The compass was not larger than a crown-piece, and perhaps not very accurate; nevertheless, it would answer the purpose for which it was required, and was accordingly given to the chief in command. Alas! short-lived were the expectations which the possession of the compass had raised. From want of care, it dropped from the fingers of the commander, disappeared between the planks of the raft, and was irrecoverably lost. There was no other guide across the deep than the rising and setting sun.

In the hurry of leaving the wreck, none had eaten any thing, and in the course of the forenoon all began to feel severely the calls of hunger. A meal was now served, consisting of a little biscuit, mixed with three-quarters of a pint of wine. Bad as it was, it was the best meal distributed on the raft. The biscuit was all consumed, and there was nothing left but wine. After this repast, and while all were as yet able to form correct conclusions, it might be supposed that some definite plan would have been executed for navigating the raft, if not to the shore of the desert, at least back to the Medusa, where there were stores of many useful materials, and an abundance of provisions. Except the erecting of a very insufficient mast and sail, nothing of this kind appears to have been done. The raft lay a hulk on the water, at the mercy of every wave. A few of the better-disposed officers preserved a degree of order, and preached patience and hope; and this is the utmost that can be said in their favor. Others employed themselves in canvassing, with the common soldiers and sailors, plans for taking revenge on those who had deserted them when they should reach the land.

With the shades of evening a better spirit prevailed. To the first feeling of despair, there now ensued a degree of resignation; and religion, with its soothing influence, contributed to the general calm. At times a sanguine spirit would try to impart hopes of succor on the morrow. Perhaps the boats would land their crews on the island of Arguin, and return to carry away those on the raft; perhaps they might return after reaching the desert; perhaps they might give intelligence of their fate to one of the vessels of the squadron with which they might fall in. These attempts at comfort were only of momentary avail. Night set in, darkness enveloped the raft, the wind rose, and the agitated sea dashed its waves and spray over the cowering mass of sufferers. The uneasy motion of the raft, and the shifting of the spars, likewise added to the horrors of the scene. With feet entangled amid the planks and cordage, many were thrown down, and deprived of the power of moving, by others falling above them. As the storm increased, numbers were obliged to lash themselves to the beams, to prevent the waves from washing them off. Cries of pain, of renewed despair, and of bitter lamentation, again rose on the blast. The faculties of many became temporarily impaired; they fancied that vessels were approaching, and, by way of holding out a signal, they fired off pistols, and set fire to small heaps of gunpowder. Among the whole on board during that awful night, there were few who did not expect that the raft would perish in the storm before morning. But these anticipations were not realized. The morning at length broke, and found the raft still buffeted on the surface of the water. It was reserved for greater horrors.

As the second day dawned, the storm gradually ceased, and the ocean calmed. When there was sufficient light, the spectacle which presented itself was most dismal. Wet, battered, sick, and wounded, the wretched sufferers were huddled confusedly together in heaps. On giving out rations of wine by way of a meal, it was found that twenty persons were missing; a greater number, however, were probably washed overboard during the night; for several, in order to increase their allowance, took rations for their dead companions. That twenty out of the hundred and fifty were gone, was at least certain. Death had taken his first installment.

During the day, which continued fine throughout, tranquillity prevailed, and sanguine hopes were entertained that the boats would shortly appear; none of them, however, made their appearance, and hope once more gave way to gloomy despair. A mutiny now broke out; the orders of the officers were disregarded, and there was reason to expect that next night, for want of the precautions hitherto adopted, many lives would be sacrificed. Night at length came, and, to add to the horrors of the scene; there was every appearance of a fresh storm approaching. The sky became covered with heavy clouds, the wind, which had been rather high all day, now rose to a gale, and the waves, again excited, rolled upon the raft in continuous masses, driving it before them as if to immediate destruction.

In this dismal condition the hearts of the mutineers quailed, and all tried to seek safety in being calm. But rest was impossible. Terrified for the fury of the waves, the mass of sufferers clung to the center of the raft, where some were actually stifled by the weight of their companions. Those who were outside, and exposed, were rolled over from side to side, and of these a number were swept into the sea. So little was the hope of surviving, that a body of sailors and soldiers resolved to drown the sense of their situation in wine, and so die while in a stupor of intoxication. The officers, clinging for safety to the mast, could offer no effectual opposition to this mad and cowardly scheme; and accordingly a wine cask was opened, and from it the mutineers drank a considerable quantity—and would have drank more, had the sea-water not entered the cask by the opening which had been made in it, and caused them to desist. Now maddened with liquor, the folly of the mutineers knew no bounds; and they proceeded to cut the lashings that held the timbers of the raft together, in order to destroy all at a blow. Roused by the proposal, the officers endeavored to avert their impending fate by more vigorous measures than they had hitherto dared to put in practice. When one of the ringleaders in the revolt made the first move to cut the ropes with a hatchet, the officers rushed upon him, and, after a desperate struggle, dispatched him, and threw his body into the sea. He was an Asiatic, of extraordinary size; and, having been troublesome and overbearing in demeanor, few lamented his loss. There was now an expectation of a battle between the two parties. The mutineers drew their swords, and were on the point of commencing an attack, when another of their number was killed, and they retreated; only, however, to make a fresh attempt to cut the ropes. One of the officers succeeded in preventing this being done, and in a scuffle which ensued, struck down a soldier and a sailor, whom he threw into the sea, where they were drowned. Their exasperated comrades now rushed to the mast, and began to cut down the ropes which supported it. The mast fell with a crash on the leg of an officer, which it nearly broke; and, far from pitying this misfortune, the enraged crowd threw the poor man into the sea, whence, however, his friends rescued him. No sooner was he on board the wretched raft, which, during the commotion, was tumbling about among the waves, than he was seized on a second time, and an attempt made to put out his eyes. Rendered desperate by these barbarous cruelties, the officers and those who supported them, made a charge on their antagonists, and put a number of them to death.

While the combat still raged, some of the mutineers took occasion to throw into the sea, together with her husband, the unfortunate woman who was on board. Correard, distressed at seeing two unoffending individuals perish, and affected by their cries for help, seized a large rope which he found on the forepart of the raft, fastened it round his waist, and plunged into the sea. He was thus able to save the female when she was in the act of disappearing below the water. Her husband was at the same time rescued by M. Lavillette. The two exhausted beings were laid on the dead bodies, and their backs were supported by a barrel: in this situation they shortly recovered their senses. The first thing the woman did was to acquaint herself with the name of the person who had saved her from drowning, and to express to him her liveliest gratitude. Finding, doubtless, that words but ill-expressed her feelings, she recollected she had in her pocket a small quantity of snuff, and instantly offered it to him—it was all she possessed. Touched with her gift, but unable to use it, M. Correard gave it to a poor sailor, who derived a solacement from it for three or four days. It is impossible to describe a still more affecting incident—the joyful recognition of the husband and wife, when they discovered that both were alive: they could scarcely credit their senses when they found themselves in one another's arms. This woman was quite a heroine of humble life. For twenty-four years she had traveled as a soldier's wife along with the French armies, in their campaigns in Italy and other places. In this vagrant life she acted as a suttler, supplying the men with articles; and often was exposed to the greatest dangers on the battle-field, in carrying assistance to the wounded soldiers. In telling her story to M. Correard, she said: "Whether the men had money or not, I always let them have my goods. Sometimes a battle would deprive me of my poor debtors; but after the victory, others would pay me double or triple for what they had consumed before the engagement. Thus I came in for a share of their victories." Unfortunate woman, to have sailed in such a miserable expedition! Little was she aware of the fate that awaited her!

Returning to the position of affairs on the raft: the mutiny was quelled by the determined attitude of the officers; nor was the humanity shown to the woman and her husband without its effect in restoring better feelings. Overcome with a momentary sense of shame, the mutineers went the length of asking pardon on their knees for their conduct. This was granted; and the officers returned to their post at the center of the raft, still, however, watchful of the movements of their infatuated companions. Toward midnight the old grudge again broke out with increased fury. Rushing on the officers, they attempted to kill them with their weapons; and those who had no arms, actually bit their adversaries in a shocking manner. One of their drunken delusions was, that Lieutenant Lozach, an officer on board, was a M. Danglas, who had deserted them on quitting the frigate; and this gentleman was with the greatest difficulty preserved from their fury. Brandishing their arms, reeling to and fro, and stumbling against each other, they continued to cry for Danglas to be delivered up to their vengeance, and by no power of reasoning could they be convinced that they were in error.

Defeated in getting hold of M. Lozach, the wretches now turned their rage upon the unfortunate M. Coudin, the wounded and distressed commander of the raft. *Coudin appears to* have been a young man worthy of a better fate than that of sailing among such a crew. During the scuffle we have been describing, he had seated himself on a small barrel, supporting in his arms a young sailor boy of twelve years of age, in whom he took an interest. Suddenly he was seized by the mutineers, who threw him into the sea, along with the barrel on which he sat, and the little boy whom he held in his arms. The other officers rushed to the rescue of their friend, and keeping off the mob with their swords, they fortunately got hold of him, and dragged him, still holding the little boy, on board. Toward morning the mutiny was finally quelled, the maddening effects of the liquor having worn off, and left the rioters dispirited.

Great suffering, and the hopelessness of their situation, had contributed, as well as wine, to render the men deranged during this eventful night. Even the strongest-minded of the officers felt themselves affected with strange illusions. M. Savigny had visions of a most agreeable kind: he fancied himself in a rich, cultivated country, surrounded by happy friends, and although reason ever and anon pointed out the fallacy, he could not divest himself of the impression. Some appeared full of hope, told their companions not to fear, and, saying that they were going to fetch succor, plunged headlong into the sea, and perished. Others thought that their companions mocked them, by holding out temptingly the wings of chickens and other delicacies, and for this they rushed on them with drawn swords. Some believed they were still in the frigate, and asked where was their hammock, for they wanted to go below to sleep. A few imagined they saw ships, or a harbor, with a noble city in the background. M. Correard at one time was under the illusion of being in Italy; and another officer mentioned gravely that he had sent off a letter to the governor describing the state of affairs on the raft, and that he would certainly send boats in the morning to take every one ashore. Such were some of the fancies of which those on board the raft were the involuntary victims; and nothing could convey a more striking testimony of their bodily and mental sufferings.

When day returned, and a reckoning could be taken, it was found that sixty-five had perished, and that the entire number was now reduced to sixty. Of those who were missing, the greater number had fallen a sacrifice to intemperance, or to ill-regulated minds. The officers were surprised to find that only two of their number were gone; and this, on consideration, they could only attribute to the comparative strength of mind they had possessed. The circumstance is a proof of the power which every man has of resisting misfortune, if he remain temperate in habits, and do not give way to panic or despair.

With the return of daylight the storm abated as formerly, and when order was restored, and a reckoning of the numbers taken, attention was directed to the stock of provisions on board. It sent a shock of fresh despair into the bosoms of the more intelligent, when it was found that the mutineers had thrown overboard two casks of wine, and the only two casks of water which remained. The loss of the water was felt to be a calamity greater than that of the wine; and the distress on the occasion was augmented by the reflection, that it was a loss caused entirely by drunken folly. Nothing now remained but one cask of wine, and it was arranged that this should be carefully served out in half allowances. The sea being calm, the solitary mast and sail were again raised, and an attempt made to direct the raft toward land. The effort was not successful; the wind drove the unruly platform hither and thither as it listed, and it was impossible to say whether the raft approached or receded from the spot where land was believed to be.

During the day the gnawings of hunger suggested the idea of catching fish, and an attempt was forthwith made. Hooks made of tags from the soldiers' clothing were tied to lines, and with baits—it is not mentioned of what—were thrown into the sea; but the current drew them under the raft, where they got entangled. A bayonet was bent to catch sharks, but a shark bit at, and straightened it; so this also failed. Fishing, in short, proved an unavailing resource; and when it was abandoned as hopeless, some tried to feed on the dead bodies of their companions, while others gnawed the soldiers' belts and cartridge-boxes. Fortunately the day was calm. The sun shone placidly on the face of the deep. Amidst the torments of hunger, therefore, hope again stole across the minds of the most desponding. They expected to see the boats make their appearance on the horizon, and with fainting eyes they looked forth to catch the first token of deliverance. Noon passed, the sun sunk beneath the world of waters, and yet relief came not. The gloom and misery of another night presented themselves.

This night was less terrible than the preceding. The weather was calm, and there was no new mutiny on board. In the darkness, nothing was heard but the groans and sobs of the sufferers, intermingled with the gurgling of the sea between the planks. The silence, broken by such sounds, was perhaps more appalling than the raging of the tempest. When the morning of the fourth day dawned on the spectral scene, it showed the dead bodies of twelve persons, who had expired during the night; and all these, with the exception of one, were thrown into the sea. The number on board was now reduced to forty-eight.

This day passed like the preceding. The weather continued fine, and despondency again gave way to feelings of hope. About four o'clock in the afternoon a joyful event occurred. A shoal of flying-fish passed under the raft, and a great number got entangled in the spaces between the timbers. All threw themselves eagerly upon them, and captured about two hundred, which they placed in an empty cask, removing only the milts. These fish were about the size of a herring, and, to men who were famishing, they were delicious. Several of the party returned thanks to God for the relief. To render the fish fit for eating, an attempt was made to boil them by means of a barrel, which served as a pot; fire being procured by a flint, steel, and a little dried gunpowder. This was the last meal they were able to cook, for the barrel took fire; and though it was soon extinguished, they were not able to save as much of it as would answer the purpose again. There was also no more gunpowder.

Night again came on, the sun set, and still there was no appearance of relief. The calm having continued, there was a prospect of a little rest, even although the greater number stood or sat constantly in water. It is distressing to know that human passions again interfered to render the scene of misery a battle-field. Some Spaniards, Italians, and negroes, who had hitherto taken no part with the mutineers, and who had been inclined to the side of the officers, formed a plot to throw all into the sea; the negroes persuading them that land was near, and that, if once there, they could conduct them in safety through Africa. It is not improbable that a wish to get possession of a small bag of money, which was tied to the mast as a common fund, to be made use of on landing, tempted them to the crime. The officers, and some sailors who refused to join the conspirators, were now obliged to take arms. They seized the Spaniard who was the ringleader, and threw him into the sea; another, when he saw that all was discovered, plunged into the water, and was drowned. The remaining conspirators now rushed forward to revenge their comrades; a desperate combat ensued; and the raft was strewn with the dead and wounded. It was evident, during the fight, that the mutineers were affected by the same delusions as before; they were, in fact, partially deranged in mind. They called for Lieutenant Danglas, in order to kill him for having deserted them, and they could not be persuaded that that person was not on the raft. During the fray the woman was again thrown into the sea, but was a second time rescued by the intrepid Coudin, assisted by some workmen. At length the battle ceased; the mutineers were repulsed; and the remainder of the night was passed without disturbance.

The morning of the fifth day dawned, and revealed the slaughter that had taken place. Since the previous morning, eighteen had, by one means or other, perished, and their number was now reduced to thirty. Among the dead were five sailors, whom the officers deeply lamented; for they were trustworthy and tractable. Of the thirty who remained alive on the raft, only twenty could stand upright or move about. The sea-water had stripped the skin from the feet and legs of nearly the whole, and every one was in a state of deplorable emaciation. If no vessel came to their assistance, they did not expect to survive more than four days, for there was wine only for that time, and scarcely a dozen fish. The fifth day passed over in melancholy mood; night came, and still there was no relief. The sixth day passed, and so did the succeeding night, in a condition equally disconsolate.

The seventh day was more eventful. Two

soldiers were discovered drinking wine clandestinely from the cask, by means of a pipe. As this had been declared to be a crime punishable with death, they were immediately seized, and thrown into the sea. One of them was a sergeant, who had fomented the last conspiracy, and had contrived to escape detection; his fate, therefore, did not cause any regret. In the course of the day died also the young boy, Leon, to whom M. Coudin had shown so much kindness. Exhausted from hunger, and delirious, he could no longer support the dreadful fatigues to which he was exposed. Before his death, his mind took the direction of his home in France; he thought his mother was near him, and till the last he cried to her for food and water. He died in the arms of his kind friend, M. Coudin.

The party were now reduced to twenty-seven; of these, twelve were so ill that there was no hope of their surviving even a few days; they had almost entirely lost their reason, and were covered with wounds; nevertheless an equal ration of the declining quantity of wine was served out to them. A consultation was now held respecting these unfortunate beings. It was represented that, as they could not possibly survive, and as their consumption of wine was daily diminishing the stock, already too low, it would be no crime to put an end to their sufferings by throwing them into the sea. This was a horrible and painful expedient, and such it was felt to be; for those who proposed and assented to it had not the cruelty to put it into execution, or see it done. Three soldiers and a sailor were commissioned to act as executioners; and while they cleared the raft of their dying companions, the others turned their backs, not to witness the afflicting spectacle. Among those thrown overboard were the woman and her husband already mentioned. Both had been grievously wounded in the different combats. The woman had a thigh broken between the beams of the raft, and the stroke of a saber had made a deep wound in the head of her husband. In terminating the existence of these hapless individuals, M. Correard observes that all felt themselves to be under a terrible necessity which knew no law. "Ye," he continues, "who shudder at the cry of outraged humanity, recollect that it was other men, fellow-countrymen, who had placed us in this awful situation." The expedient of throwing overboard their apparently-dying comrades, reduced the number on the raft to fifteen, and gave the means of subsistence for a few additional days. When the dreadful sacrifice was completed, all cast their swords into the sea, reserving but one saber, for cutting a piece of wood, or cordage, or any thing else that might be necessary.

We have now the afflicting spectacle of fifteen wretched beings in the depth of despair on this floating tomb, seated or standing constantly in water, the sun beating down upon them with tropical intensity by day, and darkness enshrouding them by night. The eighth day passed, night came, and still no friendly sail rose on the horizon. Then came the ninth day with its aggravated hunger, and thirst, and wretchedness. While hope was sunk in the feelings of the unhappy party, the eyes of all were startled on seeing a butterfly, of a kind common in France, fly over their heads and settle on the sail of the raft. This trifling incident once more raised a bright gleam of hope; the butterfly was accepted as a harbinger of deliverance, and was taken under the protection of the forlorn group. On the succeeding days more butterflies visited them, and gave rise to the belief that the land could not be far distant. While cheering with new hopes, these insects also roused the party to fresh exertions. "We had recourse," says M. Correard, "to every expedient which might lessen the miseries of our situation. We detached some planks from the raft, and made a sort of platform, on which we might lie down; this raised us above the water, which had always been from one to two feet above the surface of the raft; the waves, however, still washed over us at intervals, and frequently covered us completely. Here we endeavored to beguile the time, by recounting our different adventures. Lavillette related the various scenes he had passed through, which were indeed extraordinary; but none, he said, had brought with them such suffering from fatigue and privation as those we now endured.

"Our situation was now most distressing: the waves, which almost constantly washed over us, caused intolerable pain; and our excessive thirst, which we felt was increased by the intense heat of a tropical sun. To relieve this thirst we tried several expedients; we bathed our hands, faces, and even hair in salt water, and some even drank considerable quantities of it. One means of slaking our thirst was never thought of by us, though it has often been adopted by persons in our situation with great success. When Captain Bligh made his perilous voyage in an open boat over three thousand miles of the ocean, he and his companions used to dip their clothes in the sea, and wear them damp; the pores of the body, it is supposed, imbibing part of the moisture, and thus allaying their desire for drink. Unfortunately we had never heard of this expedient. An officer found a small melon, which he resolved to keep for himself: for a long time he refused it to the entreaties of those around him, till their threats and rage obliged him to share it. We had also a serious dispute about thirty cloves of garlic, which had escaped notice in the bottom of a sack; at another time we contended for two small vials of a liquor for cleaning the teeth; we never came, however, to extremities. This liquor was husbanded with the greatest care, two drops of it producing a delightful sensation; indeed it is difficult to conceive the agreeable effect which the most trifling relief of this kind produced. One of us had found an empty bottle, which still retained some scent of the perfume it had formerly contained; to smell at this for an instant appeared the highest enjoyment. Some kept their wine, and sucked it slowly from the goblet through a quill; the intoxication, however, it produced upon their debilitated frames was remarkable, and often produced angry disputes, and sometimes was near causing more serious consequences. On the tenth day, for example, after the wine had been distributed, MM. Clairet, Coudin, Charlot, and two others, resolved, in a fit of intoxication, to destroy themselves, and were with considerable difficulty prevented by the entreaties of their companions. Perhaps all our arguments would have been unavailing, if a number of sharks had not surrounded the raft, and turned their attention to this new danger. They came so near, that we were enabled to strike at them with the saber; but notwithstanding all the exertions of M. Lavillette, who gave them several blows, we could not kill one; the size of several appeared enormous, some of them being above thirty feet long.

"Three days now passed away in intolerable torments. We had become so careless of life, that we bathed even in the sight of the sharks, which were swimming round the raft; others were not afraid to place themselves naked on the forepart of the machine, which was then entirely under water; and though it was exceedingly dangerous, it had the effect of taking away their thirst. On the 16th July, eight of us resolved on trying to reach the coast, to which we imagined ourselves to be now very near; for this purpose we nailed some boards across a few spars, which we separated from the raft, fitted it with a mast and a sail, and made oars of barrel-staves; a certain portion of the wine remaining, which consisted but of fifteen bottles in all, was to be given to us, and our departure was fixed for the next day. Our machine being finished, however, it was necessary to try if she was able to bear us. A sailor went upon it, when it immediately upset, and showed us the rashness of our design; we therefore gave it up, resolving to wait upon the raft for the approach of death; which, unless we were immediately relieved, could not be very distant, our stock of wine being so low, and our disgust at the loathsome food we ate hourly increasing.

"On the morning of the 17th July the sun shone brightly, the sky appearing without a cloud; we addressed our prayers to God, and distributed the rations of wine. While each person was taking his portion, a captain of infantry discovered a ship in the horizon, and with a shout of joy informed us of it. We saw that it was a brig, but at such a distance that we could discern no more than the tops of her masts. It is impossible to describe the joy which we felt at the sight; each looked upon his delivery as certain, and returned repeated thanks to God. Still, in the midst of these hopes we were apprehensive that we should not be seen. We straightened some hoops, and fastened some handkerchiefs of different colors to the end. We then united our efforts, and raised a man to the top of the mast, who waved these flags. For half an hour we were suspended between hope and fear; some of us thought that the vessel was coming nearer, while others, with more accuracy, asserted that she was making sail away from us. In fact, in a short time the brig disappeared. We now resigned ourselves to despair; we even envied those whom death had taken away from the suffering we were now to undergo. We determined to seek consolation in sleep. The day before, we had suffered exceedingly from the rays of a burning sun; we now made an awning to screen us from the heat, and lay down beneath it. We agreed to carve our names on a plank, along with a short recital of our adventures, and to hang it to the mast, in the hope that it might reach our government and our families. We had passed two hours in these desponding reflections, when the master-gunner went from under the awning, in order to go to the forepart of the raft: he had scarcely, however, put his head out, when he turned toward us and uttered a loud cry. Joy was in his countenance, his hands were stretched out toward the sea, and he scarcely breathed: he could only utter, 'We are saved; the brig is near to us!' We rushed out, and found that she was in fact only a mile and a half distant, and was steering directly toward us under a press of sail. Joy now succeeded to despair; we embraced each other, and burst into tears. Even those whose wounds rendered them incapable of more exertion, dragged themselves along to the side of the raft, in order to enjoy the sight of the vessel which was to deliver them. Each laid hold on a handkerchief, or a piece of linen, to make signals to the brig, which neared us fast: a few returned thanks to Providence for their miraculous preservation. We now recognized the vessel to be the Argus, and soon after had the pleasure of seeing her shorten sail when she was within half pistol shot. The crew, dispersed through the shrouds and on the deck, waved their hats, to express their pleasure at having come to our relief. A boat was now lowered, commanded by M. Lemaigre, who ardently wished to be the person who should take us from the fatal raft. He removed the sick first, placed them beside him in his boat, and showed them all the care and attention which humanity could prompt. In a short time we were all in safety on board the brig, where we met some of our shipwrecked companions who had been saved in the boats.

"All were affected to see our miserable condition: ten out of the fifteen were scarcely able to move: the skin was stripped off our limbs, our eyes were sunk, our beards long, and we were in the most emaciated condition. As soon as we had been discovered, they prepared some excellent broth for us, and mixed in it some wine, to recruit our exhausted strength. Our wounds were dressed; and, in short, we received every attention which our miserable state required. Some became delirious; but the care of the surgeon, and the kind attention of every one on board, soon wrought in us the most favorable change."

The Argus, as has been already mentioned, had been, after some delay, sent from Senegal, with instructions to afford assistance to the crews of the boats, and afterward to look for the raft. In her course she had become aware that the crews in the boats had been saved, and had rendered them some succor while coasting the desert. Her search for the raft was at first fruitless, and after cruising about for a number of days, she had turned helm to proceed to Senegal. It was while returning that the party on the raft had seen and lost sight of her. Having reached to within forty leagues of the river, the wind veered to the south-west, and the captain said that he would steer for a short time in that direction; he tacked accordingly, and was standing toward the raft for about two hours, when those on board descried the vessel on the horizon. This change of course, as we have seen, saved the fifteen unfortunate beings, who at the time did not expect they could hold out four-and-twenty hours longer; for the last two days had been spent without food, and only a small quantity of wine was left.

As soon as the party was removed to the Argus, that vessel steered for Senegal, which it reached next day. In the evening it moored close to the shore, and on the following morning, the 19th July, anchored in the roads of St. Louis.

Thus were fifteen, all who remained alive out of a hundred and fifty individuals left on the wreck, rescued from the death which seemed to await them. Of the fifteen, five died in a short time of the injuries they had sustained; and the remainder carried on their wounded and emaciated bodies the lasting effects of their protracted and most miserable sufferings on the raft.

THE WRECK.

It will be recollected that, at the disgraceful scramble in leaving the Medusa, seventeen persons, some of them in a state of intoxication, did not depart with their companions in the boats. Lachaumareys, on quitting the vessel at one of the port-holes, promised to send out succor to them as soon as he should reach the land. To fill up the measure of his depravity, the captain falsified this as well as his other promises; and it is not less distressing to know that neither the party generally who escaped in the boats, nor those who afterward were taken from the raft, gave themselves any concern about their less fortunate brethren in the wreck. It does not appear, from the narrative of M. Correard, that they would have been thought of, but for the governor, Schmaltz, wishing to save the specie and provisions which were on board. To secure these articles a schooner was fitted out, commanded by a lieutenant, and manned by some negro traders and a few passengers. She set sail from Senegal on the 26th of July; that is, seven days after the party saved from the raft had been landed, and seventeen from the time the governor and captain had reached Senegal; but, having provisions for only eight days on board, she was obliged, when that stock was exhausted, to return without having got sight of the frigate; she was afterward furnished with a sufficiency for twenty-five days, but, being ill-found, she returned into port a second time, after having been fifteen days at sea. A delay of ten days now occurred, when she made a third attempt, with a new set of sails, and reached the Medusa fifty-two days after it had been abandoned. From the time which had elapsed, it was confidently believed that all who had been left on board the frigate would be dead; what, therefore, was the astonishment of those in the schooner, to find that three of the miserable beings had outlived all their sufferings, and now appeared like specters to welcome the approach of their countrymen!

The following is the account which these unfortunate men gave of what had occurred on the wreck. When the boats and the raft had left the frigate, the seventeen had collected a sufficient quantity of wine, biscuit, brandy, and bacon, for their subsistence during a certain number of days. While this stock lasted they were quiet; but forty-two days having passed without the arrival of the expected succor, twelve of the most resolute constructed a raft, and, endeavoring to make the land without oars or sails, and but a small quantity of provisions, were drowned. That this was their fate there is no reason for doubting, as the shattered fragments of their raft were some time afterward thrown on shore by the waves, and picked up by the Moors. Another seaman, who refused to trust for safety to the raft, adopted the strange resolution, a few days after, of placing himself on a hencoop, and in this way tried to reach the shore; at the distance of half a cable's length, however, the coop upset, and he was drowned.

Four now remained on the wreck, resolved to await death or succor, rather than brave dangers which appeared to them insurmountable. One of them had lately expired when the schooner arrived, and the others were so weak and emaciated, that in a very short time death would have put an end to all their sufferings. They lived in separate corners of the vessel, which they never quitted but to look for food, and this latterly consisted only of tallow and a little bacon. If on these occasions they accidentally met, they used to run at each other with drawn knives; so completely had selfishness and ferocity stifled that sympathy which fellow-sufferers are generally disposed to feel for one another. It is mentioned as a remarkable fact, worthy of being made known, that as long as these men abstained from strong liquor, they were able to support the hardships of their situation in a surprising manner; but when they began to drink brandy, their strength daily and rapidly diminished. How these unfortunate beings should have been driven to extremities for food, is not easily accounted for. The Medusa contained a large cargo of provisions, and why this store was not reached is not explained in the original narrative. Perhaps the men did not know of there being barrels of provisions on board; or they might not have possessed sufficient strength to reach them below other articles in the hold.

On being discovered and removed by the schooner, the three survivors received all the attention which their situation required. This having been attended to, the crew of the schooner proceeded to remove from the frigate every thing that could be taken out; and after having loaded their own vessel with wine, flour, and every thing else that was removable, whether public or private property, though without discovering the money, they returned to Senegal.

Those who had been rescued by the boats, and also from the raft, expected that the schooner, besides fetching the public property from the wreck, would bring many articles which they would claim as their own. The crew of the schooner, however, though in the service of the King of France, acted on this occasion the part of pirates: they not only kept and made sale, in the market of St. Louis, of articles of value found in the wreck, but robbed the miserable victims whom they had rescued.

The report they gave of the state of the wreck, induced the governor to permit merchants to send vessels to bring off more of the goods on board—the proceeds to be equally divided between the government and the adventurers. Four vessels thus set sail, and in a short time brought back a great quantity of flour, salt, provisions, brandy, cordage, and other articles, of which there was a fair division.

In concluding this melancholy recital, we almost feel it necessary to assure our readers that what we have been telling them is no dressed-up fiction, but a narrative drawn from authentic sources, and true in every particular. We need scarcely repeat, what must occur to every mind, that nothing in the whole annals of shipwreck equals in infamy the conduct of Lachaumareys, the captain of the Medusa, or of the governor, Schmaltz, with whom he appears to have acted in concert. Neither, we believe, did ever any disaster by sea or land present such a series of blunders, such want of concert or management, or such a deficiency among nearly all concerned, of the common feelings of humanity. Shortly after its occurrence, the shipwreck of the Medusa created a considerable sensation in Europe, and especially in France. The general feeling was that of horror; but in France, this sentiment was mingled with shame, and every effort was made to prevent the publication of the details by Correard, as well as belief in them after publication. But all was unavailing. The narrative remains trustworthy in all respects—a sad memorial of human suffering and depravity.

VI.

Mutiny of the Bounty.

THE circumstances detailed in the following narrative are altogether of so singular and romantic a character, that, but for the undeniable authenticity of every particular, the whole might be considered as the production of the ingenious brain of a Defoe. Some of the incidents, indeed, surpass in impressive interest anything to be met with in the fictitious history of Alexander Selkirk's solitary existence and adventures.

In December, 1787, the Bounty sailed from Spithead for Otaheite, under the command of Lieutenant Bligh, who had previously accompanied Captain Cook in his exploratory voyages in the Pacific Ocean. The object of the present expedition was to convey from Otaheite to the West India colonies the plants of the breadfruit-tree, which Dampier, Cook, and other voyagers, had observed to grow with the most prolific luxuriance in the South Sea Islands, and which furnished the natives with a perpetual and wholesome subsistence, without even the trouble of cultivation. The crew of the Bounty consisted of forty-four individuals, including the commander and two skillful gardeners to take charge of the plants, for the removing of which every accommodation had been provided on board, under the superintendence of Sir Joseph Banks, who had personally visited Otaheite with Captain Wallis. After a most distressing voyage, in which, after reaching Cape Horn, they were compelled to put the helm aweather, and take the route by Van Dieman's Land, the voyagers anchored in Matavia Bay, Otaheite, on the 26th October, 1788, having run over by the log, since leaving England, a space of 27,086 miles, or an average of 108 miles in twenty-four hours.

The simple natives, who had experienced much kindness from Captain Cook, testified great joy at the arrival of the strangers, and loaded them with presents and provisions of every sort. The character, condition, and habits of the islanders, as described to us even by their earliest visitors, present a most extraordinary contrast to the usual features of savage life. They were a kind, mild-tempered, social, and affectionate race, living in the utmost harmony among themselves, and their whole lives being one unvaried round of cheerful contentment, luxurious ease, and healthful exercise and amusements.

Bligh appears to have been tempted to remain at this luxurious spot much longer than was either proper or necessary, as the bread-fruit plants, and provisions of hogs, fowls, fish, and vegetables of every description, were amply supplied him by the kind natives. The liberty which he gave his crew to go on shore, and enjoy all the indulgences which the place afforded, was extremely imprudent; and this, together with the capricious harshness and unjustifiable insult with which he occasionally treated every one on board—officers as well as men—appears to have been the sole cause of the unfortunate occurrence that afterward took place. The Bounty, which, as we have mentioned, arrived October 26, 1778, did not sail till the 4th of April, 1789, when she departed, loaded with presents, and amid the tears and regrets of the natives. They continued till the 27th among the islands of that archipelago, touching at many of them, bartering and interchanging presents with the natives, many of whom remembered Bligh when he accompanied Cook in the Resolution.

The remainder of this narrative can be best detailed in Captain Bligh's own words.

About three weeks were spent among the

small islands which lie scattered round Otaheite, at some of which we touched. According to my instructions, my course was now through Endeavor Straits, to Prince's Island, in the Straits of Sunda. On the 27th of April, at noon, we were between the islands of Tofoa and Kotoo. Latitude observed, 19 degrees 18 minutes south.

Thus far the voyage had advanced in a course of uninterrupted prosperity, and had been attended with many circumstances equally pleasing and satisfactory. A very different scene was now to be experienced.

Monday, 27th April, 1789.—The wind being northerly in the evening, we steered to the westward, to pass to the south of Tofoa. I gave directions for this course to be continued during the night. The master had the first watch, the gunner the middle watch, and Mr. Christian the morning watch.

Tuesday, 28th.—Just before sunrising, while I was yet asleep, Mr. Christian, with the master-at-arms, gunner's mate, and Thomas Burkitt, seaman, came into my cabin, and seizing me, tied my hands with a cord behind my back, threatening me with instant death if I spoke or made the least noise. I, however, called as loud as I could, in hopes of assistance; but they had already secured the officers who were not of their party, by placing sentinels at their doors.

There were three men at my cabin door, besides the four within; Christian had only a cutlass in his hand, the others had muskets and bayonets. I was pulled out of bed, and forced on deck in my shirt, suffering great pain from the tightness with which they had tied my hands. I demanded the reason of such violence, but received no other answer than abuse for not holding my tongue. The master, the gunner, the surgeon, Mr. Elphinstone, master's mate, and Nelson, were kept confined below, and the fore-hatchway was guarded by sentinels. The boatswain and carpenter, and also the clerk, Mr. Samuel, were allowed to come upon deck. The boatswain was ordered to hoist the launch out, with a threat if he did not do it instantly to take care of himself.

When the boat was out, Mr. Hayward and Mr. Hallet, two of the midshipmen, and Mr. Samuel, were ordered into it. I demanded what their intention was in giving this order, and endeavored to persuade the people near me not to persist in such acts of violence; but it was to no effect. Christian changed the cutlass which he had in his hand for a bayonet that was brought to him, and holding me with a strong gripe by the cord that tied my hands, he, with many oaths, threatened to kill me immediately if I would not be quiet; the villains round me had their pieces cocked and bayonets fixed. Particular people were called on to go into the boat, and were hurried over the side, whence I concluded that with these people I was to be set adrift. I therefore made another effort to bring about a change, but with no other effect than to be threatened with having my brains blown out.

The boatswain and seamen who were to go into the boat were allowed to collect twine, canvas, lines, sails, cordage, an eight-and-twenty gallon cask of water, and Mr. Samuel got a hundred and fifty pounds of bread, with a small quantity of rum and wine, also a quadrant and compass; but he was forbidden, on pain of death, to touch either map, ephemeris, book of astronomical observations, sextant, time-keeper, or any of my surveys or drawings.

The officers were next called upon deck, and forced over the side into the boat, while I was kept apart from every one abaft the mizzen-mast.

Isaac Martin, one of the guard over me, I saw had an inclination to assist me, and, as he fed me with shaddock—my lips being quite parched—we explained our wishes to each other by our looks; but this being observed, Martin was removed from me. He then attempted to leave the ship, for which purpose he got into the boat; but with many threats they obliged him to return. The armorer, Joseph Coleman, and two of the carpenters, M'Intosh and Norman, were also kept contrary to their inclination; and they begged of me, after I was astern in the boat, to remember that they declared they had no hand in the transaction. Michael Byrne, I am told, likewise wanted to leave the ship.

It appeared to me that Christian was some time in doubt whether he should keep the carpenter or his mate; at length he determined on the latter, and the carpenter was ordered into the boat. He was permitted, but not without some opposition, to take his tool-chest. The officers and men being in the boat, they only waited for me, of which the master-at-arms informed Christian; who then said, "Come, Captain Bligh, your officers and men are now in the boat, and you must go with them; if you attempt to make the least resistance, you will instantly be put to death:" and without further ceremony, with a tribe of armed ruffians about me, I was forced over the side, where they untied my hands. Being in the boat, we were veered astern by a rope. A few pieces of pork were thrown to us, and some clothes, also four cutlasses; and it was then that the armorer and carpenters called out to me to remember that they had no hand in the transaction. After having undergone a great deal of ridicule, and been kept some time to make sport for these unfeeling wretches, we were at length cast adrift in the open ocean.

I had eighteen persons with me in the boat. There remained on board the Bounty twenty-five hands, the most able men of the ship's company. Having little or no wind, we rowed pretty fast toward Tofoa, which bore north-east about ten leagues from us. While the ship was in sight, she steered to the west-north-west; but I considered this only as a feint; for when we were sent away, "Huzza for Otaheite!" was frequently heard among the mutineers.

It will very naturally be asked, What could be the reason for such a revolt? In answer to which, I can only conjecture that the mutineers had flattered themselves with the hopes of a more happy life among the Otaheitans than they could possibly enjoy in England; and this, joined to some female connections, most probably occasioned the whole transaction. The women at Otaheite are handsome, mild and cheerful in their manners and conversation, possessed of great sensibility, and have sufficient delicacy to make them admired and beloved. The chiefs were so much attached to our people, that they rather encouraged their stay among them than otherwise, and even made them promises of large possessions. Under these, and many other attendant circumstances equally desirable, it is now perhaps not so much to be wondered at, though scarcely possible to have been foreseen, that a set of sailors, most of them void of connections, should be led away: especially when, in addition to such powerful inducements, they imagined it in their power to fix themselves in the midst of plenty, on one of the finest islands in the world, where they need not labor, and where the allurements of dissipation are beyond any thing that can be conceived.

My first determination was to seek a supply of bread-fruit and water at Tofoa, and afterward to sail for Tongataboo, and there risk a solicitation to Poulaho, the king, to equip our boat, and grant us a supply of water and provisions, so as to enable us to reach the East Indies. The quantity of provisions I found in the boat was a hundred and fifty pounds of bread, sixteen pieces of pork, each piece weighing two pounds, six quarts of rum, six bottles of wine, with twenty-eight gallons of water, and four empty barrecoes.

We got to Tofoa when it was dark, but found the shore so steep and rocky that we could not land. We were obliged, therefore, to remain all night in the boat, keeping it on the lee-side of the island with two oars. Next day—Wednesday, April 29—we found a cove, where we landed. I observed the latitude of this cove to be 19 degrees 41 minutes south. This is the north-west part of Tofoa, the north-westernmost of the Friendly Islands. As I was resolved to spare the small stock of provisions we had in the boat, we endeavored to procure something toward our support on the island itself. For two days we ranged through the island in parties, seeking for water, and any thing in the shape of provisions, subsisting, meanwhile, on morsels of what we had brought with us. The island at first seemed uninhabited, but on Friday, May 1, one of our exploring parties met with two men, a woman, and a child: the men came with them to the cove, and brought two cocoa-nut shells of water. I endeavored to make friends of these people, and sent them away for bread-fruit, plantains, and water. Soon after, other natives came to us; and by noon there were thirty about us, from whom we obtained a small supply. I was much puzzled in what manner to account to the natives for the loss of my ship: I knew they had too much sense to be amused with a story that the ship was to join me, when she was not in sight from the hills. I was at first doubtful whether I should tell the real fact, or say that the ship had overset and sunk, and that we only were saved: the latter appeared to be the most proper and advantageous for us, and I accordingly instructed my people, that we might all agree in one story. As I expected, inquiries were made about the ship, and they seemed readily satisfied with our account; but there did not appear the least symptom of joy or sorrow in their faces, although I fancied I discovered some marks of surprise. Some of the natives were coming and going the whole afternoon.

Toward evening, I had the satisfaction to find our stock of provisions somewhat increased; but the natives did not appear to have much to spare. What they brought was in such small quantities, that I had no reason to hope we should be able to procure from them sufficient to stock us for our voyage. At night, I served a quarter of a bread-fruit and a cocoa-nut to each person for supper; and a good fire being made, all but the watch went to sleep.

Saturday, 2*d.*—As there was no certainty of our being supplied with water by the natives, I sent a party among the gullies in the mountains, with empty shells, to see what could be found. In their absence the natives came about us, as I expected, and in great numbers; two canoes also came in from round the north side of the island. In one of them was an elderly chief, called Macca-ackavow. Soon after, some of our foraging party returned, and with them a good-looking chief, called Egijeefow, or Eefow.

Their affability was of short duration, for the natives began to increase in number, and I observed some symptoms of a design against us. Soon after, they attempted to haul the boat on shore, on which I brandished my cutlass in a threatening manner, and spoke to Eefow to desire them to desist; which they did, and every thing became quiet again. My people, who had been in the mountains, now returned with about three gallons of water. I kept buying up the little bread-fruit that was brought to us, and likewise some spears to arm my men with, having only four cutlasses, two of which were in the boat. As we had no means of improving our situation, I told our people I would wait till sunset, by which time, perhaps, something might happen in our favor; for if we attempted to go at present, we must fight our way through, which we could do more advantageously at night; and that, in the mean time, we would endeavor to get off to the boat what we had bought. The beach was lined with the natives, and we heard nothing but the knocking of stones together, which they had in each hand. I knew very well this was the sign of an attack. At noon I served a cocoa-nut and a bread-fruit to each person for dinner, and gave some to the chiefs, with whom I continued to appear intimate and friendly. They frequently importuned me to sit down, but I as constantly refused; for it occurred both to Nelson and myself that they intended to seize hold of me, if I gave them such an opportunity. Keeping, therefore, constantly on our guard, we were suffered to eat our uncomfortable meal in some quietness.

After dinner, we began, by little and little, to get our things into the boat, which was a troublesome business, on account of the surf. I carefully watched the motions of the natives, who continued to increase in number; and found that, instead of their intention being to leave us, fires were made, and places fixed on for their stay during the night. Consultations were also held among them, and every thing assured me we should be attacked. I sent orders to the master that, when he saw us coming down, he should keep the boat close to the shore, that we might the more readily embark.

The sun was near setting when I gave the word, on which every person who was on shore with me boldly took up his proportion of things and carried them to the boat. The chiefs asked me if I would not stay with them all night. I said, "No, I never sleep out of my boat; but in the morning we will again trade with you, and I shall remain till the weather is moderate, that we may go, as we have agreed, to see Poulaho, at Tongataboo." Macca-ackavow then got up and said, "You will not sleep on shore, then, Mattie?"—which directly signifies we will kill you—and he left me. The onset was now preparing: every one, as I have described before, kept knocking stones together; and Eefow quitted me. All but two or three things were in the boat, when we walked down the beach, every one in a silent kind of horror. We all got into the boat except one man, who, while I was getting on board, quitted it, and ran up the beach to cast the sternfast off, notwithstanding the master and others called repeatedly and vehemently to him to return, while they were hauling me out of the water.

I was no sooner in the boat than the attack began by about two hundred men; the unfortunate poor man who had run up the beach was knocked down, and the stones flew like a shower of shot. Many Indians got hold of the stern rope, and were near hauling the boat on shore; which they would certainly have effected, if I had not had a knife in my pocket, with which I cut the rope. We then hauled off to the grappel, every one being more or less hurt. At this time I saw five of the natives about the poor man they had killed, and two of them were beating him about the head with stones in their hands.

We had no time to reflect, for, to my surprise, they filled their canoes with stones, and twelve men came off after us to renew the attack; which they did so effectually, as nearly to disable us all. We were obliged to sustain the attack without being able to return it, except with such stones as lodged in the boat. I adopted the expedient of throwing overboard some clothes, which, as I expected, they stopped to pick up; and as it was by this time almost dark, they gave over the attack, and returned toward the shore, leaving us to reflect on our unhappy ituation.

The poor man killed by the natives was John Norton: this was his second voyage with me as a quarter-master, and his worthy character made me lament his loss very much. He left an aged parent, I am told, whom he supported.

We set our sails, and steered along shore by the west side of the island of Tofoa, the wind blowing fresh from the eastward. My mind was employed in considering what was best to be done, when I was solicited by all hands to take them toward home; and when I told them that no hopes of relief for us remained, except what might be found at New Holland, till I came to Timor, a distance of full twelve hundred leagues, where there was a Dutch settlement, but in what part of the island I knew not, they all agreed to live on one ounce of bread and a quarter of a pint of water per day. Therefore, after examining our stock of provisions, and recommending to them, in the most solemn manner, not to depart from their promise, we bore away across a sea where the navigation is but little known, in a small boat, twenty-three feet long from stem to stern, deep laden with eighteen men. I was happy, however, to see that every one seemed better satisfied with our situation than myself.

Our stock of provisions consisted of about one hundred and fifty pounds of bread, twenty-eight gallons of water, twenty pounds of pork, three bottles of wine, and five quarts of rum. The difference between this and the quantity we had on leaving the ship was principally owing to our loss in the bustle and confusion of the attack. A few cocoa-nuts were in the boat, and some bread-fruit, but the latter was trampled to pieces.

Sunday, 3d.—At daybreak the gale increased; the sun rose very fiery and red—a sure indication of a severe gale of wind. At eight it blew a violent storm, and the sea ran very high, so that between the seas the sail was becalmed, and when on the top of the sea it was too much to have set; but we could not venture to take in the sail, for we were in very imminent danger and distress, the sea curling over the stern of the boat, which obliged us to bail with all our might. A situation more distressing has perhaps seldom been experienced.

Our bread was in bags, and in danger of being spoiled by the wet: to be starved to death was inevitable, if this could not be prevented. I therefore began to examine what clothes there were in the boat, and what other things could be spared; and having determined that only two suits should be kept for each person, the rest was thrown overboard, with some rope and spare sails, which lightened the boat considerably, and we had more room to bail the water out. Fortunately the carpenter had a good chest in the boat, in which we secured the bread the first favorable moment. His tool-chest also was cleared, and the tools stowed in the bottom of the boat, so that this became a second convenience.

I served a teaspoonful of rum to each person—for we were wet and cold—with a quarter of a bread-fruit, which was scarce eatable, for dinner. Our engagement was now strictly to be carried into execution, and I was fully determined to make our provisions last eight weeks, let the daily proportion be ever so small.

Monday, 4th.—At daylight our limbs were so benumbed, that we could scarcely find the use of them. At this time I served a teaspoonful of rum to each person, from which we all found great benefit. Just before noon, we discovered a small, flat island, of a moderate hight, bearing west-south-west four or five leagues. I observed our latitude to be eighteen degrees fifty-eight minutes south; our longitude was, by account, three degrees four minutes west from the island of Tofoa, having made a north seventy-two degrees west course, distance ninety-five miles, since yesterday noon. I divided five small cocoa-nuts for our dinner, and every one was satisfied. During the rest of that day we discovered ten or twelve other islands, none of which we approached. At night I served a few broken pieces of bread-fruit for supper, and performed prayers.

Tuesday, 5th.—The night having been fair, we awoke after a tolerable rest, and contentedly breakfasted on a few pieces of yams that were found in the boat. After breakfast we examined our bread, a great deal of which was damaged and rotten; this, nevertheless, we were glad to keep for use. We passed two islands in the course of the day. For dinner I served some of the damaged bread, and a quarter of a pint of water.

Wednesday, 6th.—We still kept our course in the direction of the north of New Holland, passing numerous islands of various sizes, at none of which I ventured to land. Our allowance for the day was a quarter of a pint of cocoa-nut milk, and the meat, which did not exceed two ounces to each person. It was received very contentedly, but we suffered great drouth. To our great joy we hooked a fish, but we were miserably disappointed by its being lost in trying to get it into the boat.

As our lodgings were very miserable, and confined for want of room, I endeavored to remedy the latter defect by putting ourselves at watch and watch; so that one-half always sat up while the other lay down on the boat's bottom, or upon a chest, with nothing to cover us but the heavens. Our limbs were dreadfully cramped, for we could not stretch them out; and the nights were so cold, and we so constantly wet, that, after a few hours' sleep, we could scarcely move.

Thursday, 7th.—Being very wet and cold, I served a spoonful of rum and a morsel of bread for breakfast. We still kept sailing among islands, from one of which two large canoes put out in chase of us; but we left them behind. Whether these canoes had any hostile intention against us must remain a doubt: perhaps we might have benefited by an intercourse with them ; but, in our defenseless situation, to have made the experiment would have been risking too much.

I imagined these to be the islands called Feejee, as their extent, direction, and distance from the Friendly Islands answers to the description given of them by those islanders. Heavy rain came on at four o'clock, when every person did their utmost to catch some water, and we increased our stock to thirty-four gallons, besides quenching our thirst for the first time we had been to sea; but an attendant consequence made us pass the night very miserably, for being extremely wet, and having no dry things to shift or cover us, we experienced cold shiverings scarcely to be conceived. Most fortunately for us, the forenoon, Friday 8th, turned out fair, and we stripped and dried our clothes. The allowance I issued to-day was an ounce and a half of pork, a teaspoonful of rum, half a pint of cocoa-nut milk, and an ounce of bread. The rum, though so small in quantity, was of the greatest service. A fishing-line was generally towing from the stern of the boat, but though we saw great numbers of fish, we could never catch one.

In the afternoon we cleaned out the boat, and it employed us till sunset to get every thing dry and in order. Hitherto I had issued the allowance by guess, but I now made a pair of scales with two cocoa-nut shells, and having accidentally some pistol-balls in the boat, twenty-five of which weighed one pound, or sixteen ounces, I adopted one* as the proportion of weight that each person should receive of bread at the times I served it. I also amused all hands with describing the situation of New Guinea and New Holland, and gave them every information in my power, that, in case any accident happened to me, those who survived might have some idea of what they were about, and be able to find their way to Timor, which at present they knew nothing of more than the name, and some not even that. At night I served a quarter of a pint of water and half an ounce of bread for supper.

Saturday, *9th.*—About nine in the evening the clouds began to gather, and we had a prodigious fall of rain, with severe thunder and lightning. By midnight we caught about twenty gallons of water. Being miserably wet and cold, I served to the people a teaspoonful of rum each, to enable them to bear with their distressed situation. The weather continued extremely bad, and the wind increased; we spent

---

* It weighed two hundred and seventy-two grains.

a very miserable night, without sleep, except such as could be got in the midst of rain. The day brought no relief but its light. The sea broke over us so much, that two men were constantly bailing; and we had no choice how to steer, being obliged to keep before the waves, for fear of the boat filling.

The allowance now regularly served to each person was one-twenty-fifth of a pound of bread, and a quarter of a pint of water, at eight in the morning, at noon, and at sunset. To-day I gave about half an ounce of pork for dinner, which, though any moderate person would have considered only as a mouthful, was divided into three or four.

All Sunday, Monday, Tuesday, Wednesday, Thursday, and Friday, the wet weather continued, with heavy seas and squalls. As there was no prospect of getting our clothes dried, my plan was to make every one strip, and wring them through the salt water, by which means they received a warmth that, while wet with rain, they could not have. We were constantly shipping seas and bailing, and were very wet and cold during the night. The sight of the islands which we were always passing served only to increase the misery of our situation. We were very little better than starving, with plenty in view; yet to attempt procuring any relief was attended with so much danger, that prolonging of life, even in the midst of misery, was thought preferable, while there remained hopes of being able to surmount our hardships. For my own part, I consider the general run of cloudy and wet weather to be a blessing of Providence. Hot weather would have caused us to have died with thirst, and probably being so constantly covered with rain or sea protected us from that dreadful calamity.

Saturday, 16th.—The sun breaking out through the clouds gave us hopes of drying our wet clothes; but the sunshine was of short duration. We had strong breezes at south-east by south, and dark, gloomy weather, with storms of thunder, lightning, and rain. The night was truly horrible, and not a star to be seen, so that our steerage was uncertain.

Sunday, 17th.—At dawn of day I found every person complaining, and some of them solicited extra allowance, which I positively refused. Our situation was miserable; always wet, and suffering extreme cold during the night, without the least shelter from the weather. Being constantly obliged to bail, to keep the boat from filling, was perhaps not to be reckoned an evil, as it gave us exercise.

The little rum we had was of great service. When our nights were particularly distressing,

I generally served a teaspoonful or two to each person; and it was always joyful tidings when they heard of my intentions.

The night was dark and dismal, the sea constantly breaking over us, and nothing but the wind and waves to direct our steerage. It was my intention, if possible, to make New Holland, to the southward of Endeavor Straits, being sensible that it was necessary to preserve such a situation as would make a southerly wind a fair one; that we might range along the reefs till an opening should be found into smooth water, and we the sooner be able to pick up some refreshments.

Monday and Tuesday were terrible days, heavy rain, with lightning. We were always bailing. On Wednesday, the 20th, at dawn of day, some of my people seemed half dead. Our appearance was horrible, and I could look no way but I caught the eye of some one in distress. Extreme hunger was now too evident; but no one suffered from thirst, nor had we much inclination to drink—that desire, perhaps, being satisfied through the skin. The little sleep we got was in the midst of water, and we constantly awoke with severe cramps and pains in our bones.

Thursday, Friday, and Saturday, we were in the same distressed condition, and I began to fear that such another night or two would put an end to us. On Saturday, however, the wind moderated in the evening, and the weather looked much better, which rejoiced all hands, so that they ate their scanty allowance with more satisfaction than for some time past. The night also was fair; but being always wet with the sea, we suffered much from the cold.

Sunday, 24*th*.—A fine morning, I had the pleasure to see produce some cheerful countenances; and the first time, for fifteen days past, we experienced comfort from the warmth of the sun. We stripped, and hung our clothes up to dry, which were by this time become so threadbare that they would not keep out either wet or cold.

This afternoon we had many birds about us, which are never seen far from land, such as boobies and noddies. As the sea began to run fair, and we shipped but little water, I took the opportunity to examine into the state of our bread, and found that, according to the present mode of issuing, there was a sufficient quantity remaining for twenty-nine days' allowance, by which time I hoped we should be able to reach Timor; but as this was very uncertain, and it was possible that, after all, we might be obliged to go to Java, I determined to proportion the allowance so as to make our stock hold out six weeks. I was apprehensive that this would be ill received, and that it would require my utmost resolution to enforce it; for small as the quantity was which I intended to take away for our future good, yet it might appear to my people like robbing them of life; and some, who were less patient than their companions, I expected would very ill brook it. However, on my representing the necessity of guarding against delays that might be occasioned in our voyage by contrary winds or other causes, and promising to enlarge upon the allowance as we got on, they cheerfully agreed to my proposal. It was accordingly settled that every person should receive one-twenty-fifth of a pound of bread for breakfast, and the same quantity for dinner; so that, by omitting the proportion for supper, we had forty-three days' allowance.

Monday, 25*th*.—At noon some noddies came so near to us, that one of them was caught by hand. This bird was about the size of a small pigeon. I divided it, with its entrails, into eighteen portions, and by a well-known method at sea, of "Who shall have this?"* it was dis-

* One person turns his back on the object that is to be divided; another then points separately to the portions, at each of them asking aloud, "Who shall have this?" to which the first answers by naming somebody. This impartial method of division gives every man an equal chance of the best share.

tributed, with the allowance of bread and water for dinner, and ate up, bones and all, with salt water for sauce. I observed the latitude 13 degrees 32 minutes south; longitude made 35 degrees 19 minutes west; course north 89 degrees west, distance one hundred and eight miles.

In the evening several boobies flying very near to us, we had the good fortune to catch one of them. This bird is as large as a duck. I directed the bird to be killed for supper, and the blood to be given to three of the people who were most distressed for want of food. The body, with the entrails, beak, and feet, I divided into eighteen shares, and with an allowance of bread, which I made a merit of granting, we made a good supper, compared with our usual fare.

Sailing on, Tuesday, Wednesday, and Thursday, I at length became satisfied that we were approaching New Holland. This was actually the case; and after passing the reefs which bound that part of the coast, we found ourselves in smooth water. Two islands lay about four miles to the west by north, and appeared eligible for a resting-place, if for nothing more; but on our approach to the nearest island, it proved to be only a heap of stones, and its size too inconsiderable to shelter the boat. We therefore proceeded to the next, which was close to it, and toward the main. We landed to examine if there were any signs of the natives being near us; we saw some old fireplaces, but nothing to make me apprehend that this would be an unsafe situation for the night. Every one was anxious to find something to eat, and it was soon discovered that there were oysters on these rocks; for the tide was out; but it was nearly dark, and only a few could be gathered. I determined, therefore, to wait till the morning, when I should know better how to proceed.

Friday, 29th.—As there were no appearances to make me imagine that any of the natives were near us, I sent out parties in search of supplies, while others of the people were putting the boat in order. The parties returned, highly rejoiced at having found plenty of oysters and fresh water. I had also made a fire, by the help of a small magnifying glass; and, what was still more fortunate, we found among the few things which had been thrown into the boat, and saved, a piece of brimstone and a tinder-box, so that I secured fire for the future.

One of the people had been so provident as to bring away with him from the ship a copper pot. By being in possession of this article, we were enabled to make a proper use of the supply we now obtained; for, with a mixture of bread, and a little pork, we made a stew that might have been relished by people of far more delicate appetites, and of which each person received a full pint. The general complaints of disease among us were a dizziness in the head, great weakness of the joints, and violent tenesmus.

The oysters which we found grew so fast to the rocks, that it was with difficulty they could be broken off, and at length we discovered it to be the most expeditious way to open them where they were fixed. They were of a good size, and well tasted. To add to this happy circumstance, in the hollow of the land there grew some wire-grass, which indicated a moist situation. On forcing a stick about three feet long into the ground, we found water, and with little trouble dug a well, which produced as much as our necessities required.

As the day was the anniversary of the restoration of King Charles II, I named the island Restoration Island. Our short stay there, with the supplies which it afforded us, made a visible alteration for the better in our appearance. Next day, Saturday the 30th, at four o'clock, we were preparing to embark, when about twenty of the natives appeared, running and hallooing to us, on the opposite shore. They were each armed with a spear or lance, and a short weapon which they carried in their left hand. They made signs for us to come to them, but I thought it prudent to make the best of our way. They were naked, and apparently black, and their hair or wool bushy and short.

Sunday, 31*st*.—Many small islands were in sight to the north-east. We landed at one of a good hight, bearing north one-half west. The shore was rocky, but the water was smooth, and we landed without difficulty. I sent two parties out, one to the northward, and the other to the southward, to seek for supplies, and others I ordered to stay by the boat. On this occasion fatigue and weakness so far got the better of their sense of duty, that some of the people expressed their discontent at having worked harder than their companions, and declared that they would rather be without their dinner than go in search of it. One person, in particular, went so far as to tell me, with a mutinous look, that he was as good a man as myself. It was not possible for me to judge where this might have an end, if not stopped in time; therefore, to prevent such disputes in future, I determined either to preserve my command, or die in the attempt; and seizing a cutlass, I ordered him to take hold of another and defend himself, on which he called out that I was going to kill him, and immediately made concessions. I did not allow this to interfere further with the harmony of the boat's crew, and every thing soon became quiet. We here procured some oysters and clams, also some dog-fish, caught in the holes of the rocks, and a supply of water.

Leaving this island, which I named Sunday Island, we continued our course toward Endeavor Straits. During our voyage Nelson became very ill, but gradually recovered. Next day we landed at another island, to see what we could get. There were proofs that the island was occasionally visited by natives from New Holland. Encamping on the shore, I sent out one party to watch for turtle, and another to try to catch birds. About midnight the bird party returned, with only twelve noddies, birds which I have already described to be about the size of pigeons; but if it had not been for the folly and obstinacy of one of the party, who had separated from the other two, and disturbed the birds, they might have caught a great number. I was so much provoked at my plans being thus defeated, that I gave the offender a good beating. This man afterward confessed that, wandering away from his companions, he had eaten nine birds raw. Our turtling party had no success.

Tuesday and Wednesday we still kept our course north-west, touching at an island or two for oysters and clams. We had now been six days on the coast of Holland, and but for the refreshment which our visits to its shores afforded us, it is all but certain that we must have perished. Now, however, it became clear that we were leaving it behind, and were commencing our adventurous voyage through the open sea to Timor.

On Wednesday, June 3d, at 8 o'clock in the evening, we once more launched into the open ocean. Miserable as our situation was in every respect, I was secretly surprised to see that it did not affect any one so strongly as myself. I encouraged every one with hopes that eight or ten days would bring us to a land of safety, and after praying to God for a continuance of his most gracious protection, I served an allowance of water for supper, and directed our course to the west-south-west, to counteract the southerly winds in case they should blow strong. For six days our voyage continued; a dreary repetition of those sufferings which we had experienced before reaching New Holland. In the course of the night we were constantly wet with the sea, and exposed to cold and shiverings; and in the day-time we had no addition to our scanty allowance, save a booby and a small dolphin that we caught, the former on Friday the 5th, and the latter on Monday the

8th. Many of us were ill, and the men complained heavily. On Wednesday the 10th, after a very comfortless night, there was a visible alteration for the worse in many of the people, which gave me great apprehensions. An extreme weakness, swelled legs, hollow and ghastly countenances, a more than common inclination to sleep, with an apparent debility of understanding, seemed to me the melancholy presages of an approaching dissolution.

Thursday, 11*th*.—Every one received the customary allowance of bread and water, and an extra allowance of water was given to those who were most in need. At noon I observed in latitude 9 degrees 41 minutes south; course south 77 degrees west, distance 109 miles; longitude made 13 degrees 49 minutes west. I had little doubt of having now passed the meridian of the eastern part of Timor, which is laid down in 128 degrees east. This diffused universal joy and satisfaction.

Friday, 12*th*.—At three in the morning, with an excess of joy, we discovered Timor bearing from west-south-west to west-north-west, and I hauled on a wind to the north-north-east till daylight, when the land bore from south-west by south to north-east by north; our distance from the shore two leagues. It is not possible for me to describe the pleasure which the blessing of the sight of land diffused among us. It appeared scarcely credible to ourselves that, in an open boat, and so poorly provided, we should have been able to reach the coast of Timor in forty-one days after leaving Tofoa, having in that time run, by our log, a distance of 3,618 miles, and that, notwithstanding our extreme distress, no one should have perished in the voyage.

I have already mentioned that I knew not where the Dutch settlement was situated, but I had a faint idea that it was at the south-west part of the island. I therefore, after daylight, bore away along shore to the south-south-west, which I was the more readily induced to do, as the wind would not suffer us to go toward the north-east without great loss of time.

We coasted along the island in the direction in which I conceived the Dutch settlement to lie, and next day, about two o'clock, I came to a grapnel in a small sandy bay, where we saw a hut, a dog, and some cattle. Here I learned that the Dutch governor resided at a place called Coupang, which was some distance to the north-east. I made signs for one of the Indians who came to the beach to go in the boat and show us the way to Coupang, intimating that I would pay him for his trouble; the man readily complied, and came into the boat. The

Indians, who were of a dark tawny color, brought us a few pieces of dried turtle and some ears of Indian corn. This last was the most welcome, for the turtle was so hard, that it could not be eaten without being first soaked in hot water. They offered to bring us some other refreshments, if I would wait; but, as the pilot was willing, I determined to push on. It was about half-past four when we sailed.

Sunday, 14*th*.—At one o'clock in the morning, after the most happy and sweet sleep that ever men enjoyed, we weighed, and continued to keep the east shore on board, in very smooth water. The report of two cannon that were fired gave new life to every one; and soon after, we discovered two square-rigged vessels and a cutter at anchor to the eastward. After hard rowing, we came to a grapnel near daylight, off a small fort and town, which the pilot told me was Coupang.

On landing, I was surrounded by many people, Indians and Dutch, with an English sailor among them. A Dutch captain, named Spikerman, showed me great kindness, and waited on the governor, who was ill, to know at what time I could see him. Eleven o'clock having been appointed for the interview, I desired my people to come on shore, which was as much as some of them could do, being scarce able to walk;

they, however, were helped to Captain Spikerman's house, and found tea, with bread and butter, provided for their breakfast.

The abilities of a painter, perhaps, could seldom have been displayed to more advantage than in the delineation of the two groups of figures which at this time presented themselves to each other. An indifferent spectator would have been at a loss which most to admire—the eyes of famine sparkling at immediate relief, or the horror of their preservers at the sight of so many specters, whose ghastly countenances, if the cause had been unknown, would rather have excited terror than pity. Our bodies were nothing but skin and bone, our limbs were full of sores, and were clothed in rags: in this condition, with tears of joy and gratitude flowing down our cheeks, the people of Timor beheld us with a mixture of horror, surprise, and pity

The governor, Mr. William Adrian Van Este, notwithstanding extreme ill health, became so anxious about us, that I saw him before the appointed time. He received me with a great affection, and gave me the fullest proofs that he was possessed of every feeling of a humane and good man. Though his infirmity was so great that he could not do the office of a friend himself, he said he would give such orders as I might be certain would procure us every supply we wanted. A house should be immediately prepared for me, and with respect to my people, he said that I might have room for them either at the hospital or on board of Captain Spikerman's ship, which lay in the road.

On returning to Captain Spikerman's house, I found that every kind relief had been given to my people. The surgeon had dressed their sores, and the cleaning of their persons had not been less attended to, several friendly gifts of apparel having been presented to them.

I desired to be shown to the house that was intended for me, which I found ready, with servants to attend. It consisted of a hall, with a room at each end, and a loft overhead, and was surrounded by a piazza, with an outer apartment in one corner, and a communication from the back part of the house to the street. I therefore determined, instead of separating from my people, to lodge them all with me; and I divided the house as follows: One room I took to myself; the other I allotted to the master, surgeon, Mr. Nelson, and the gunner; the loft to the other officers; and the outer apartment to the men. The hall was common to the officers, and the men had the back piazza. Of this disposition I informed the governor, and he sent down chairs, tables, and benches, with bedding and other necessaries, for the use of every one. At noon a dinner was brought to the house, sufficiently good to make persons more accustomed to plenty eat too much. Yet I believe few in such a situation would have observed more moderation than my people did. Having seen every one enjoy this meal of plenty, I dined myself with Mr. Wanjon, the governor's son-in-law; but I felt no extraordinary inclination to eat or drink. Rest and quiet I considered as more necessary to the re-establishment of my health, and therefore retired soon to my room, which I found furnished with every convenience. But instead of rest, my mind was disposed to reflect on our late sufferings, and on the failure of the expedition; but, above all, on the thanks due to almighty God, who had given us power to support and bear such heavy calamities, and had enabled me at last to be the means of saving eighteen lives.

In our late situation it was not the least of my distresses to be constantly assailed with the melancholy demands of my people for an increase of allowance, which it grieved me to refuse. The necessity of observing the most rigid economy in the distribution of our provisions was so evident, that I resisted their solicitations, and never deviated from the agreement we made at setting out. The consequence of this care was, that at our arrival we had still remaining sufficient for eleven days, at our scanty allowance: and if we had been so unfortunate as to have missed the Dutch settlement at Timor, we could have proceeded to Java, where I was certain that every supply we wanted could be procured.

We remained at Coupang about two months, during which time we experienced every possible kindness. On the 20th of July, David Nelson, who had been ill during our voyage, died of an inflammatory fever, and was buried in the European cemetery of the place. Having purchased a small schooner, and fitted her out under the name of his Majesty's schooner Resource, I and my crew set out for Batavia on the 20th of August. We reached that settlement on the 1st of October, where I sold the schooner, and endeavored to procure our passage to England. We were obliged, however, to separate, and go home in different ships. On Friday, the 16th October, before sunrise, I embarked on board the Vlydte packet, commanded by Captain Peter Couvret, bound for Middleburg. With me likewise embarked Mr. John Samuel, clerk, and John Smith, seaman. Those of our company who staid behind, the governor promised me should follow in the first ships, and be as little divided as possible. On the 13th of March, 1790, I left the packet, and was landed at Portsmouth by an Isle of Wight boat.

Those of my officers and people whom I left at Batavia were provided with passages in the earliest ships, and, at the time we parted, were apparently in good health. Nevertheless, they did not all live to quit Batavia. Thomas Hall, a seaman, had died while I was there. Mr. Elphinstone, master's mate, and Peter Linkletter, seaman, died within a fortnight after my departure; the hardships they had experienced having rendered them unequal to cope with so unhealthy a climate as that of Batavia. The remainder embarked on board the Dutch fleet for Europe, and arrived safe in this country, except Robert Lamb, who died on the passage, and Mr. Ledward, the surgeon, who has not yet been heard of. Thus, of nineteen who were forced by the mutineers into the launch, it has pleased God that twelve should surmount the difficulties and dangers of the voyage, and live to revisit their native country.

FATE OF THE MUTINEERS—COLONY OF PITCAIRN'S ISLAND.

The intelligence of the mutiny, and the sufferings of Bligh and his companions, naturally excited a great sensation in England. Bligh was immediately promoted to the rank of commander, and Captain Edwards was dispatched to Otaheite, in the Pandora frigate, with instructions to search for the Bounty and her mutinous crew, and bring them to England. The Pandora reached Matavai Bay on the 23d of March, 1791; and even before she had come to anchor, Joseph Coleman, formerly armorer of the Bounty, pushed off from shore in a canoe, and came on board. In the course of two days afterward, the whole of the remainder of the Bounty's crew—in number sixteen—then on the island, surrendered themselves, with the exception of two, who fled to the mountains, where, as it afterward appeared, they were murdered by the natives.

From his prisoners, and the journals kept by one or two of them, Captain Edwards learnt the proceedings of Christian and his associates after turning Bligh and his companions adrift in the boat. It appears that they steered in the first instance to the island of Toobouai, where they intended to form a settlement; but the opposition of the natives, and the want of many necessary materials, determined them to return in the mean time to Otaheite, where they arrived on the 25th of May, 1789. In answer to the inquiries of Tinah, the King, about Bligh and the rest of the crew, the mutineers stated that they had fallen in with Captain Cook, who was forming a settlement in a neighboring island, and had retained Bligh and the others to assist him, while they themselves had been dispatched to Otaheite for an additional supply of hogs, goats, fowls, bread-fruit, and various other articles. Overjoyed at hearing their old friend Cook was alive, and about to settle so near them, the humane and unsuspicious islanders set about so actively to procure the supplies wanted, that in a few days the Bounty received on board three hundred and twelve hogs, thirty-eight goats, eight dozen of fowls, a bull, and a cow, and a large quantity of bread-fruit, plantains, bananas, and other fruits. The mutineers also took with them eight men, nine women, and seven boys, with all of whom they arrived a second time at Toobouai, on the 26th of June, where they warped the ship up the harbor, landed the live stock, and set about building a fort fifty yards square. Quarrels and disagreements, however, soon broke out among them. The poor natives were treated like slaves, and upon attempting to retaliate, were mercilessly put to death. Christian, finding his authority almost entirely disregarded, called a consultation as to what steps were next to be taken, when it was agreed that Toobouai should be abandoned; that the ship should once more be taken to Otaheite, where those who might choose it would be put ashore, while the rest, who preferred remaining in the vessel, might proceed wherever they had a mind. This was accordingly done. Sixteen of the crew went ashore at Matavai—fourteen of whom, as already stated, were received on board the Pandora, and two were murdered—while Christian, with his eight comrades, and taking with them seven Otaheitan men and twelve women, finally sailed from Matavai on the 21st of September, 1789, from which time they had never been more heard of.

Captain Edwards instituted a strict search after the fugitives among the various groups of islands in the Pacific, but finding no trace of them, he set sail, after three months' investigation, for the east coast of New Holland. Here, by some mismanagement, the Pandora struck upon the singular coral reef that runs along that coast called the "Barrier Reef," and filled so fast, that scarcely were the boats got out when she foundered and went down, thirty-four of the crew and four of the prisoners perishing in her. The concurring testimony of the unfortunate prisoners exhibits the conduct of Captain Edwards toward them, both before and after the wreck, as having been cruel in the extreme. After reaching a low, sandy, desert island, or rather *key*, as such are nautically termed, Captain Edwards caused his men to form tents out of the sails they had saved, under which he and his men reposed in comparative comfort; but he refused the same indulgence to his miserable captives, whose only refuge, therefore, from the scorching rays of the sun was by burying themselves up to the neck among the burning sand, so that their bodies were blistered as if they had been scalded with boiling water. The Pandora's survivors reached Batavia in their boats, whence they obtained passage to England in Dutch vessels. A court-martial was soon afterward held—September, 1792—when six of the ten mutineers were found guilty and condemned to death—the other four were acquitted. Only three of the six, however, were executed.

Nearly twenty years elapsed after the period of the above occurrences, and all recollection of the Bounty and her wretched crew had passed away, when an accidental discovery, as interesting as unexpected, once more recalled public attention to that event. The captain of an American schooner having, in 1808, accidentally touched at an island up to that time supposed to be uninhabited, called Pitcairn's Island, found a community speaking English, who represented themselves as the descendants of the mutineers of the Bounty, of whom there was still one man, of the name of Alexander Smith, alive among them. Intelligence of this singular circumstance was sent by the American captain—Folger—to Sir Sydney Smith at Valparaiso, and by him transmitted to the Lords of the Admiralty. But the Government was at that time perhaps too much engaged in the events of the continental war to attend to the information, nor was any thing further heard of this interesting little society till 1814. In that year two British men-of-war, cruising the Pacific, made Pitcairn's Island, and on nearing the shore, saw plantations regularly and orderly laid out. Soon afterward they observed a few natives coming down a steep descent, with their canoes on their shoulders, and in a few minutes perceived one of these little vessels darting through a heavy surf, and paddling off toward the ships. But their astonishment may be imagined when, on coming along side, they were hailed in good English with, "Won't you heave us a rope now?" This being done, a young man sprang up the side with extraordinary activity, and stood on the deck before them. In answer to the question, "Who are you?" he replied that his name was Thursday October Christian, son of the late Fletcher Christian, by an Otaheitan mother; that he was the first born on the island, and was so named because he was born on a Thursday in October. All this sounded singular and incredible in the ears of the British captains, Sir Thomas Staines and Mr. Pipon; but they were soon satisfied of its truth. Young Christian was at this time about twenty-four years old, a tall, handsome youth, fully six feet high, with black hair, and an open, interesting English countenance. As he wore no clothes, except a piece of cloth round his loins, and a straw-hat ornamented with black cock's feathers, his fine figure and well-shaped, muscular limbs were displayed to great advantage, and attracted general admiration. His body was much tanned by exposure to the weather; but although his complexion was somewhat brown, it wanted that tinge of red peculiar to the natives of the Pacific. He spoke English correctly both in grammar and pronunciation; and his frank and ingenuous deportment excited in every one the liveliest feelings of compassion and interest. His companion was a fine, handsome youth, of seventeen or eighteen years of age, named George Young, son of one of the Bounty's midshipmen.

The youths expressed great surprise at every thing they saw, especially a cow, which they supposed to be either a huge goat or a horned sow, having never seen any other quadrupeds. When questioned concerning the Bounty, they referred the captains to an old man on shore, the only surviving Englishman, whose name, they said, was John Adams, but who proved to be the identical Alexander Smith before-mentioned, having changed his name from some caprice or other. The officers went ashore with the youths, and were received by old Adams—as we shall now call him—who conducted them to his house, and treated them to an elegant repast of eggs, fowls, yams, plantains, bread-fruit, etc. They now learned from him an account of the fate of his companions, who, with himself, preferred accompanying Christian in the Bounty to remaining at Otaheite—which account agreed with that he afterward gave at greater length to Captain Beechey in 1828. Our limits will not permit us to detail all the interesting particulars at length, as we could have wished, but they are in substance as follows:

It was Christian's object, in order to avoid the vengeance of the British law, to proceed to some unknown and uninhabited island, and the Marquesas islands were first fixed upon. But Christian, on reading Captain Cartaret's account of Pitcairn's Island, thought it better adapted for the purpose, and shaped his course thither. Having landed and traversed it, they found it every way suitable to their wishes, possessing water, wood, a good soil, and some fruits.

Having ascertained all this, they returned on board, and having landed their hogs, goats, and poultry, and gutted the ship of every thing that could be useful to them, they set fire to her, and destroyed every vestige that might lead to the discovery of their retreat. This was on the 23d of January, 1790. The island was then divided into nine equal portions among them, a suitable spot of neutral ground being reserved for a village. The poor Otaheitans now found themselves reduced to the condition of mere slaves; but they patiently submitted, and every thing went on peaceably for two years. About that time, Williams, one of the seamen, having the misfortune to lose his wife, forcibly took the wife of one of the Otaheitans, which, together with their continued ill-usage, so exasperated the latter, that they formed a plan for murdering the whole of their oppressors. The plot, however, was discovered, and revealed by the Englishmen's wives, and two of the Otaheitans were put to death. But the surviving natives soon afterward matured a more successful conspiracy, and in one day murdered five of the Englishmen, including Christian. Adams and Young were spared at the intercession of their wives, and the remaining two, M'Koy and Quintal — two desperate ruffians — escaped to the mountains, whence, however, they soon rejoined their companions. But the farther career of these two villains was short. M'Koy, having been bred up in a Scottish distillery, succeeded in extracting a bottle of ardent spirits from the *tee root;* from which time he and Quintal were never sober, till the former became delirious, and committed suicide by jumping over a cliff. Quintal being likewise almost insane with drinking, made repeated attempts to murder Adams and Young, till they were absolutely compelled, for their own safety, to put him to death, which they did by felling him with a hatchet.

Adams and Young were at length the only surviving males who had landed on the island, and being both of a serious turn of mind, and, having time for reflection and repentance, they became extremely devout. Having saved a Bible and prayer-book from the Bounty, they now performed family worship morning and evening, and addressed themselves to training up their own children and those of their unfortunate companions in piety and virtue. Young, however, was soon carried off by an asthmatic complaint, and Adams was thus left to continue his pious labors alone. At the time Captains Staines and Pipon visited the island, this interesting little colony consisted of about forty-six persons, mostly grown-up young people, all living in harmony and happiness together; and not only professing, but fully understanding and practicing, the precepts and principles of the Christian religion. Adams had instituted the ceremony of marriage, and he assured his visitors that not one instance of debauchery and immoral conduct had occurred among them.

The visitors having supplied these interesting people with some tools, kettles, and other articles, took their leave. The account which they transmitted home of this newly-discovered colony was, strange to say, as little attended to by Government as that of Captain Folger, and nothing more was heard of Adams and his family for nearly twelve years, when, in 1825, Captain Beechey, in the Blossom, bound on a voyage of discovery to Behring Strait, touched at Pitcairn's Island. On the approach of the Blossom, a boat came off under all sail toward the ship, containing old Adams and ten of the young men of the island. After requesting and obtaining leave to come on board, the young men sprung up the side, and shook every officer cordially by the hand. Adams, who was grown very corpulent, followed more leisurely. He was dressed in a sailor's shirt and trowsers, with a low-crowned hat, which he held in his hand in sailor fashion, while he smoothed down his bald forehead when addressed by the officers of the Blossom. The little colony had now increased to about sixty-six, including an English sailor of the name of John Buffet, who, at his own earnest desire, had been left by a whaler. In this man the society luckily found an able and willing schoolmaster. He instructed the children in reading, writing, and arithmetic, and devoutly co-operated with old Adams in affording religious instruction to the community. The officers of the Blossom went ashore, and were entertained with a sumptuous repast at young Christian's, the table being spread with plates, knives, and forks. Buffet said grace in an emphatic manner; and so strict were they in this respect, that it was not deemed proper to touch a morsel of bread without saying grace before and after it. The officers slept in the house all night, their bedclothing and sheets consisting of the native cloth made of the native mulberry-tree. The only interruption to their repose was the melody of the evening hymn, which was chanted together by the whole family after the lights were put out; and they were awakened at early dawn by the same devotional ceremony. On Sabbath the utmost decorum was attended to, and the day was passed in regular religious observances.

In consequence of a representation made by Captain Beechey, the British Government sent out Captain Waldegrave in 1830, in the Seringapatam, with a supply of sailors' blue jackets and trowsers, flannels, stockings, and shoes, women's dresses, spades, mattocks, shovels, pickaxes, trowels, rakes, etc. He found their community increased to about seventy-nine, all exhibiting the same unsophisticated and amiable characteristics as we have before described. Other two Englishmen had settled among them; one of them, called Nobbs, a low-bred, illiterate man, a self-constituted missionary, who was endeavoring to supersede Buffet in his office of religious instructor. The patriarch Adams, it was found, had died in March, 1829, aged sixty-five. While on his death-bed, he had called the families together, and urged upon them to elect a chief; which, however, they had not yet done; but the greatest harmony still prevailed among them, notwithstanding Nobbs's exertions to form a party of his own. Captain Waldegrave thought that the island, which is about four miles square, might be able to support a thousand persons, upon reaching which number they would naturally emigrate to other islands.

Such is the account of this most singular colony, originating in crime and bloodshed. Of all the repentant criminals on record, the most interesting, perhaps, is John Adams; nor do we know where to find a more beautiful example of the value of early instruction than in the history of this man, who, having run the full career of nearly all kinds of vice, was checked by an interval of leisurely reflection, and the sense of new duties awakened by the power of natural affections.

VII.

Destruction of the Ship Ann Alexander by a Whale.

THE ship Ann Alexander, Captain John S. Deblois, sailed from New Bedford, Massachusetts, June 1, 1850, for a cruise in the South Pacific in search of sperm-whales. After cruising some months in the Atlantic, and capturing several whales, the vessel proceeded to the South Pacific; and finally, on the 20th of August, 1851, she reached a favorable spot, in latitude 5 degrees 50 minutes south, longitude 102 degrees west. In the morning of that day, at about nine o'clock, whales were discovered in the neighborhood, and about noon the same day they succeeded in making fast to one. Two boats had gone after the whales—the larboard and the starboard; the former commanded by the first mate, and the latter by Captain Deblois. The whale which they had struck was harpooned by the larboard boat. After running some time, the whale turned upon the boat, and, rushing at it with tremendous violence, lifted open its enormous jaws, and taking the boat in, actually crushed it into fragments as small as a common-sized chair! Captain Deblois immediately struck for the scene of the disaster with the starboard-boat, and succeeded, against all expectation, in rescuing the whole of the crew of the demolished boat, nine in number! How they escaped from instant death, when the whale rushed upon them with such violence and seized the boat in its ponderous jaws, it is impossible to say.

There were now eighteen men in the starboard-boat, consisting of the captain, the first-mate, and the crews of both boats. The frightful disaster had been witnessed from the ship, and the waist-boat was called into readiness and sent to their relief. The distance from the ship was about six miles. As soon as the waist-boat arrived the crews were divided, and it was determined to pursue the same whale, and make another attack upon him. Accordingly they separated, and proceeded at some distance from each other, as is usual on such occasions, after the whale. In a short time they came up to him, and prepared to give him battle. The waist-boat, commanded by the first mate, was in advance. As soon as the whale perceived the demonstration being made upon him, he turned his course suddenly, and made a tremendous dash at this boat, seized with his wide-spread jaws, and crushed it into atoms, allowing the men barely time to escape his vengeance by throwing themselves into the ocean.

Captain Deblois again seeing the perilous condition of his men, at the risk of meeting the same fate, directed his boat to hasten to their rescue, and in a short time succeeded in saving them all from a death little less horrible than that from which they had twice so miraculously escaped. He then ordered the boat to put for the ship as speedily as possible; and no sooner had the order been given, than they discovered the monster of the deep making toward them with his jaws widely extended. Escape from death now seemed totally out of the question. They were six or seven miles from the ship; no aid even there to afford them necessary relief, and the whale, maddened by the wounds of the harpoons and lances which had been thrown into him, and seemingly animated with the prospect of speedy revenge, within a few cable's length. Fortunately, the monster came up and passed them at a short distance. The boat then made her way to the ship, and they all got on board in safety.

After reaching the ship, a boat was dispatched for the oars of the demolished boats, and it was determined to pursue the whale with the ship.

As soon as the boat returned with the oars, sail was set, and the ship proceeded after the whale. In a short time she overtook him, and a lance was thrown into his head. The ship passed on by him, and immediately after they discovered that the whale was making for the ship. As he came up near her, they hauled to the wind, and suffered the monster to pass her. After he had fairly passed, they kept on to overtake and attack him again. When the ship had reached within about fifty rods of him, they discovered that the whale had settled down deep below the surface of the water, and as it was near sundown, they concluded to give up the pursuit. Subsequent events proved, however, that the whale had formed a deadly resolution to destroy the ship which had given him so much annoyance.

While Captain Deblois was waiting on deck for the reappearance of the whale, he suddenly saw it approaching at the rate of fifteen miles an hour. In an instant the determined monster struck the ship with tremendous violence, shaking her from stem to stern. She quivered under the violence of the shock as if she had struck upon a rock. Captain Deblois immediately descended into the forecastle, and there, to his horror, discovered that the whale had struck the ship about two feet from the keel, abreast the foremast, knocking a great hole entirely through her bottom, through which the water roared and rushed in impetuously. Springing to the deck, he ordered the mate to cut away the anchors and get the cables overboard to keep the ship from sinking. In doing this, the mate succeeded in relieving only one anchor and getting one cable clear, the other having been fastened around the foremast. The ship was then sinking very rapidly. The captain went into the cabin, where he found three feet of water; he, however, succeeded in procuring a chronometer, sextant, and chart. Reaching the decks, he ordered the boats to be cleared away, to get water and provisions, as the ship was keeling over. He again descended to the cabin, but the water was rushing in so rapidly that he could procure nothing. He then came upon deck, ordered all hands into the boats, and was the last to leave the ship, which he did by throwing himself into the sea, and swimming to the nearest boat. The ship was on her beam-ends, her topgallant-yards under water. They then pushed off some distance from the ship, expecting her to sink in a very short time. Upon an examination of the stores they had been able to save, it was discovered that they had only twelve quarts of water, and not a mouthful of provisions of any kind.

The boats contained eleven men each, were leaky, and night coming on, they were obliged to bail them all night, to keep them from sinking.

Next day, at daylight, they returned to the ship, no one daring to venture on board but the captain, their intention being to cut away the masts, and fearful that the moment the masts were cut away the ship would go down. With a single hatchet the captain went on board, and cut away the mast, when the ship righted. The boats then came up, and the men, by the sole aid of spades, cut away the chain-cable from around the foremast, which got the ship nearly on her keel. The men then tied ropes around their bodies, got into the sea, and cut holes through the decks to get out provisions. They could procure nothing but about five gallons of vinegar and twenty pounds of wet bread. The ship threatened to sink, and they deemed it imprudent to remain by her longer; so they set sail in her boats, and left her.

They were then in a dreadful state of anxiety, as it was doubtful whether they should be able to reach land or see any vessel. With faint hopes of being rescued, they directed their course northerly, and on the 22d of August, at about 5 o'clock, P. M., they had the indescribable joy of discerning a ship in the distance. They made a signal, and were soon answered, and in a short time they were reached by the good ship Nantucket, of Nantucket, Massachusetts, Captain Gibbs, who took them all on board, clothed and fed them, and extended to them in every way the greatest possible hospitality.

On the succeeding day, Captain Gibbs went to the wreck of the ill-fated Ann Alexander, for the purpose of trying to procure something from her, but as the sea was rough, and the attempt considered dangerous, he abandoned the project. The Nantucket then set sail for Paita, where she arrived on the 15th of September, and where she landed Captain Deblois and his men. Captain Deblois was kindly and hospitably received and entertained at Paita by Captain Bathurst, an English gentleman residing there, and subsequently took passage on board the schooner Providence, Captain Starbuck, for New Bedford, which was reached on the 12th of August, and where the account of the strange disaster created the deepest surprise and interest.

VIII.

Silvio Pellico in the Austrian Dungeons.

SILVIO PELLICO, the story of whose wrongs has created a sympathizing interest over Europe, was born at Saluzzo, in Piedmont, a province of the Italian kingdom of Sardinia, in 1789, at which time his father, Honorato Pellico, held a situation in the post-office. He was afterward promoted to a seat in the ministry of war at Turin, to which place he removed with his family. Silvio was at that time six years of age, and had already given token of his poetical feelings. Ossian was the bard to whom his earliest years were consecrated. In his sixteenth year he accompanied his twin sister, to whom he was devotedly attached, to Lyons in France, where he remained till some verses of Foscolo, the most eminent of modern Italian poets, awakened in his breast so passionate a reminiscence of his native country, that he hastened toward it, and rejoined his father, then settled at Milan. The latter was in the war department, under the government of Napoleon, as king of Italy. The restoration of Lombardy to the emperor of Austria, on the overthrow of Bonaparte, displaced Honorato Pellico, who then returned to Turin, accompanied by all the members of his family, excepting Silvio, who manifested a disposition to remain at Milan.

Young Silvio, with a poetic temperament and love of letters, had formed an intimacy with Monti, Foscolo, and other eminent literary characters residing in Milan, the whole forming a brilliant society, who sighed over the abased condition of the country under a foreign yoke. Silvio himself became known as the author of a tragedy, which was acted in all the theaters of Italy with the highest applause, and is stated to have been translated into English by Lord Byron, though not published among his works. Pellico had become acquainted with Byron at Milan, and partaking the admiration, which was felt in Italy and Germany much more intensely than in Britain, for the poems of that noble personage, he translated into Italian prose the poetical drama of Manfred. Upon presenting it to Byron, the latter expressed his surprise that he should have turned a poem into prose; and as Pellico maintained it was impossible to translate it properly into poetry, Byron presented to him, upon a subsequent meeting, his own tragedy in an English poetical dress, as a practical refutation of the opinion advanced by him.

The great acquirements of Pellico, and his amiable and pleasing manners, rendered his society much sought after in Milan. The Count Briche committed to his care one of his sons, and subsequently he became tutor to the sons of Count Porro Lambertenghi, one of the wealthiest of the Lombardian nobility, in whose house he associated with persons of the first distinction. With the Count Porro himself he was united in the closest friendship.

Distressed with the general want of enlightenment among the people, and conceiving that the establishment of a literary and scientific journal might improve the public mind, Silvio, in 1819, broached the idea to Porro and some of his literary companions. All were delighted with it; Count Porro advanced the funds necessary for the purpose, and the plan was put in execution. The journal was called "The Conciliator," and had for contributors men of the greatest eminence in Italy. Besides those resident in Milan, were Romagnosi, of Venice, a celebrated jurisconsult; Melchior Gioja, a political economist; Manzoni, at once a poet and prose writer of the first order; Grossi, the author of Ildagonda; and Brechet. Maroncelli, fated to be Pellico's future companion in captivity, was also one of the contributors.

The press was under the strictest censorship. The Austrian government seemed to tremble at the least symptom of liberality of opinion. The Conciliator was soon exposed to the corrections of the censor. Though politics were not discussed, the liberal tone of some of its articles on literature was offensive. They were erased, and the journal went forth with half its columns blank. It was therefore given up.

In 1820 the unfortunate revolution of Naples took place. The jealous government of Austria had its fears more than ever excited. A proclamation was issued, attaching the penalty of death to the offense of belonging to a secret society. The party in Italy, whose object it was to cast off the galling yoke of foreigners, was styled that of the Carbonari, for the suppression of whom every Italian government diligently labored. The emperor of Austria was not in the rear. Numberless arrests were made, upon the merest suspicion of disaffection, throughout what he designated "the Lombardo-Venetian Kingdom." Two distinguished citizens of Milan were exposed to the jealousy of the government, from the enlightened efforts they had made for the improvement of their country. These were the Counts Porro and

Confalonieri, who appropriated a great part of their possessions to the truly-patriotic designs of founding infant and other schools, of promoting the arts, and of introducing into Italy the great discoveries of modern times. Confalonieri visited Paris and London to study the modes of instruction in the schools of France and England, in order to institute them in Italy. He also sent from London the necessary apparatus for the manufacture of gas, for lighting the streets of Milan, the expense of which he and Porro bore jointly. They also, in conjunction with Alexander Visconti, constructed the first steamboat which appeared in Italy. These were exertions that rendered them objects of hatred and suspicion to the Austrians. The contributors to The Conciliator, established at the expense of Porro, were also looked upon with an evil eye. Orders for the arrest of them all were issued. Porro was the only person who escaped, by a timely flight into a foreign country. Confalonieri was taken from a sick-bed, and the arms of an affectionate wife. Pellico and the others were all arrested. Alas! poor Pellico. Let us follow him to prison, and hear him tell the story of his sufferings.*

---

* What follows is an abridgment of Pellico's narrative, translated from the original Italian.

IMPRISONMENT AT MILAN.

On Friday, the 13th of October, 1820, I was arrested at Milan, and conducted to Santa Margherita—formerly a convent, and now the head office of the extensive police establishment. It was about three o'clock in the afternoon, and, after an examination, I was consigned to the charge of the jailer, who having conducted me to the apartment destined for me, politely invited me to deliver into his hands, to be restored at the fitting time, my watch, purse, and any thing else I might have in my pockets; which, having obtained, he with some ceremony wished me good evening.

In less than half an hour my dinner arrived; I ate a few mouthfuls, drank a glass of water, and was left alone. My room was on the ground, and opened on a court-yard, with cells all around, cells on the right and on the left, opposite and above me. I leaned against the window, and stood some time listening to the tramp of the jailers as they went to and fro, and to the dissolute songs of some of the prisoners.

I fell into reflection: a century ago, this prison was a nunnery. Could the holy penitents who inhabited it have ever believed that a day would come when their chambers would resound no longer with the prayers and lamentations of devout women, but with blasphemies and detestable ribaldry, and would hold within them the refuse of society—wretches destined to the hulks or the gallows? And in another century who will breathe in these cells? Alas for the swiftness of time, and the instability of things! Should any one complain that fortune ceases to smile upon him, or grieve that he is cast into a prison and threatened with the gibbet? But yesterday I was one of the happiest of men; to-day I have lost every thing that conduced to the joy of my existence—liberty, friends, hope! It would be absurd to delude myself. I leave this place only for a dungeon more horrible, or for the hands of the executioner. Be it so. When I am dead, it will signify little whether I yielded my last sigh in a dungeon, or am borne to the tomb in all the grandeur of funereal pomp.

It was thus my mind found strength in thinking of the inexorable sweep of time; but shortly the remembrance of my father, my mother, my sisters, my brothers, and of a family which I loved as tenderly as if it were my own, came to assail me, and the arguments of philosophy were powerless. Tenderer thoughts came over me, and I wept like a child.

During the night I slept a little. I became

gradually resigned to my unhappy fate. Toward morning my agitation was calmed, and I was astonished at the change. I yet thought upon my parents, and upon all those whom I loved; but I no longer despaired of their strength of mind. The recollection of those virtuous sentiments which I had known sustain them in previous calamities, consoled me on their behalf.

In the course of the day which followed I was again called to an examination; and it was renewed during several successive days, without any other interval than that allowed for my meals.

While the process thus continued, the days passed rapidly, owing to the constant exercise in which my mind was kept, from the necessity of answering, without intermission, the most varied questions, and of collecting my energies during the intervals of the examination in recalling all that had been asked of me, what answers I had given, and in reflecting upon all those things upon which I would probably be next interrogated.

At the end of the first week a most cruel misfortune happened to me. My poor friend Piero, equally eager with myself to establish a communication between us, wrote me a letter, and sent it, not by a *secondino*—officer of the prison—but by an unfortunate prisoner who was employed in performing services in our rooms. He was a man of from sixty to seventy years of age, condemned to I know not how many months of imprisonment. With a needle which I had, I pricked my finger and wrote a few lines in reply with my blood, which I gave to the messenger. He had the misfortune to be observed, was seized with the note upon him, and, if I am not mistaken, scourged. I heard frightful cries, which struck me as coming from the poor old man. I never saw him afterward.

Called to the bar, I shuddered at having presented to me my little letter covered with blood, although, thanks to Heaven, it contained no dangerous matter, for there were only a few words of friendly salutation. I was asked with what I had drawn blood. The needle was taken from me, and the ruffians laughed in derision. But I could not laugh! I could not forget the countenance of the old messenger. I would willingly have suffered any punishment to have procured his pardon; and when I heard those cries, which I believed were his, my heart was dissolved in tears.

It was in vain that I repeatedly asked the jailer and his *secondino* after him. They shook their heads, and said, "He has paid dearly for his fault; he will not do the like again; he is now somewhat more quiet." And they refused to give any further explanation. Did they refer by that to the narrow prison in which the wretched man was confined, or did they mean that he had died under the blows inflicted upon him, or from the consequences of those blows?

One day I thought I saw him beyond the court-yard beneath the portico with a load of wood upon his shoulders, and my heart beat as if I had seen a brother. When I had no longer to undergo the torment of answering interrogatories, and there was nothing to occupy the day, I found in all its bitterness the weight of solitude.

I was allowed to have a Bible and a copy of Dante; the jailer placed his whole library at my disposition, which contained some romances by Scuderi, Piazzi, and others worse than they; but my mind was too agitated to devote itself to reading any thing. I got by heart every day a canto of Dante; but this exercise was so mechanical, that, in pursuing it, I thought less of the verses than of my misfortunes. It was the same when I read any other thing, except at certain passages of the Bible, which deeply affected my feelings, and inspired me with fortitude and resignation. To live free is a thing infinitely more pleasant than to live in prison; and yet even in the gloom of a prison, when one reflects that God is present, that the joys of this world are transitory, that true happiness consists in a good conscience, and not in exterior objects, there is a charm in living. In less than a month I resigned myself to my fate with a tranquillity which, if not perfect, was at least tolerable. I was aware that, being resolved not to commit the infamous action of purchasing impunity by the destruction of others, my lot could be no other than the gibbet or a long imprisonment. It behooved me, therefore, to conform to destiny: I will breathe, said I, as long as they grant me a puff of air; and when they take it away, I will do what all others do at the last gasp—I will die.

I did all in my power to be satisfied with every thing, and to let my mind have all possible enjoyment. My most ordinary plan consisted in making the enumeration of the advantages which had brightened my existence: an excellent father, an excellent mother, excellent brothers and sisters, such and such for friends, a good education, a love of letters, etc.; who had had more happiness than I? Why not render thanks to God, although this happiness was at present interrupted by misfortune! Sometimes, in making this enumeration, I grew tender-hearted, and wept for a moment; but my courage and my satisfaction soon returned.

During the first days I had made a friend: it

was not the jailer, nor any of his *secondini*, nor any of those conducting my process. I speak, nevertheless, of a human creature. Who was it, then? A deaf and dumb child of from five to six years old. The father and the mother were felons, and the law had disposed of them. The unfortunate little orphan was reared by the state with several other children in the same condition. They all lived together in one room opposite mine, and at certain hours they came out to take the air in the court-yard.

The deaf and dumb boy came under my window, smiled at me, and made some gesticulations. I threw to him a lump of bread; he took it up, made a few gambols from joy, ran to his companions, gave some to all, and came afterward to eat his small portion by my window, expressing to me his gratitude with a smile from his beautiful eyes.

The other children looked at me from a distance, but durst not approach. The deaf and dumb one had a great sympathy for me, which was sufficiently disinterested. Sometimes he did not know what to do with the bread I threw to him, and he made signs to me that he and his comrades had eaten enough, and could not swallow any more. If he saw a *secondino* going into my room, he gave him the bread that he might restore it to me.

Yet although he expected nothing from me, he continued to play before my window with a grace perfectly delightful, placing his happiness upon being seen by me. Once a *secondino* permitted him to enter my prison. The boy had no sooner entered than he ran to me to embrace my knees, uttering a cry of joy. I took him in my arms, and I can not describe the transports with which he caressed me. How much love was there in that dear little breast! How I should have wished to educate him, and to have saved him from his abject state!

I never knew his name; he himself did not know he had one. He was always cheerful, and I never saw him weep but once, when he was beaten, I know not wherefore, by the jailer. Strange! we look upon it as the hight of misfortune to live in such places, and yet this child found certainly as much happiness there, as could the son of a prince at his age.

In the solitude of my dungeon, and with a yearning desire for something to love, I looked forward with pleasure to my intercourse with the poor child; but I was doomed to disappointment. One day I was removed to a cell on the opposite side of the court-yard, but, alas! no longer on the ground-floor, no longer in a place where it was possible for me to converse with my little mute. Traversing the court, I saw the dear child seated on the ground, terrified and sad. He had comprehended he was about to lose me. In a moment he sprang up and ran toward me: the *secondini* wished to remove him: I took him in my arms, and, dirty as he was, embraced him with affection, and separated from him—shall I say it?—with my eyes full of tears.

In my new chamber, so gloomy and so unclean, deprived of the companionship of my little mute, I was overpowered by sadness. I remained several hours at the window, which opened upon a gallery, and whence I could see the bottom of the court-yard and the window of my former lodging. Who, then, had replaced me there? I saw a prisoner walking up and down with the rapid step of a person highly agitated. Two or three days after, I saw that they had given him writing materials, and then he remained all the day at his table.

At last I recognized him. He issued from his chamber in company with the jailer, and went to the examination. It was Melchior Gioja, an amiable man, and the most profound thinker that the economical sciences have had in Italy in these latter times. My heart was seized with agony. And thou, too, worthy man, art here!

After spending some time in looking at him,

in speculating, from his movements, whether his mind was calm or agitated, in giving him my best wishes, I found myself more fortified, more rich in ideas, more contented with myself. This shows that the appearance even of a human creature for whom one experiences a sympathy, is sufficient to relieve the tedium of solitude. Such a benefit I had first received from a poor dumb boy; at present I experienced it from the distant view of a man of great merit.

Some *secondini* told him, doubtless, where I was. One morning, in opening his window, he waved his handkerchief as a salutation to me; I used the same signal to reply to him. O, what joy filled my bosom at that moment! It appeared that all distance was annihilated—that we were together: my heart beat like a lover's when he meets his mistress; we gesticulated without comprehending each other, and with the same vivacity as if we were perfectly conscious of each other's meaning. In reality we did understand one another; those gestures expressed all that our souls felt, and the one was not ignorant of what was passing in the mind of the other.

O what consolation this intercourse seemed to promise me for the future! The future came; but our signals were not repeated! Every time that I again saw Gioja at the window I waved my kerchief, but in váin! The *secondino* told me that he had been commanded not to provoke my signals, or to reply to them. Nevertheless, he looked at me frequently, and I as frequently at him; and we thus knew how to say a good many things to each other. In a few weeks I was consoled in knowing that the worthy man had been set at liberty.

One morning an official who had taken down my examination entered my cell, and announced to me, with some mystery, that I should prepare myself for a visit which would be agreeable to me; and when he thought he had sufficiently prepared me, he said, "It is your father; be good enough to follow me." I followed him into the office, agitated with joy and tenderness, and striving to preserve a serene air, to tranquilize my father.

When he learned my arrest, he hoped that it had taken place from suspicions of little importance, and that I should soon regain my liberty; but seeing that my captivity was prolonged, he solicited the Austrian Government for my discharge. Deplorable illusion of paternal love! My father could not conceive me rash enough to expose myself to the vengeance of the laws; and the studied contentment with which I spoke to him, convinced him that I was under no apprehension of evil.

The short conversation which was allowed us agitated me more than I can tell, so much the more, that I compelled myself to repress every symptom of it. The most difficult task was to conceal it when the moment of separation came.

In the circumstances of Italy at that period, I was convinced that Austria would make examples with extraordinary rigor, and that I should be doomed to death or to a long imprisonment. To conceal this conviction from a father; to flatter him with the hope of my approaching liberty; to refrain from tears while embracing him, or talking of my mother, my brothers, my sisters, whom I thought, at least, I should never see again in this world; to beseech him, without my voice being choked with sobs, to return to see me if he were able—O, never, never did I do myself such violence!

He quitted me, almost consoled, and I returned to my prison with my heart torn. Scarcely did I find myself alone, than I endeavored to ease my emotions by abandoning myself to tears: this relief was denied me. I burst into sobs, but could not shed a tear. Not being able to weep in excessive grief is the most deplorable of misfortunes, and it is what I have often suffered.

I was seized with a burning fever, accompanied by a horrible headache. I could not swallow during the whole day a mouthful of soup. Next day I had recovered my fortitude, and my feelings were more composed.

On New-Year's day, 1821, the Count Luigi Porro obtained permission to see me. The close and tender friendship which united us, the numberless things we wished to say to each other, the obstacle which the presence of an officer presented to the overflowing of our minds, the short period which was allowed us to be together, the gloomy presentiments which oppressed me, the mutual efforts we made to appear tranquil—there was in all these things enough to raise in my heart a terrible tempest. Severed from a friend so dear, I felt myself calm; much affected, but still calm. Such is the efficacy of precautions against strong emotions!

IMPRISONMENT AT VENICE.

Nothing remarkable occurred till the night between the 18th and 19th of February, when I was awakened by the noise of bolts and keys, and I saw several men enter with a lantern. My first idea was, that they had come to murder me; but while I was looking at them with anxiety, I saw advancing toward me the Count B., who politely requested me to take the trouble of dressing myself as quickly as possible, with a view to an immediate departure.

This intimation surprised me, and I was foolish enough to hope that they were going to conduct me to the frontiers of Piedmont. Was it possible that so threatening a storm should thus be dissipated?—that I should again enjoy the sweets of liberty?—that I should once more embrace my beloved parents, my brothers, and my sisters?

Such delusions agitated me a few moments. I dressed in haste, and followed my companions. "Where are we going?" said I to the Count, as I got into a carriage with him and an officer of gendarmerie.

"I can not tell you till we are a mile beyond Milan," he replied. I did not speak. It was a beautiful night, and the moon shone serenely. I looked upon those well-known streets, which I had traversed for so many years in happiness; upon the houses and the churches. All brought back to me a thousand sweet recollections!

The public gardens, where I had so often walked with Monti, Ludovico di Breme, Pietro Borsieri, Porro, and his sons, and with others who were dear to me, conversing full of life and hope—alas! as I looked upon them for the last time, as we drove rapidly past, I felt that I had loved them, and loved them still! As we went out of the eastern gate, I pulled my hat over my eyes and wept unobserved.

I allowed more than a mile to be passed, when I said to the Count B., "I suppose we are going to Verona?" "A good deal farther," answered he; "we are going to Venice, where I have to consign you to a special commission."

We traveled without stopping, and on the 20th of February we reached Venice. In the month of September of the preceding year, a month before my arrest, I was at Venice, and had dined with a numerous and joyful company at the Hotel "della Luna." It was strange enough that the Count and the gendarme conducted me to the very same hotel.

A servant of the hotel trembled when he recognized me, and perceived that I was in the hands of the police, in spite of the disguise assumed by the gendarme and his satellites, who were dressed as servants. I was glad at this meeting, for I was sure the servant would inform several persons of my arrival.

We dined, after which I was conducted to the palace of the doge, where the tribunals now sit. On arriving at the palace, the Count delivered me over to the jailer, and in taking leave of me embraced me with emotion.

I followed the jailer in silence. After having traversed several galleries and rooms, we reached a small stair which led us under the Leads, celebrated as state prisons since the time of the Venetian republic. There the jailer took a note of my name, and shut me up in the chamber destined for me. The Leads are the highest part of the ancient palace of the doge, which is entirely covered with lead.

My room had a large window, with enormous iron bars, and looked upon the roof of the church of St. Mark, also covered with lead. Beyond the church, I saw in the distance the extremity of the Piazza, and on all sides an infinity of cupolas and steeples. The gigantic steeple of St. Mark was only separated from me the length of the church, and I heard the people on the summit talking when they at all raised their voices. I could see also, on the left of the church, part of the great court of the palace, and one of the entrances. In this part of the court was a public well, to which was a perpetual resort for water. But at the hight I was, those whom I perceived below appeared like children, and I could only distinguish their words when they happened to shout. I thus found myself yet more solitary than in the prison of Milan.

For the first few days, the anxieties of the criminal process which was instituted against me by the special commission produced a degree of sadness, which was increased, perhaps, by the bitter sensation of more complete loneliness. I was, besides, at a greater distance from my family, and no longer received any tidings from them. The new faces which I saw did not create in me antipathy; but there was a seriousness upon them which caused me alarm. Report had exaggerated the plots of the Milanese, and the rest of Italy, to achieve independence. In their eyes I was, doubtless, one of the least worthy of pardon among the instigators of this frenzy. My slight literary celebrity was known to the jailer, to his wife, his daughter, his two sons, even to the two *secondini*. Who knows but they looked upon a maker of tragedies as a species of magician? They were grave, distrustful, eager to learn every thing connected with me, but at the same time full of politeness.

After a certain period they were less reserved and appeared good enough people. The woman was the best calculated to maintain the air and character of a jailer. Her visage was of a peculiarly-harsh expression, bearing the marks of forty years or thereabouts; her words were few; and she gave no symptoms of benevolence but for her own sons.

She was accustomed to bring my coffee in the morning and after dinner, as well as water, linen, etc. She was generally accompanied by her daughter, a girl of fifteen, who was not pretty, but who had compassion in her looks.

and by her two sons, of whom one was thirteen and the other ten. They retired, following their mother, and turned their young countenances mildly toward me as the door was closing. The jailer never entered my room except when he had to conduct me to the hall, where the commission met to interrogate me. The *secondini* rarely came, as they had to take charge of the prisons of the police, situated a story below, where there were always plenty of robbers. One of these *secondini* was an old man of seventy years of age, but still quite fit for so fatiguing a life, which consists in running without relief from one cell to another, first up stairs and then down; the other was a young man, twenty-four or twenty-five years old.

My examinations were now renewed. I was distracted with the questions put to me, and the suspicions entertained of my motives. I should have been driven mad, but for the consolations of religion.

My loneliness, in the mean time, increased. The two sons of the jailer, who at first occasionally visited me, were sent to school, and remaining afterward only a short time at home, came to see me no more. The mother and daughter, who, when the boys were there, often stopped to talk with me, appeared only to bring my coffee, and immediately retired. For the mother I cared little, as she did not show much compassion; but the daughter had a softness in her looks and words which was not without value to me. When she brought my coffee, and said, "I have made it myself," I was sure to find it excellent; when she said, "It is mamma's," it was hot water.

Seeing human creatures so rarely, I turned my attention to some ants which came upon my window, and I fed them so sumptuously, that they brought a whole army of their companions, and my window was soon filled. I occupied myself likewise with a spider, which spun its web on one of the walls; I gave it gnats and flies, and it became so familiar as to come upon my bed and into my hand to seize its prey.

Would that these insects had been the only ones to visit me! It was yet spring, and the gnats increased frightfully in numbers. The winter had been peculiarly mild, and after some winds in March, the heat came on. It is not possible to imagine how heated the air in my den became; placed to the south under a leaden roof, with a window opening to the roof of St. Mark, likewise of lead, the refraction was terrific. I could scarcely breathe. I had no idea of a heat so overpowering. To this torment, in itself so sufficient, were added such swarms of gnats, that if I made the least movement, and disturbed them, I was completely covered—the bed, the table, the chair, the floor, the walls, the ceiling, the whole room was filled with them—a countless multitude, which went and came through the window with an intolerable buzzing. The bites of these insects are very painful; and when one is punctured with them from morning to night, and from night to morning, and the attention is incessantly occupied in devising means to lessen the infliction, there is enough of suffering, in all conscience, for both mind and body.

When I found by experience the misery of this visitation, and could not obtain a change of room, I felt arise within me once more an inclination for suicide, and sometimes I feared I should become mad. But, thanks to God, such frenzies did not last long, and religion continued to sustain me. It convinced me that man ought to suffer, and to suffer with firmness; it made me feel in my grief a certain joy, a voluptuous satisfaction in not being vanquished, in rising superior to every evil.

To strengthen and occupy my mind, I conceived the idea of committing my thoughts to writing. The misfortune was, that the commission, in granting me pen, ink, and paper, ordered the sheets to be counted, and prohibited me from destroying any, reserving to themselves the right of examining to what use I had applied them. To supply the want of paper I had recourse to the innocent artifice of polishing with a piece of glass a rough table that I had, and there I recorded every day my lengthy meditations upon the duties of mankind, and especially upon my own.

I do not exaggerate when I say that the hours thus occupied appeared to me delightful, in spite of the difficulty I experienced in breathing, from the excessive heat, and the painful stings of the gnats. To diminish the number of these, I was compelled, notwithstanding the heat, to envelop my head and limbs, and to write not only with gloves, but my wrists bandaged, so as to prevent the little animals from getting up the sleeves.

These meditations of mine took a biographical form. I composed the history of every thing that had operated for good or for evil within me since my infancy. I discussed questions within myself, ascertained, as far as practicable, all my knowledge and all my ideas upon every matter.

When all the disposable surface of the table was covered with writing, I read and re-read, I meditated upon my own meditations; and at last I resolved, often with regret, to scratch out with the glass what I had written, so as to render the surface fit to receive the fresh impress of my thoughts. Thus I continued my history, often interrupted by digressions of all sorts, by an analysis of some point in metaphysics, morals, politics, or religion; and when all was full, I recommenced reading, re-reading, and then effacing.

In order to avoid any impediment to my justly and freely accounting with myself for the facts which I recollected, and for my opinions, as well as to avert the consequences of any inquisitorial visit, I wrote in a sort of jargon; that is to say, with transpositions of letters, and abbreviations, which were quite familiar to myself. However, no such visit was ever made to me, and no one had any idea that this sad period passed so tranquilly for me. When I heard the jailer or any other person open the door, I covered the table with a cloth, and placed upon it the inkstand and the *legalized* quire of paper.

This quire had also some of my hours devoted to it, frequently extending to a whole day or an entire night. I wrote several literary works, dramatic and poetical.

As it was not easy for me to get, as promptly as I could wish, the supply of paper renewed when it was finished, I cast my first ideas in composition upon the table or the waste paper in which I had dried figs or other fruits brought to me. Sometimes, by giving my dinner to one of the *secondini*, and persuading him that I had no appetite, I induced him to bring me as a present a few sheets of paper. I availed myself of this scheme only when the table was already crammed with writing, and I could not prevail upon myself though I often made the effort to erase it.

With these efforts at amusement the summer vanished. In the latter part of September the heat diminished. October came, and I rejoiced at having a room which in winter would be agreeable. But one morning the jailer came, and announced to me that he had received orders to change my abode.

Although I had suffered much in this chamber, I was sorry to quit it, not only because it would be comfortable in cold weather, but for many other reasons. I, first of all, had those ants, which I loved and nourished with a solicitude which might be called paternal, if the expression were not ridiculous. A few days previously, a spider, which had become familiarized with me, departed, I know not for what reason; but who knows, thought I, but it will remember me, and return? And now that I am going away, if it return, it will find the prison empty; or if it meet with a new host, he will be, perchance, an enemy to spiders, who will sweep away with his slipper this goodly web, and crush the poor animal.

The room they put me in was also under the Leads, but to the north and west, with a window on each side—a place for perpetual colds, and of horrible chillness in the winter months.

The window fronting the west was very large, that to the north small and high, and placed immediately above my bed.

I looked out at the first, and found that it opened upon the palace of the patriarch. Other cells were near mine in a wing of small extent to the right, and in a prolongation of the building in front of me. In this prolongation were two prisons, one above the other. The lower one had an enormous window, through which I saw a man walking about in very splendid attire. It was the Signor Caporali di Cesena. He saw me, made a sign to me, and we communicated to each other our names.

I wished afterward to examine where the other window looked to. I put the table on the bed, and on the table a chair, on which I climbed, and saw myself on a level with part of the palace roof. Beyond the palace appeared a fine view of the city and the canal.

I stood viewing this beautiful prospect, and hearing the door open, I did not stir. It was the jailer, who, seeing me in so elevated a position, and forgetting that I could not pass, like a magician, through the bars, imagined I was about to escape, and, in the first impulse of his alarm, jumped upon the bed, in spite of a sciatica which tormented him, and seizing me by the legs, screeched like an eagle.

"Do you not see," said I, "most stupid man, that the iron bars are here to prevent me escaping? Can you not comprehend that I have mounted here through curiosity?"

"I see, sir, I see; I understand; but come down, I pray you, come down: there is a great temptation to escape." So I descended, laughing.

At the windows of the side prisons I recognized six others detained for political causes. Thus, then, at the moment when I was preparing for a solitude more perfect than the past, I found myself in a sort of world, and was occasionally able to exchange words and signs of civility and compassion.

The month of October brought round a most cruel anniversary. I had been arrested on the 13th of that month the preceding year. Many recollections equally sad tormented me during this month. Two years before, also in October, a man of merit, whom I greatly esteemed, had been unfortunately drowned in the Ticino. Six years before, still in October, Odoardo Briche, a youth whom I loved as if he had been my son, had shot himself involuntarily. In my early youth, in an October, another heavy affliction had occurred to me. Although I am not superstitious, so fatal a concourse of bitter recollections springing from this month weighed upon my spirits.

I took up the pen to compose verses, or to follow some other literary bent, but an irresistible force seemed to compel me into another channel. Into what? Into writing long letters, which I could not send—long letters to my beloved family, in which I poured out my whole heart. I wrote them on the table, and then obliterated them. They were the warm expressions of my tenderness, of my recollections of the felicity I had enjoyed with my indulgent and affectionate parents, brothers, and sisters. The love which drew me to them, inspired me with a thousand impassioned sentiments. And after writing hours and hours, there were always thoughts which remained for expression.

These recreations at length affected my mind, and in my dreams, or rather in my delirium, I saw my father, my mother, or some other of those whom I loved, lamenting my unhappy lot. I heard their distressing sobs, and I was suddenly aroused, also sobbing and affrighted.

Sometimes, during these short hallucinations, I

thought I heard my mother consoling the others, coming with them into my prison, and addressing to me solemn exhortations to resignation; and at the moment that I was rejoicing at her fortiude, and that of the others, she burst into tears, and they all wept together. No one can conceive how, at such times, my heart was lacerated.

At night, my imagination was excited to such a pitch that I seemed to hear, although wide awake, groans and stifled laughter in my room. In my infancy I had never believed in witchcraft or in ghosts, and yet now these groans and laughs terrified me, and I could not explain the cause. I was forced to doubt whether I were not the sport of some mysterious and malevolent power.

I often took the light, with a trembling hand, and looked under the bed, to see if no one were concealed there; and it frequently occurred to me that I had been removed from my first chamber into this, because the latter had a trap-door, or some hole in the wall, by which my keepers saw all that I did, and diverted themselves by frightening me.

Seated at my table, it sometimes seemed to me that I was pulled by the coat, sometimes that a hidden hand pushed away my book, till I saw it falling on the ground; sometimes that some one came behind me to blow out the candle. Then I started to my feet with precipitation, I looked around me, I trod with apprehension, and I asked myself if I were mad, or in my proper senses.

I know how absurd such aberrations of the mind appear to others, but to me, who have experienced them, they were so hurtful that I yet shudder at them.

In the morning they always vanished; and so long as the light of day lasted, I felt my mind so braced against these terrors, that I thought it impossible they should again pursue me. But when the sun set, I recommenced my trembling, and each night brought back the extravagant phantoms of its predecessors.

One morning, after coffee, I was seized with diarrhea and vomitings. I thought I was poisoned, but it was only an effort of nature. After the attack had passed off, I found myself well, and the illusions that had haunted me disappeared.

On the 24th of November, Dr. Foresti was removed from the prisons of the Leads, and taken I knew not whither. The jailer, his wife, and the *secondini*, were in terror, but none of them would explain to me the mystery. At length one of them told me that poor Foresti had been taken to the criminal prisons. The reader may imagine the agitation I was in all that day and the following night, and during several days, that I could learn no further intelligence.

This uncertainty lasted a month. At length the sentences of a number of persons were made public; but no names were as yet given. Nine were condemned to death, but their sentence would perhaps be commuted into imprisonment for twenty years; others were to be imprisoned for fifteen—and in both cases they had to undergo their sentence in the fortress of Spielberg, near the city of Brunn, in Moravia—and some for ten years at the least—these last in the fortress of Lubiana. Was I among the number who had been condemned to death? If the term of my existence is come, thought I, am I not more happy that it comes in a manner to allow me time to collect myself, and to purify my conscience by repentance? Judging with the vulgar, the gibbet is of all modes of death the worst. But, in the opinion of the wise, is not this death preferable to many others which ensue after long disease, in which the intellect is debilitated, and the mind has not force to cast aside petty thoughts?

The justice of this reasoning was so firmly fixed in my mind, that the horror of death, and of this mode of death, was entirely dissipated. I meditated deeply on the sacraments, for which all the strength of my mind was required at this solemn moment, and I thought myself in a state to receive them in a beneficial manner. The dignity and peace of mind, the placid affection for those who hated me, the joy of sacrificing my life to the will of God, all which I seemed now to feel; could I have preserved them if I had been led forth to the last punishment? Alas! how many contradictions in man! Alas! when he appears the most sanctified and firm, an instant can precipitate him into weakness and crime! God only knows whether I were then fit for death: I have not confidence in myself to affirm it. I had attained a degree of firmness, as I thought, which would overcome the pang of dissolution, when, one evening, seated at my table studying, quite chilled with cold, some voices near me—they were the voices of the jailer, his wife, his sons, and the *secondini*—exclaimed: "Fire! fire! we are lost!" The chillness quitted me in a moment. I sprang to my feet in a sudden perspiration, and looked all round to see where the flames were: they were not to be seen.

The fire was, however, in the palace, in some offices adjoining the prisons. One of the *secondini* shouted out: "But, master, what are we to do with the prisoners if the fire advances?" The jailer answered, "I haven't the heart to let them be roasted. However, we can not open the prison without the consent of the commission. Go, then, I say, run as quick as you can to ask for leave." "I will run, master; I will run; but the answer will not come in time, recollect!"

And where, then, was that heroic resignation that I believed myself so sure of possessing, while thinking on death? Why did the idea of being burned alive put me in a fever? As if there were more pleasure in being suffocated by the throat than consumed by fire? I made this reflection, and was ashamed at my terror. I was about to cry to the jailer to open the door for the love of God, but I checked myself. Nevertheless, I was in a fear.

After a lengthened disturbance the noise subsided, and I doubted not that the fire had been extinguished. The following morning I learned from one of the jailers the particulars of this fire, and I laughed at the terror it had excited in him, as if mine had not equaled, perhaps surpassed his.

On the 11th of February, 1822, about nine o'clock in the morning, I was informed that I was to be immediately removed to a prison in the island of St. Michael of Murano, not far from Venice; but for what purpose was not mentioned. A moment after the jailer entered, accompanied by the *secondini*, and a man whom I had never seen before. The jailer appeared confused, and the new-comer took the word: "Signor, the commission orders you to follow me." "I am ready," I answered; "and you, who are you?" "I am keeper of the prison of St. Michael, where you are about to be transferred."

The jailer of the Leads handed over to the latter my money which he had in his hands. I asked and obtained permission to make some present to the *secondini;* I put my clothes in order, took the Bible under my arm, and departed.

We went out a door which opened on the canal, where a gondola, with two *secondini* of the new jailer, awaited us. I entered the gondola, a prey to a thousand inconsistent feelings. On the whole, I felt happy at finding myself in the open air, after so long a seclusion—at seeing the sky, the waters, and the city, without the sad intervention of close bars—at the remembrance of the joyous gondola which in a more happy time bore me on this same canal, of the gondolas of the Lake of Como, of the Lake Maggiore, of the light barks of the Po, the Rhone, and the Saone! O smiling years, forever gone! Who in the world had enjoyed a happiness equal to mine?

In the midst of these reflections I arrived at St. Michael, where they shut me up in a room which looked upon a court, upon the canal, and the beautiful island of Murano. I sought intelligence respecting Maroncelli from the jailer, his wife, and the four *secondini*. But they made me only short visits, and, full of distrust, would tell me nothing.

I lived in ignorance of my fate till the 21st of February. On that day the jailer came for me about ten o'clock in the morning; he led me into the hall of the commission, and retired. I found upon their seats the president, the inquisitor, and the two assessors, who all rose.

The president, with a tone of dignified commiseration, told me that the sentence had arrived; that it was a terrible one, but that the Emperor had already mitigated it.

The inquisitor read this sentence—Condemned to death. Then he read the imperial rescript—The penalty is commuted to fifteen years of imprisonment in the fortress of Spielberg. I replied: "God's will be done!"

I had, in truth, the disposition to receive, like a Christian, this horrible annunciation, and neither to testify nor to cherish resentment against any one. The president applauded my moderation, and counseled me always to preserve it, adding that, at the end of two or three years, this resignation would perhaps render me worthy of a great favor.

The other judges also addressed me with words of consolation and hope. "To-morrow," said the inquisitor, "we shall have the disagreeable duty of announcing the sentence to you in public, but it is an indispensable formality."

"Be it so," I replied.

"From this moment," he resumed, "we allow you the society of your friend."

And, having called the jailer, they consigned me into his hands, and ordered him to put me with Maroncelli.

How sweet a moment was that, for my friend and myself, in which we saw each other again, after a separation of a year and three months, after so many afflictions! The ecstasies of friendship made us almost forget, for the moment, our condemnation.

I soon tore myself, however, from the arms of Maroncelli, to take the pen and write to my father. I ardently desired that the news of my sad lot should reach my family through me, rather than through others, in order that the grief of those beloved hearts should be mitigated by the pious calmness of my language. The judges promised to expedite my letter without delay.

Maroncelli talked to me afterward of his

process, and I of mine. We related by turns our prison adventures; and then, going to the window, we saluted three of our friends who were at theirs. They were Canova and Rezia, who were together, each condemned to imprisonment, the first to six years, and the second to three. The third was the Doctor Cesare Armari, who, during the previous months, had been my neighbor in the Leads. No judgment had been pronounced against him, and he was not long in being liberated as guiltless.

We conversed together all the day and all the evening. It was for both an agreeable distraction. But when in bed, the light extinguished, and silence established, I felt it impossible to sleep. My brain was on fire, and my heart bled on thinking of my family. Could my poor old parents bear up against so great a misfortune? Would their other sons suffice to console them? They were all as much beloved as myself, and more worthy to be so; but do a father and a mother ever find, in the children who are spared to them, a compensation for those who are lost?

At nine in the morning, Maroncelli and I were made to enter a gondola, to be conducted into the city. The gondola stopped at the palace of the doge, and we ascended to the prisons. We were put into the chamber which

Signor Caporali had occupied a few days before. I am ignorant of his fate. Nine or ten officers were seated there to guard us, and we walked about, waiting for the moment when we had to appear in the Piazza. We waited a very long time. It was already noon when the inquisitor came to announce that we had to proceed. The physician came also, and recommended us to drink a glass of mint-water; we followed his advice, and were grateful to him, not so much for this attention, as for the profound pity the good old man testified for us. His name was Doctor Dosmo. The head officer afterward appeared, and put manacles on us. We followed him, accompanied by the other officers.

Walking between two rows of Austrian soldiers, we arrived at the scaffold, and then looking around us, saw in the immense crowd nothing but expressions of terror. In the distance were other soldiers, drawn up at various points. We were told that cannons were fixed, with the matches ready lighted.

The Austrian commander ordered us to turn toward the palace and raise our eyes. We obeyed, and saw an official of the court upon the terrace holding a paper in his hand. It was the sentence. He read it aloud. Every one could hear and understand.

There was a profound silence, till the expression—*condemned to death.* Then arose a general murmur of compassion. Silence was restored to hear the rest, and a new murmur greeted these words—*Condemned to close imprisonment; Maroncelli for twenty years, and Pellico for fifteen.*

The captain made us a sign to descend; we did so, after casting another glance around us. We returned to the palace, remounted the staircase, and entered again the chamber from which we had been taken. Having removed our manacles, we were conducted back to Saint Michael.

Those who had been condemned before us had already departed for Lubiana or Spielberg, under the conduct of a commissary of police. They now waited the return of this same commissary, he being intrusted also with the duty of convoying us to our destination. We waited for him a month.

When he arrived and visited us, "I have the pleasure," said he, "of being able to afford you some consolation. In returning from Spielberg, I saw his imperial majesty, the emperor, at Vienna, who told me that your days of imprisonment should be twelve hours long, and not twenty-four. It is a mode of intimating to you that the punishment is reduced one-half."

This intelligence was never officially confirmed to us; but there is no probability that the commissary spoke falsely, the more especially as he did not communicate it in secret, but with the consent of the commission. And yet I could not rejoice at it. In my mind seven years and a half in irons were not much less horrible than fifteen. It seemed to me impossible that I could live so long. My health had become affected. I suffered much in the chest, attended with coughing, and I thought my lungs attacked. I ate very little, and that little was indigestible.

IMPRISONMENT AT SPIELBERG.

Our departure from Venice took place in the night of the 25th and 26th March. We were permitted to embrace our friend Doctor Armari. Then an officer fastened on us a chain, passing transversely from the right hand to the left foot, so as to render flight impossible. We entered a gondola, and the guards rowed us toward Fusina.

At Fusina we found two carriages ready. Rezia and Canova got into one, Maroncelli and I into another. In the first sat the commissary, and in the second a sub-commissary, each with two prisoners. Six or seven police guards completed the convoy, armed with sabers and muskets; some behind the carriages, others on the drivers' seats.

Being forced to quit one's country is always

a cruel calamity; but to quit it in chains, and to be carried to a horrible climate, there to languish for years, surrounded by jailers, is a misfortune so dreadful that I have not words to describe it.

Before passing the Alps, my country became every hour more dear to me, from the sympathy which every-where the persons we met expressed for us. In every town, in every village, in every solitary hamlet, we were looked for, as our condemnation had been known for several weeks. In some places the commissary and the guards could with difficulty remove the crowd which surrounded us. The interest which was manifested on our account was surprising.

In traveling through Austria the same compassion followed us, and the consolation which I derived from these marks of kindness diminished my resentment against those whom I deemed my enemies. On the 10th April we reached the place of our destination.

The town of Brunn is the capital of Moravia, and the residence of the governor of the two provinces of Moravia and Silesia. It is situated in a fertile valley, and has the appearance of being opulent. Several cloth manufactories were then in a state of prosperity, which have since fallen to decay. The population was about 30,000. Near its walls, on the west, stands a hill on which is erected that fatal fortress of Spielberg, formerly the palace of the lords of Moravia, and at present the most rigorous place of imprisonment in the Austrian dominions. The citadel was of great strength, but the French bombarded and took it at the time of the famous battle of Austerlitz—the village of Austerlitz is at a short distance. Since then it has not been restored so as to serve as a citadel, but they have contented themselves with rebuilding a part of the outer wall, which was thrown down. About three hundred condemned persons, chiefly robbers and murderers, are detained there; some subjected to hard labor—*carcere duro*—others to the hardest labor—*carcere durissimo.*

The *carcere duro* consists in being obliged to work, to drag a chain at the feet, to sleep upon naked boards, and to be fed upon the poorest imaginable nourishment. The *carcere durissimo* consists in being chained, in a manner yet more horrible, with an iron girdle round the loins, and a chain fixed in the wall, scarcely affording scope to turn round on the plank which serves for a bed. The food is the same, although the law prescribes *bread and water.* We, as prisoners of state, were condemned to the *carcere duro.*

On reaching the summit of the hill, we turned

our eyes behind, to bid adieu to the world, ignorant whether the gulf which was about to swallow us alive would ever open again to let us out. Outwardly I appeared calm, but within me raged a tempest. In vain I had recourse to philosophy to tranquilize my mind; the reasonings of philosophy were insufficient.

Having left Venice in bad health, the journey had been attended with wretched fatigue; my head, my whole body, was distracted with pain—and I burned with fever. Physical distemper contributed to the irritation of my mind, which in turn doubtless aggravated my bodily ills.

We were delivered into the hands of the superintendent of the fortress, who inscribed our names among those of the malefactors. On quitting us, the imperial commissary embraced us with affection. "I recommend you to be docile," said he to us; "the least infraction of discipline will receive from the superintendent a severe punishment." The ceremony of delivery being completed, they conducted Maroncelli and me into a subterranean corridor, in which two dark cells were open for us, at a distance from each other. Each was locked up in his den.

The bitterest of all calamities surely occurs when, after bidding adieu to so many objects, and two friends equally unfortunate are left alone, these friends are forcibly separated. Such a separation is the bitterest of calamities. Maroncelli, on quitting me, saw me ill, and wept for me as a man whom, without doubt, he should never behold again. I wept for him, blooming in the vigor of health, torn, perhaps forever, from the refreshing light of the sun. And, like a beautiful flower cast into darkness, how has he in reality drooped and faded! He has again emerged into light, but, alas! in what a state.

When I found myself in this horrible cavern, and heard the bolts drawn—when, by the feeble light which fell from a narrow window above, I perceived the naked plank which was given for a bed, and an enormous chain fixed to the wall—I seated myself shuddering on the bed, and taking up the chain, I measured its length, thinking it destined for me.

Half an hour afterward I heard the keys rattle, and the door opened. A jailer, whose name was Schiller, entered, and delivered me a pitcher of water. He was an old man, and I could observe that he felt compassion for my fate.

In this horrible dungeon I very soon became exceedingly ill, which being perceived by the superintendent of the prison in his daily visits of inspection, the physician of the establishment was requested to see me, and report on my case. Doctor Bayer found me in a fever, ordered me a straw pallet, and insisted upon their removing me from this subterranean vault to the story above. They could not, as there was no room. But a report upon the subject having been addressed to the Count Mitrovski, governor of the two provinces of Moravia and Silesia, who resided at Brunn, the Count replied that, in consequence of the severity of the illness, the orders of the doctor should be followed.

Into the chamber which they gave me a little daylight penetrated; and creeping to the bars of the narrow window, I could see the valley which the fortress commanded, a part of the town of Brunn, a suburb with a multitude of small gardens, the necropolis, the small lake of the charter-house, and the woody hills which separated us from the celebrated hills of Austerlitz. This view enchanted me. O, how I should have rejoiced to partake it with Maroncelli!

They were preparing, in the mean time, our prison-dresses, and at the end of five days they brought me mine. These were a pair of pantaloons of rough cloth, the right side gray and the left side a brown color; a close coat of two colors, disposed in the same manner; a vest similarly variegated, with the slight difference of the gray color being to the left and the capuchin to the right. The stockings were of thick wool, the shirt of unwoven flax, stinging to the skin like a true haircloth; for the neck was a cravat of the same stuff as the shirt. A pair of laced half-boots of untanned leather, and a white hat, completed the wardrobe.

This livery was accompanied by irons to the feet—that is to say, a chain that extended from one leg to the other, the rings of which were fastened by nails riveted upon an anvil. A few minutes after the blacksmith had gone, I heard the hammer upon the anvil sounding from below—doubtless they were riveting the irons on poor Maroncelli.

From the window of my new cell I found that I could converse with the prisoner in an adjoining apartment, the Count Antonio Oroboni. This intercourse was frequently interrupted by the sentinels; but by habituating ourselves to speak in whispers, and at certain intervals, we contrived in a great measure to elude the vigilance of our guards. We thus became united in a tender friendship. Oroboni narrated to me his life, and I mine to him; the sorrows and consolations of the one became the sorrows and consolations of the other. O how greatly we comforted each other!—how many times, after a sleepless night, did each of us feel his sadness alleviated, and his courage fortified, by our morning salutation and interchange of words! Each of us felt himself indispensable to the other, and this persuasion incited us to an emulation in amiability, and produced that delicious feeling which a man experiences, even in distress, when he can gladden the heart of a fellow-being.

The physician perceiving that none of us could eat the food which they gave us during the first days, put us on a diet which was called "*a quarter portion*"—that is to say, a hospital regimen. It consisted of three very light soups each day, a very small morsel of roast lamb, which could be swallowed at a bite, and about three ounces of white bread. As my health grew stronger every day, my appetite kept in creasing, and I felt this *quarter* verily too little. I tried to return to the allowance of those who were in health, but I took nothing by the attempt: it disgusted me so effectually, that I could not eat it. I was driven back to the "quarter." For more than a year I learned what the pangs of hunger were. Many of our companions suffered these pangs yet more violently; for, being of robuster constitutions than I, they were accustomed to a more ample nourishment. I know several of them accepted bread from Schiller, whose kind-heartedness was exceedingly remarkable, though he had an exterior not in any sense prepossessing.

Several times this good man brought me a piece of boiled meat, begging me to eat it, and assuring me it cost him nothing—that it was left from his own dinner—that he could do nothing with it except to give it to others, if I would not take it. I would willingly have flown to devour it; but if I had taken it, would not Schiller bring me something every day?

Twice only I yielded. One day he brought me a plate of cherries, and another some pears. The sight of these fruits was irresistible. I repented of having accepted them, because he did not cease to offer me more.

From the first period of our confinement, it had been established that each of us should have twice a week an hour's walking; afterward this consolation was extended to us every other day; and at last every day, except festivals.

We each went separately to the promenade between two guards, with muskets on their shoulders. As I lodged at the extremity of the corridor, I passed, in going out, the cells of all the Italian political prisoners, except that of Maroncelli, who alone languished beneath.

"A pleasant walk!" murmured each of them through the loophole of his door; but I was not permitted to stop to exchange salutations with any one. We descended the staircase, and traversed a court which led us to a terrace with a southern aspect, whence we could see the town of Brunn, and a considerable part of the surrounding country.

In the court of which I speak was always a great number of ordinary criminals, who went and came from their work, or walked about conversing. Among them were several Italian robbers, who saluted me with much respect, saying among themselves, "This is not a rogue like us, and yet his punishment is more severe than ours." They had, in fact, much more liberty than I. These words and many others I heard, and I cordially returned their salutation.

The constraint of the irons at the feet, by preventing sleep, contributed to ruin my health. Schiller wished me to remonstrate, maintaining that it was the duty of the physician to cause their removal.

For some time I did not follow his advice; but at last I yielded, and I begged the physician that he would order me to be relieved of the chain, at least for a few days, so that I might procure a little sleep.

The physician answered that the fever had not yet arrived at such a hight that he could grant my request, and that it was necessary I should accustom myself to the irons. I was vexed with having made the request.

I was still able, however, to take my usual walk, and one morning, on returning from my promenade, I observed that the door of Oroboni's cell was open. Schiller, who was within, had not heard me coming. My guards wished to advance a pace to close the door; but I got before them, sprang into the room, and was instantly in the arms of Oroboni.

Schiller stood in astonishment; he raised his finger in a menacing attitude; but his eyes were filled with tears, and with sobs he cried, "O, my God! show mercy to these poor young men, and to me, and to all the unfortunates who have been wretched on this earth!"

The two guards wept also. The sentinel in the corridor, attracted from his post, was also in tears. Oroboni said, "Silvio, Silvio, this is one of the happiest days of my life!" I did not know what to reply: I was beside myself with joy and emotion.

When Schiller conjured us to part, alleging the necessity of obedience, Oroboni burst into a flood of tears, and faltered out, "Shall we never see each other again in this world?"

We did not see each other again. Some months after, his cell was vacant, and Oroboni lay in the cemetery which I had before my eyes.

I was able to move about up till the 11th January, 1823. On that morning I arose with a slight headache, and a disposition to faint. My limbs trembled, and I could scarcely draw breath.

Oroboni also, for the last two or three days, had been ill, and did not rise.

They brought me the soup: I scarcely took a spoonful, when I fell, deprived of sensation. The sentinel of the corridor looked by chance through a wicket of the door a few moments after, and seeing me extended on the floor, with the pot upside down lying near me, he judged me dead, and called Schiller.

The superintendent came also; the physician was likewise called, and I was put to bed. It was with difficulty I recovered. The physician declared my life in danger, and caused my chains to be removed. He ordered me some sort of a cordial, but my stomach would retain nothing. The headache grew to an intolerable hight. A report to the governor was immediately made as to my condition, and he dispatched a courier to Vienna to ask how I should be treated. He was ordered in reply not to send me to the infirmary, but to cause me to be attended to in the prison with the same care as if I had been in the infirmary. Farther, the superintendent was authorized to furnish me with soups and pottages from his own kitchen as long as the malady should continue serious.

The last precaution was quite useless to me at first. Neither meat nor drink passed my lips. For a whole week I got worse and worse; I was delirious day and night.

Kral and Kubitzky were given me as attendants, and they served me with affection. Each time that I resumed a little consciousness Kral repeated to me, "Have confidence in God, sir; God alone is good."

"Pray to Him for me," said I to him; "not that he will cure me, but that my misfortunes and my death may be received in expiation of my sins."

He suggested to me the idea of calling for the sacraments.

"If I have not demanded them already," I answered, "attribute it to the weakness of my head, but it will be a great consolation for me to receive them."

He reported my words to the superintendent, who brought the chaplain of the prison. I was pleased with this priest; his name was Sturm. The reflections which he delivered to me upon the justice of God, the injustice of mankind, the duty of forgiveness, the vanity of all the things of this world, were not commonplaces. They bore the stamp of a high and cultivated intellect, and of a lively sentiment of the love due to God and our neighbor.

The effort which I was called upon to make in receiving the sacraments, seemed at first to exhaust the slight remains of life; but it afterward served to assist me, by plunging me into a lethargy, which produced some hours of repose.

I awoke a little relieved, and seeing Kral and Schiller near me, I took their hands in mine, and thanked them for all their care.

Toward the end of the second week a crisis occurred in the malady, and all danger vanished.

I was about to rise one morning, when my door opened, and the superintendent, Schiller, and the physician, entered with smiling countenances. The first of them ran to me and said: "We have received permission to give you Maroncelli for a companion, and to allow you to write to your parents." Maroncelli was conducted to my arms.

O what a moment was that! "Thou yet livest, my friend, my brother!" we each exclaimed. "How happy a day we have been reserved to see! Praise be to God!"

But our joy, great as it was, was soon damped by mutual compassion. Maroncelli was necessarily less struck at finding me so wasted, knowing from how severe an illness I had just escaped. But I, with all my knowledge of what he had undergone, could not have imagined so great a difference from what he was before—I scarcely recognized him. His beautiful countenance, so radiant with health, was withered from grief, from hunger, from the bad air of his gloomy prison.

However, it was a source of consolation to see and hear each other, to be assured we should not again be separated. It was likewise consolatory to write to my parents, which I now did, and the letter was duly forwarded.

The disposition of Maroncelli and myself harmonized perfectly together. The courage of the one sustained the courage of the other. If either of us was seized with melancholy, or excited to anger by the hardships of our condition, the other restored his friend's equanimity by some pleasantries or appropriate reasonings. A smile generally tempered our sorrows.

As long as we had books, though we had read them often enough to know them by heart, we possessed an agreeable means of mental cultivation, because they were a perpetual excitation to fresh examinations, comparisons, criticisms, and corrections. We read, or meditated in silence, the greatest part of the day, and we gave to conversation the times of dinner and of the promenade, and all the evening.

Maroncelli, in his dungeon, had composed a great many verses of superior beauty. He recited them to me, and composed others; while I also composed some which I recited to him, and our memories were exercised in retaining all this. We acquired by these means a wonderful facility in the composition, from memory, of long poems, a power of polishing and improving them at repeated intervals, and of bringing them to as high a state of perfection as we could have done by writing them. Maroncelli thus composed by degrees, and delivered to memory, several thousands of lyric and epic verses. As for me, I composed the tragedy of "Leoniero da Dertyna," and various other pieces.

At the commencement of 1824 a number of additional prisoners were brought to Spielberg, among whom were some of our unfortunate acquaintances; and the rigors of our confinement were increased. How did we pass all the years of 1824, 1825, 1826, and 1827! We were refused the use of our books, which the governor had granted provisionally. The prison became for us a real tomb, in which, however, we were not allowed even the tranquillity of the tomb. Each month, on an indeterminate day, the director of the police, accompanied by a lieutenant and his guards, came to make a severe inspection. They stripped us naked, examined all the seams of our clothes, and in the fear that any paper or other thing was concealed therein, they opened our mattresses to search the insides. Although it was impossible they could find any thing clandestine with us, this visit, made in so hostile a manner, so suddenly, and so often repeated, irritated me to a great extent, and always threw me into a fever.

The preceding years had appeared to me so sad, and *now*, I looked back with regret upon those years, as to a time of enjoyment!

By making the punishment commence not at the epoch of my arrest, but at that of my condemnation, the seven years and a half finished in 1829, in the first days of July, if they were dated from the signature of the Emperor, or on the 22d of August, if dated from the publication of the sentence. But this term passed like the others, and all hope was extinguished.

Up to that time, Maroncelli and I sometimes imagined that it might yet be possible we should once more see the world, our beloved Italy, and our relations; and it was for us a subject of conversation replete with anxiety, emotion, and love.

But when we saw August pass, then September, then that whole year, we accustomed ourselves to hope nothing more on this earth except the unvarying continuance of our mutual friendship, and the aid of God to perform worthily what remained to accomplish of our long sacrifice.

Ah! friendship and religion are two inestimable benefits! They embellish even the hours of prisoners for whom all hope of mercy has expired. God is indeed with the unfortunate—with the unfortunate who love him!

The first day of August, 1830, appeared. It was not far from ten years since I had lost my liberty, and eight and a half since I had been subjected to the *carcere duro.*

It was a Sunday. We went, as on other holidays, to the usual inclosure, and looked again, from the low wall running round it, upon the valley and the graveyard in which Oroboni and Villa lay, talking to each other of the repose which our bones would one day find in the same place.

This day, after returning from the chapel, and when preparing to eat our wretched dinner, the sub-intendant entered the cell. "I am very sorry to disturb your dinner," said he, "but have the goodness to follow me; the director of the police is here."

As this latter personage never came but for disagreeable purposes, such as searches or inquiries, we followed the sub-intendant, in very bad humor, to the room of audience.

We found there the director of police and the superintendent; the former moved to us more graciously than usual.

He took a paper in his hand, and, in disconnected words, as if he were afraid of producing upon us too great a sensation of surprise by a more rapid delivery, said to us: "Gentlemen, I have the pleasure—I have the honor—to inform you—that his Majesty, the Emperor—has performed another act of mercy——"

And he hesitated to inform us in what the mercy consisted. We thought that it referred to some mitigation of our punishment, such as exempting us from the tiresomeness of labor, permitting us some more books, or granting us less disgusting food. "Do you not understand?" added the director.

"No, sir; have the goodness to explain to us what sort of mercy is meant."

"It is liberty for you both, and for a third, whom you are about to embrace."

Apparently our joy should have broken forth in loud jubilee. But our thoughts immediately ran upon our parents, of whom we had no intelligence for so long a time. Should we still find them on earth? This doubt occurred to us in such force, that it certainly destroyed the pleasure the news of our freedom should have given us.

"You remain mute," said the police-director. "I expected to have seen you jump for joy."

"I beseech you," answered I, "to be good enough to transmit our gratitude to the Emperor. But if no account is given us of our families, it is impossible not to fear that some very dear individuals are now lost to us. This uncertainty overpowers us, even in the moment which should be that of supreme joy."

He then gave to Maroncelli a letter from his brother, which consoled him. He told me there was none from my family, and that redoubled my fear that some misfortune had happened.

"Return into your chamber," resumed the director, "and before long I will show the other prisoner who has also received pardon."

We retired, and waited for this third person with anxiety. We would have taken with us all the others, but there could only be one. Might it be the poor Munari? or such a one? or such another? It was not one of those for whom we offered our prayers. At last the door opened, and we saw that our companion was the Signor Andrea Tonelli da Brescia. We embraced. We could eat no dinner. We conversed till the evening, compassionating the lot of those dear friends who remained behind us.

At nightfall the director of police returned to take us from this place of misfortune. Our hearts were lacerated as we passed before the cells of so many beloved beings, without being able to take them with us. Who knows how long they must still languish there! How many of them would become the slow victims of death!

They cast on the shoulders of each of us a soldier's great-coat, and a cap on our heads; and thus, in the clothing of galley-slaves, with the exception of chains, we descended that disastrous hill, and were conducted into the city to the prisons of the police. It was a beautiful moonlight night. The streets, the houses, the persons whom we met, all appeared to me so strange and pleasant, after the many years I had passed without beholding a similar scene!

We waited in the prisons of the police for an imperial commissary, who was to come from Vienna to accompany us to the frontier. In the mean time, as our trunks had been sold, we provided ourselves with linen and clothes, and laid aside the prison livery.

At the end of five days the commissary arrived, and the director of police delivered us into his hands. He handed over to him at the same time the money that we had brought to Spielberg, and that which resulted from the sale of our portmanteaus and books, all of which was restored to us at the frontier. The expense of our journey was defrayed by the Emperor, and nothing was spared. I was far from well, and when we arrived at Vienna I was in a fever. For eight days I was under medical treatment, and at length I recovered. Being now comparatively well, I was anxious to depart, the more especially as the news of the *three days* of Paris had just reached us.

The Emperor had signed the decree for our liberty the very day that revolution broke out. He assuredly would not now revoke it; but it was very probable that, as the crisis was becoming critical for all Europe, and as popular movements were feared also in Italy, Austria would not at such a moment allow us to return to our country. We were well convinced they would not take us back to Spielberg, but we were afraid it might be suggested to the Emperor to consign us to some town of the empire far removed from the peninsula.

At last we left Vienna, and I was able to get as far as Brash. There I again became ill; but at the end of two days I insisted on resuming the journey. We traversed Austria and Styria, and reached Carinthia without accident; but when we arrived at a village called Feldkirchen, a short distance from Klagenfurt, there came a counter order. We were commanded to halt in this place till further directions.

I leave to be imagined how disagreeable this

event was to us. I had, in addition, the unpleasant reflection of being the cause of so great a calamity to my companions. My fatal malady was the reason they were debarred from returning to their country. We remained five days at Feldkirchen, and during that time the commissary did all in his power to amuse us. There was a small theater of poor players, and he took us to it. Another day he procured for us the diversion of a hunt. Our host, and several young people of the country, with the proprietor of a fine forest, were the hunters, and we, placed in a favorable position, enjoyed the sport as spectators.

At length a courier arrived from Vienna with orders for the commissary to conduct us to our destination. This good news filled me with joy, as well as my companions; but at the same time I trembled to see approaching the hour of a fatal discovery—the hour which would unfold to me that I had no longer either father or mother, nor several other connections, I knew not how many! Thus my melancholy increased as we advanced toward Italy.

From this side the approach to Italy is not agreeable, and the sterile aspect of the country contributed to increase my sadness. To see again our own sky, to meet human faces having no longer the northern expression, to hear on all lips the words of our language, affected me much; but the emotion produced tears rather than smiles. How often I covered my face with my hands, feigning to sleep, but shedding tears! How many nights I passed, unable to close an eye, and burning with fever, sometimes bestowing the most impassioned benedictions upon my sweet Italy, and thanking Heaven for having restored me to it; sometimes tormenting myself with the absence of intelligence concerning my family, and conjuring up imaginary ills; sometimes in reflecting that I should shortly have to separate, perhaps forever, from a friend who had passed through so many sufferings with me, and had given me such proofs of fraternal affection!

At Mantua it was necessary to bid farewell to Maroncelli, for here we were to separate. It was a parting of the most tender kind, not unaccompanied with tears. At Brescia I left behind my other companion in misfortune, Andrea Tonelli. On the 9th of September, two days after, I arrived at Milan, where I was detained for several days, and then set out for Piedmont in charge of a brigadier of gendarmerie.

The state of my feelings may be judged on once more finding myself on the Piedmontese soil. Ah! much as I love all nations, God knows that Italy is dearest to me! and much as I dote upon Italy, God knows how infinitely sweeter to me than the name of every other country in Italy, is the name of Piedmont, the land of my fathers!

I was still not free. The brigadier, on leaving me, handed me over to the Piedmontese carabineers. After a short delay, a gentleman appeared, who begged me to permit him to accompany me to Novara. He had missed another opportunity, and now there was no carriage but mine; he was much obliged that I allowed him to take advantage of it.

This disguised carabineer was of a jovial turn, and kept me good company as far as Novara. When we arrived at that town, pretending to conduct me to a hotel, he directed the carriage to the barracks of the carabineers, and there I was told there was a bed for me in the apartment of a brigadier, where I was to wait for higher orders.

Expecting to resume my journey on the following day, I went to bed, and, after conversing a moment with my host, I sunk into a profound sleep. I had not slept so well for a long time. I awoke toward morning, immediately arose, and got through some very long hours. I breakfasted, chatted, walked about the room and on the terrace, and cast a look on my host's books. At last a letter arrived from my father.

O, what joy to see again those much-loved

characters! What joy to learn that my mother, my dearest mother, still lived—that my two brothers and my eldest sister were also still alive! Alas! the youngest, the Marietta, who had entered the convent of the Visitation, as I had clandestinely learned in prison, had ceased to breathe nine months ago. It is sweet to think that I owe my liberty to those who loved me, who never ceased to intercede for me.

Days passed, and permission to leave Novara did not come. On the morning of the 16th September this permission was at last given me, and then I was freed from the tutelage of the carabineers. O, how many years it was since I had been able to go where I pleased, without the incumbrance of guards!

I obtained some money, received the greetings of a few persons, acquaintances of my father, and about three in the afternoon I departed. I had as companions on the journey a lady, a merchant, a sculptor, and two young painters, one of whom was deaf and dumb. We passed the night at Vercelli. The fortunate sun of the 17th September arose. We continued our journey, and did not reach Turin till the evening.

Who, who could describe the emotion of my heart, of the hearts of those so endeared to me, when I beheld, when I embraced my father, my mother, my brothers! My sister, my dear Josephine, was not present, as her duties detained her at Chieri; but at the first news of my return, she hastened home to pass a few days in the bosom of the family. Restored to these five objects of my tenderest affection, I was, I am, the most enviable of mortals.

CONCLUSION.

After his restoration to his native country, Silvio Pellico remained in tranquillity and retirement, surrounded by his family, the recollection of which forms so frequent a source of inspiration to him in the memoir of his imprisonment. His reappearance in the field of literature, in which he early gained so brilliant a renown, was, in a great measure, prevented by the captious censorship which weighs upon the Italian press, and must ever be a serious impediment to the effusions of genius. One of the works he composed beneath the Leads of Venice, "Ester d'Engaddi," which was considered, even by the commission appointed by the Emperor of Austria to conduct the process against him, as unobjectionable, was acted at Turin in 1831, the year after his liberation, with the highest applause, as well as another piece entitled "Gismonda." Both were immediately interdicted by the jealousy of Italian despotism.

The Count Arrivabene, who is mentioned by

Silvio Pellico as having been discharged from the prison of Saint Michael as innocent, found himself, shortly after, exposed to the suspicions of the government, and judged it expedient to fly. His only crime was having received Porro, Pellico, and some others at his country-house, near Mantua, as they returned from a trip in Porro's steamboat from Pavia to Venice. He fled from Mantua to Brescia, where he imparted his and their danger to his friends Ugoni and Scalvini, who joined him in his endeavor to escape into Switzerland. Gendarmes had been dispatched on all the routes to arrest Arrivabene as soon as his departure was known. He and his friends effected their retreat into Switzerland, disguised as cattle-drovers, but were very nearly caught. They had to pass an inn in which three gendarmes, lying in wait for them, were asleep; and at the moment they reached the Swiss frontier, they were so exhausted, from having had no interval of repose for sixty hours, that they fell upon the ground in the presence of the Austrian soldiers, who were close upon their heels when they crossed the line which separated tyranny from freedom. They were, however, safe. Count Porro also effected his escape from Italy. The gendarmes entered his house at one door as he left it by another. Confalonieri was prevented from executing the same maneuver by finding a door locked, the key of which had been altered by his intendant without his knowledge.

The events here narrated took place during the reign of Francis I, Emperor of Austria. They are a fair illustration of the illiberality and cruelty of despotism.

IX.

Alexander Selkirk, the Original of Robinson Crusoe.

ALEXANDER SELKIRK, the undoubted original of Defoe's celebrated character, Robinson Crusoe, was born in the year 1676, in the village of Largo, on the southern coast of Fife, in Scotland. John, the father of Alexander, was a thriving shoemaker, who lived in a house of his own, which has since been pulled down, at the west end of the town. He seems to have been a man of strict temperance, respected for his steady and religious character, and, like the majority of the Scottish parents at that time, a severe disciplinarian in his family. The name of his wife, the mother of our hero, was Euphan Mackie, also, it would seem, a native of Largo, and reported by tradition to have been the very contrast of her husband in her parental conduct—as yielding and indulgent as he was rigorous. In the case of Alexander, however, there was a special reason why Mrs. Selkirk should prove a kind and pliant mother.

Not only was she considerably advanced in years at the time of his birth, but, by a chance not very common, he was her seventh son, born without an intermediate daughter, and therefore destined, according to an old Scottish superstition, to come to great fortune, and make a figure in the world. Mrs. Selkirk, good, easy woman, firmly believed this, and made no doubt that her son, Sandie, was to be the great man of the family. He was therefore her pet; and the greater part of her maternal care, in respect to his education, consisted in confidential discourses with him by the fireside when the rest of the family were absent, and in occasional consultations how they should screen some little misdemeanor from the eyes of his father.

Young Selkirk was a clever enough boy, and quickly learned all that was taught at the school of his native town. Besides reading, writing, and arithmetic, he is said to have made considerable progress in navigation—a branch of knowledge likely to be of some repute in Largo, not only on account of its being a sea-coast town, with a considerable fishing population, but also in consequence of its having been the birthplace and property of Sir Andrew Wood, a distinguished Scottish admiral of the preceding century, whose nautical fame and habits must have produced considerable impression on it.

At all events, whether owing to the ideas he received at school, or to the effect on his mind of the perpetual spectacle of the sails in Largo Bay, and of his constant association with the Largo fishermen, Selkirk early determined to follow a seafaring life. Either out of a disposition to let the boy have his own will, or as thinking the life of a sailor the likeliest way to the attainment of the great fortunes which she anticipated for her son, his mother favored his intention; his father, however, opposed it strenuously, and was anxious, now that his other sons were all settled in life, that his youngest should remain at home, and assist him in his own trade. This, and young Selkirk's wayward and obstinate conduct, seem to have kept him and his father perpetually at war; and a descendant of the family used to show a walking-stick which the old man is said to have applied to the back of his refractory son, with the affirmation, "A whip for the horse, a bridle for the ass, and a rod for the fool's back." Notwithstanding the boy's restless character, respect for his father's wishes kept him at home for a considerable time: a father's malediction being too awful a thing for even a seventh son to brave with impunity.

The first thirteen years of Selkirk's life coincide with the hottest period of the religious persecutions in Scotland. He would be about three years of age at the time of the assassination of Archbishop Sharp, which took place at not a very great distance from Largo; and the chief subject of interest, during his boyhood, in Fife, as in the other counties of Scotland, was the position of the Church; then filled by Episcopalian and indulged clergy, greatly to the disgust of the people. What part old Selkirk and his family may have taken during the time when it was dangerous to show attachment to Presbytery—whether they professed themselves Covenanters, or whether, as is more probable, they yielded a reluctant attendance at the parish church—can not be ascertained; but the following entry in the parish records of Largo, referring to the year 1689, immediately after the Revolution had sealed the restoration of Presbytery in Scotland, will show that if they did attend the parish church, it was not out of lukewarmness to the popular cause, or affection for the established clergyman: "Sabbath, —— 1689.—Which day, the minister being obstructed in his duty, and kept out of the church by a great mob armed with staves and bludgeons, headed by John Selkirk, divided what money there was among the poor, and retired from his charge." John Selkirk, who thus signalized himself by heading the mob for the expulsion of the conforming clergyman, was the eldest brother of our hero, who, however, is reported himself to have testified his enthusiasm by flourishing a stick with the other boys. This outburst of Presbyterian zeal freed Largo from the unpopular clergyman, and in a short time in it, as well as in the other parishes of Scotland, the Presbyterian rule was re-established.

One of the first youths in Largo to experience the stricter discipline of Presbytery, whose restoration he had celebrated, was Alexander Selkirk. His high spirits, and want of respect for any control, led him, it would appear, to be guilty of frequent misbehavior during Divine service; for under date the 25th August, 1695, is the following entry in the parish records: "Alexander Selcraig, [the ancient mode of spelling Selkirk,] son of John Selcraig, elder, cited to appear before the session for indecent conduct in church." This seems to have been more than our hero, now in his nineteenth year, could submit to. The elder's son to appear before the session, and be rebuked for laughing in church! Within twenty-four hours after this terrible citation the young shoemaker was gone; he had left Largo and the land of kirk-sessions behind him, and was miles away at sea. When the kirk-session met, they were obliged to be content with inserting the following paragraph in the record: "August 27th.—Alexander Selcraig called out; did not appear, having gone to sea." Resolved, however, that he should not escape the rebuke which he had merited, they add, "Continued until his return."

The return which the kirk-session thus looked forward to did not take place for six years, during which time we have no account of Selkirk's adventures, although the probability is, that he served with the buccaneers, who then scoured the South Seas. To have persisted in calling the young sailor to account for a fault committed six years before, would have been too great severity. The kirk-session, accordingly, do not seem to have made any allusion to the circumstance which had driven him to sea; but it was not long before a still more disgraceful piece of misconduct than the former brought him under their censure. The young sailor, coming home, no doubt, with his character rendered still more reckless and boisterous than before by the wild life to which he had been accustomed at sea, was hardly a fit inmate for a sedate and orderly household, and quarrels and disturbances became frequent in the honest shoemaker's cottage. One of these domestic uproars brought the whole family before the session: the peace and good order of families being one of the things which were then taken cognizance of by the ecclesiastical authorities in every parish. The circumstances are thus detailed in the session records: "November, 1701.—The same day, John Guthrie delated John Selcraig, elder, and his wife, Euphan Mackie, and his son, Alexander Selcraig, for disagreement together; and also, John Selcraig, Alexander's eldest brother, and his wife, Margaret Bell. All of them are ordered to be cited against next session, which is to be on the 25th instant."

Agreeably to this citation the parties appeared—the father, the mother, the eldest son and his wife, and our hero. On this occasion, John Selcraig, the elder, "being examined what was the cause of the tumult that was in his house, said he knew not; unless that Andrew Selcraig—another of the old man's sons who lived in the house, and who was but half-witted—having brought in a can full of salt-water, of which his brother Alexander did take a drink through mistake, and he, Andrew, laughing at him for it, his brother Alexander came and beat him, upon which he ran out of the house, and called his brother John—John and his wife, Margaret Bell, would appear to have lived in a neighboring house; and Andrew had run into it to call his brother. Being again questioned what made him—Selkirk, the father—sit upon the floor with his back at the door, he said it was to keep down his son Alexander, who was seeking to go up to get down his pistol. And being inquired what he was going to do with it, said he could not tell." Such was the tenor of the old man's evidence. On the same day the culprit Alexander was called; but he had contrived to go to Cupar, to be out of the way. Directing a second citation to be issued against him for next session, the court proceeded to examine the other witnesses. The younger John Selkirk gave his evidence as follows: "On the 7th of November last, he being called by his brother Andrew, came to his father's house; and when he entered it, his mother went out; and he, seeing his father sitting upon the floor, with his brother at the door, was much troubled, and offered to help him up; at which time he did see his brother Alexander in the other end of the house casting off his coat, and coming toward him; whereupon his father did get up, and did get betwixt them—Alexander and John—but he did not know what he did besides, his—John's—head being borne down by his brother Alexander; but afterward, being liberated by his wife, he made his escape." Margaret Bell, John's wife, who thus courageously rescued her husband from the clutches of Alexander, was next examined. She declared that her husband being called out by his brother Andrew to go to his father's house, she followed him, "and coming into the house, she found the said Alexander gripping both his father and her husband, and she, laboring to loose his hands from her husband's head and breast, her husband fled out of doors, and she followed him, but called back, 'You false loon, will you murder your father and my husband both?' whereupon he—Alexander—followed her to the door; but whether he beat her or not, she was in so great confusion she can not distinctly say, but ever since she hath had a sore pain in her head." The last witness examined was Andrew Selkirk, whose laughter at his brother's mistake had been the original cause of the quarrel. Andrew, however, was able to say "nothing to purpose in the business," and the further investigation of the matter was adjourned till the next meeting.

The session met again on the 29th of November; and this time the culprit was present. The following is the entry regarding the interview between the future Robinson Crusoe and his ecclesiastical judges: "Alexander Selcraig, scandalous for contention and disagreeing with his brothers, compeared, and being questioned concerning the tumult that was in his house, whereof he was said to be the occasion, confessed that he, having taken a drink of salt water out of a can, his brother Andrew laughing at him for it, he did beat him twice with a staff. He confessed also that he had spoken very ill words concerning his brother; and particularly that he had challenged his elder brother John to a combat of *dry nieves*, [dry fists,] as he called it, else then, he said, he would not care even to do it now, which afterward he did refuse. [The meaning seems to be, that at first he told the session to their face that he would not care even then to challenge his brother, but afterward retracted the expression.] Moreover he said several things; whereupon the session appointed him to compear before the face of the congregation for his scandalous carriage." This punishment, the greatest disgrace which could be inflicted on a Scotchman of that day, the young sailor actually underwent; for on the next day, Sunday, November 30, 1701, "Alexander Selcraig, according to the session's appointment, compeared before the pulpit, and made acknowledgment of his sin in disagreeing with his brothers, and was rebuked in the face of the congregation for it, and promised amendment in the strength of the Lord, and so was dismissed."

Probably Selkirk would not have staid to undergo the punishment inflicted on him by the session, but would have gone off to sea, as on the former occasion, had the season not been too far advanced for him to find a ship. He therefore remained at Largo during the winter; whether assisting his father at his trade, or going about idle, we do not know. In the spring of 1702 he seized an opportunity of going to England; and a short time afterward we find him engaged to proceed with the celebrated Dampier on a buccaneering expedition to the South Seas. That our readers may understand the nature of this expedition, during which that extraordinary event happened to Selkirk which has made his name so famous, it will be necessary to give a brief account of the people called the buccaneers.

THE BUCCANEERS—SELKIRK JOINS A PRIVATEERING EXPEDITION UNDER DAMPIER—ACCOUNT OF THE VOYAGE.

As is well known, the Spaniards were the first to discover and take possession of the lands in the new world, including the choicest islands of the West Indies, and the rich coasts of South America and Mexico. It was not long, however, before adventurers of other nations, especially French, English, and Dutch, pressed into the newly-discovered seas, and attempted to procure a share of the good things with which the American islands and shores abounded. The Spaniards, whose savage cruelties to the unfortunate natives of the lands they had discovered had made them absolute lords of every portion of American ground on which they had planted themselves, resisted the new-comers with all their strength; attacked their ships, drove them out of the spots where they endeavored to found their small settlements, and in a hundred other ways annoyed and injured them. The consequence was, that the English, French, and Dutch adventurers who had congregated in the West Indian Archipelago were unable to settle down permanently in any place, but were obliged to keep up a continual war with the Spaniards, in order to maintain their existence. Hayti or St. Domingo, being the earliest and most flourishing of the Spanish settlements, became the principal haunt of these rivals and enemies of the Spaniards. A number of French adventurers, whom the Spaniards in their narrow jealousy had driven out of the island of St. Christophers, took up their headquarters in the small island of Tortuga, adjoining the northern coast of St. Domingo, and convenient as a station from which they could make expeditions into the latter island, for the purpose of hunting the wild cattle and swine with which it swarmed.

This, of course, increased the animosity of the Spaniards, who resented these incursions upon their territory, and attacked the intruders without mercy whenever they surprised them in the woods of St. Domingo.

Compelled thus to associate themselves for mutual safety in bands of considerable force, and joined by adventurers of other nations, the *Bucaniers*, as the French were called, from the custom of *bucanning*, or drying and smoking the flesh of the animals which they killed, became a formidable body. Many of them, tired of the miserable life which they led on shore, embarked in vessels, and sought a desperate but congenial occupation in attacking and plundering the richly-laden ships which were constantly sailing from the Spanish colonies to the mother country. Allured by the charms of this lawless mode of life, fresh adventurers arrived from France and England in ships fitted out for the purpose, with the permission of the French and English governments, both of which were eager to damage the Spanish interests; and thus, toward the close of the seventeenth century, the West Indian Archipelago, and the shores of South America, swarmed with crews of pirates, who, under the name of privateers, chased every merchant vessel that made its appearance. When they came up with such a vessel quitting an American harbor, they boarded her with the most reckless audacity, either murdered the sailors and passengers, or made them prisoners, and shared the cargo according to their own rules of equity. In consequence of their ravages, the Spanish colonists in the new world became less and less disposed to risk their property in commerce, and the intercourse which had hitherto been kept up between the colonies and the mother country was greatly interrupted.

Disappointed of prizes at sea, the buccaneers did not hesitate to make up for the loss by storming and plundering the Spanish settlements on the American coasts. Landing in the night-time on the beach, close by some ill-guarded town or village, they would surprise the inhabitants while asleep, and either carry off all the wealth they could find, or sell back their own property to the wretched inhabitants for a heavy ransom. The buccaneers were, in fact, a floating nation of robbers—a revival, in more modern times, of the Norwegian sea-kings. They had their own rude notions of justice; they even professed religion in the midst of their licentiousness; and many of them never gave chase to a flag without falling down on their knees on the deck to pray God that he would grant them the victory and a valuable cargo. The more respectable among them defended their mode of life, by saying that the injuries they perpetrated upon the Spaniards were a just retribution upon that nation for their cruelties to the Indians, or sought shelter under the general usage of the time, which authorized the various governments of Europe to grant licenses to private adventurers to harass and destroy the ships and ports belonging to nations with which they were at war. These excuses, joined with the love of adventure and the desire of wealth, the prospect of attaining which was so great in the buccaneering mode of life, operated as motives sufficient to induce a number of persons belonging to families of good repute to engage in the trade; nor did they incur disgrace by so doing. As we have already seen, young Selkirk, although he was the son of a stanch Scottish Presbyterian, and had been subject from his infancy to the wholesome impressions of respectable society, had not scrupled to join the rovers of the South Seas. His experience of the toils and dangers of such a life had not cured him of his propensity to adventure; and now, for the second time, he leaves his father's house to become a privateer.

William Dampier, the originator and commander of the expedition which Selkirk now joined, was an Englishman, who had gone to sea at an early age, and for upward of thirty years had been enduring the innumerable hardships and vicissitudes incident to the life of a sailor in those times. He was a man of ardent mind and great abilities, as the accounts of his voyages which he has left testify; and he had gained more knowledge of the South Seas than any man then living. He had not, however, with all his energy and skill, been very successful in improving his own fortunes; and now, at the age of fifty years, he was planning another expedition, which he hoped would issue in the acquisition of immense riches for all concerned. He found little difficulty in persuading some merchants to fit out two vessels, the St. George and the Fame, each of twenty-six guns, the former to be commanded by himself, the latter by a Captain Pulling; and as war had just been declared against France and Spain, in consequence of a dispute regarding the succession to the crown of the latter, in which Great Britain, Holland, and several other countries ranged themselves against France, he easily obtained the necessary commissions from Prince George, then high admiral of England, authorizing the crews of the two ships to attack and plunder the French and Spaniards for their own profit. Thus entitled, so far as the lord high admiral's warrant could entitle them, to grow rich by robbing Frenchmen and Spaniards all over the world, the adventurers listened eagerly to the plans which Dampier proposed as most sure to succeed. The first of these was, that they should sail to the south-eastern coast of South America, proceed up the river La Plata as far as Buenos Ayres, and earn £600,000 at one stroke by capturing the Spanish galleons usually stationed there. Should this plan fail, they were to sail round Cape Horn, and make a privateering cruise as far as the coast of Peru, where they would be likely to fall in with some valuable prizes; and should they fail also in this, they could still find profitable occupation in plundering the Spanish towns along the western coast of South America, waiting for the ship which periodically sailed from the Mexican port of Acapulco, and which would be a splendid capture. Such were the hopes which Dampier held out to the crews. The vessels were victualed for nine months; "and the articles of agreement were, *no purchase, no pay;* or, in other words, the merchants risked the vessels, and the crews their limbs and lives."*

All was prepared for sailing, and the vessels were already in the Downs, when, in conse-

* Howell's Life of Alexander Selkirk.

quence of a quarrel between Dampier and Pulling, the latter went off alone, intending, he said, to make for the Canary Islands. Neither he nor the ship was ever heard of afterward. Dampier, on Pulling's departure, lost no time in procuring the equipment of another vessel instead of the Fame. The name of the new vessel was "The Cinque Ports," of about ninety tuns burden, with a crew of sixty-three, and carrying sixteen guns. This ship joined the St. George in the Bay of Kinsale, on the Irish coast, on the 18th of May, 1703, and made all haste to proceed on their voyage. Still it was not till the 11th of September that they left Kinsale. The following is the list of the officers of the ships respectively as given by Mr. Howell: In the St. George—William Dampier, captain; John Clipperton, chief mate; William Funnel, second mate; and John Ballet, surgeon. In the Cinque Ports—Charles Pickering, captain; Thomas Stradling, lieutenant; and *Alexander Selkirk*, sailing-master. The appointment of our hero to so responsible a situation as that of sailing-master indicates considerable confidence in his abilities and seamanship.

On the 25th of September the vessels reached Madeira, and here Dampier had the disappointment of learning that his delay, in consequence of Pulling's desertion, had deprived them of the chance of capturing the galleons in the La Plata river, these ships having already arrived at Teneriffe. The crews then resolved to trust to the chances which the other plans proposed by Dampier might afford. Accordingly, they made straight for the South American coast. The only incident of consequence on the way was the disagreement of Captain Dampier with some of his crew. On the 2d of November they passed the equator, and on the 8th they saw the coast of Brazil.

On the 24th of November they anchored at the island of Le Grand, in latitude twenty-three degrees thirty minutes south. "It produces," says William Funnel, the second mate of the St. George, who wrote a narrative of the voyage, "rum, sugar, and several kinds of fruit, but all very dear, on account of supplying the inland town of St. Paul with necessaries. Here we wooded, watered, and refitted our ships; and nine of our men falling out with Captain Dampier, left us, and went ashore." Another incident which happened at Le Grand, and which exercised a bad effect on the remainder of the expedition, was the death of Captain Pickering, of the Cinque Ports, who was succeeded by his lieutenant, Stradling, a man of ferocious and quarrelsome temper. The death of Pickering, the appointment of Stradling, the frequent altercations between Dampier and his crew, the difference of views which began to be manifested among the sailors as to the best plan for rendering the rest of the voyage successful, all preyed upon the mind of Selkirk to such a degree, as to render him disgusted with his situation. He had a dream, it is said, off the coast of Le Grand, which left the firm impression on his mind that the expedition was to be disastrous, and that he ought to take the first opportunity of giving up all connection with it. It was not till some time afterward, however, that he resolved finally to do so.

Leaving Le Grand on the 28th of December, the vessels continued their voyage southward; passed the Falkland Isles on the 29th, and were encountered by such a storm in rounding Cape Horn, that they lost sight of each other on the 4th of January, 1704. They did not fall in with each other again till the 10th of February, when the St. George, anchoring at the island of Juan Fernandez, after a tedious voyage along the coasts of Patagonia and Chili, found that the Cinque Ports had been waiting there for her three days. "We anchored," says Funnel, "in the great bay, in thirty-five fathoms. At this island we wooded, watered, and refitted our ships, giving them a heel, to clean their sides as low as we could, which took up much time, and occasioned both companies to be much on shore. In this island there are an abundance of cabbage-trees, which are excellent, though small. The cabbage-tree, which is a species of palm, has a small, straight stem, often ninety or a hundred feet long, with many knots or joints, about four inches asunder, like a bamboo cane. It has no leaves, except at the top, in the midst of which the substance called cabbage is contained. The branches of this tree are commonly twelve or thirteen feet in length; and at about a foot and a half from the tree the leaves begin, which are about four feet long, and an inch and a half broad—the leaves growing so regularly, that the whole branch seems one entire leaf. The cabbage, when cut out from among the roots of the branches, is usually a foot long, and six inches in diameter, and as white as milk. From the bottom of the cabbage there spring out several large bunches of berries, like grapes, each bunch being five or six pounds weight. The berries are red, and about the size of cherries, each having a large stone in the middle, and the pulp tastes like that of haws. On the island we saw also the sea-lion, which is so called, as I suppose, because he roars somewhat like a lion, and his head has also some resemblance to that animal, having four large teeth in front, all the rest being short, thick, and stubbed. Instead of feet and legs, he has four fins, the two foremost serving him, when he goes ashore, to raise the fore-part of the body, and he then draws the hind-part after him. The two hinder fins are of no use on land, but only in the water. The animal is very fat; for which reason we killed several of them, from which we made a tun of oil for our lamps, and while at this island, made use of it also for frying our fish. They have short, light-colored hair when young, becoming sandy when old. Their food is fish, and they prey altogether in the water, but come on land to sleep, when five, six, or more of them huddle together like swine, and will often lie still three or four days if not molested. They are much afraid of men, and make off as fast as they can into the water. If hard pressed, they will turn about, raising their bodies on their fore-fins, and face you with their mouths wide open; so that we used to clap a pistol to their mouths and fire down their throats. Sometimes five or six of us would surround one of these monsters, each having half a pike, and so prick him dead, which commonly was the sport of two or three hours."* Selkirk little thought, while cutting

* Funnel's Narrative.

the branches of the cabbage-trees, and hunting sea-lions with Funnel and the other sailors on the beach of Juan Fernandez, that in a short time this island was to be his solitary home.

The life of comparative idleness which the crews of the two ships were leading on the island was not favorable to good-humor or harmony, especially as, hitherto, they had not succeeded in attaining the object of their expedition. The sailors of the Cinque Ports quarreled with their captain, Stradling; and the dispute at length ran so high, that forty-two men, or more than two-thirds of the crew, went ashore, and threatened to remain. Whether Selkirk, who, as sailing-master, was next in rank to Stradling on board the Cinque Ports, was one of those who revolted, is not ascertained; but the sequel renders it probable that he was. At length Dampier succeeded in reconciling the sailors with their captain, order was restored, and matters went on as usual.

On the 29th of February the idle crews were roused to activity by the sight of a sail. In their hurry to give chase, they left behind them one of their boats, their anchors, a quantity of oil, and other materials, and, what was more alarming, five sailors and a negro, who happened to be straggling in a part of the island distant from the beach at the time when the sail was seen. Bearing out to sea, they found the strange ship to be a Frenchman of thirty guns. After a long pursuit, they came up with her next day, and engaged her very close, the St. George keeping her broadside to broadside for seven hours. A gale then sprang up, and the Frenchman escaped, disappointing the privateers of their expected booty. Nine of the St. George's men had been killed, and many more wounded in the action. The crews were, nevertheless, exceedingly anxious to continue the chase; but Dampier opposed them, saying it was not worth while, and "they did not need to care for merchantmen, as he could get them a prize of £500,000 any day of the year." They therefore returned, in no very good humor to Juan Fernandez, which they came in sight of on the 3d of March. To their surprise they found two French vessels at anchor off the island, each of thirty-six guns; a sight which made them glad to sheer off, leaving the boat, the anchors, the oil, and the six sailors to their fate. It afterward appeared that the Frenchmen, on landing, had taken possession of all the stores they found on the island, and made prisoners of four of the six men, the other two managing to conceal themselves.

Prevented from again taking up their station at Juan Fernandez, the St. George and the

Cinque Ports bore away north-east for the coast of Peru, which they came in sight of on the 11th of March. "Coasting northward along the shore," says Funnel, "which is the highest and most mountainous I ever saw, we were surprised, on the 19th of March, to see the waves changed to a red color for seven or eight leagues, though, on sounding, we had no ground at one hundred and seventy fathoms; but, on drawing up some of the water, we found the color to be owing to a vast quantity of fish-spawn swimming on the surface." Keeping a constant look-out for vessels to attack, they saw, on the 22d of March, two at some distance, the sternmost of which proved to be the Frenchman which they had chased and fought off Juan Fernandez. They were very eager to capture this vessel, not merely on account of her value, but because, if she reached Lima—the port which she seemed to be bound for—her crew would communicate the intelligence that two buccaneering ships were on the coast, and so prevent the merchantmen in that port from sailing. Dampier, however, was averse to attacking her; and she escaped, greatly to the discontent of the men, whose fears were in great part realized, and who were only kept from breaking out in rebellion by the capture of two considerable prizes a few days afterward. Clearing these vessels of the valuable part of their cargo, as well as a bark laden with plank and cordage, which they fell in with on the 11th of April, they let them go, and began to meditate a descent upon some settlement on the coast north of Lima. Santa Maria was the town they resolved to attack, as they expected there to find a great quantity of gold collected from the adjacent mines. On their way to this town from the island of Gallo, which they left on the 17th of April, they captured a small Spanish vessel, on board of which they found a Guernsey man, who had long been a prisoner among the Spaniards. In high spirits with their success, they sailed for Santa Maria, Captain Dampier telling them that, on a former occasion, one hundred and twenty pounds weight of gold had been carried off by a buccaneer from that town, and, that, as it was now much larger, the quantity of gold in it must be enormous. They reached the town, and commenced the attack in the night-time. "The design, however," says Funnel, "miscarried, whether from fear, confusion, or the enemy having early intelligence of our motions, which enabled them to cut off many of our men. This is certain, that we became quite sick of our fruitless attempts before the 1st of May, and immediately re-embarked. We were now so short of provisions that five boiled green plantains were allotted for six men; but when almost out both of hope and patience, a vessel came and anchored close beside us at midnight, which we took without resistance. This proved a most valuable prize, being a ship of one hundred and fifty tuns, laden with flour, sugar, brandy, wine, about thirty tuns of marmalade of quinces, a considerable quantity of salt, and several tuns of linen and woolen cloth; so that we had now a sufficient supply of provisions even for four or five years." On board of this rich prize, to secure an equitable division of the spoil among the crews of the two ships, were placed William Funnel and Alexander Selkirk—the former on behalf of the crew of the St. George, the latter on behalf of the crew of the Cinque Ports.

The buccaneers carried their prize into the Bay of Panama, and anchored with her under the island of Tobago, on the 14th of May. "Here," says Funnel, "Captains Dampier and Stradling disagreed, and the quarrel proceeded to such a length, that they could not be reconciled, so that at last it was determined to part company, all the men of both crews being at liberty to go with which captain they pleased. Five of our men went over to Captain Stradling and five of his men came to us." It would therefore seem that our hero, Selkirk, had here an opportunity of changing his captain; and as it is certain that he had no special friendship for Stradling, his not availing himself of the opportunity would indicate that, bad as Stradling was, he preferred him to Dampier. Probably he thought that, by remaining with Stradling, who was more unhesitating in his measures than Dampier, he would sooner grow rich. At all events, he and Funnel, on quitting the prize, resumed their old stations in their respective ships. The prize was abandoned after all that was considered valuable had been taken out of her; and on the 19th of May, 1704, the two ships parted company, never to meet again, the St. George sailing away in quest of more prizes, the Cinque Ports remaining behind. It is with the fate of the latter that we are now to be further concerned; and as Funnel went with the St. George, we have no longer his narrative to guide us.

For three months the Cinque Ports kept cruising along the shores of Mexico, Guatemala, and Equatorial America, like a villainous vulture watching the horizon for its prey. No ships, however, appeared to reward the greedy activity of the crew; and at length, in the end of August, Stradling resolved to turn southward, and make for Juan Fernandez, to take in provisions and refit. Meanwhile, as was natural among so many men of savage character, cooped up idle in a vessel, all was dissension on board. Stradling and Selkirk especially were, to use a common phrase, at dagger-drawing; now in loud and angry dispute below, now scowling sullenly at each other on deck. Selkirk resolved to leave the vessel as soon as an opportunity offered. Accordingly, when, in the beginning of September, they came in sight of Juan Fernandez, and the two men who had been living on the island since the beginning of March—when, it will be remembered, the St. George and Cinque Ports had been obliged to sheer off without being able to pick them up—made their appearance, healthy and strong as ever, and delighting their old companions with an account of how they had spent the seven months of their solitary reign, eating fruit in abundance, chasing goats, and hunting seals, the idea flashed across his mind that he would take their place, and leaving the vessel to sail away without him, remain the possessor of Juan Fernandez. By what process of imagination he flattered himself that such a life would be agreeable; whether he finally adopted his resolution in a fit of unthinking enthusiasm, such as sometimes leads to strange and whimsical acts, or whether his differences with Stradling, and his disgust with his situation on board the Cinque Ports, were really such that escape by any method seemed advisable, can not now be known; but, at all events, the conclusion was, that when the vessel was ready to leave the island, Selkirk signified his intention of remaining. Stradling made no objections; a boat was lowered, Selkirk descended into it with all his effects, three or four men rowed him ashore under the direction of the captain, the crew of the Cinque Ports looking on from the deck. Selkirk leaped on the beach, his effects were lifted out after him by the sailors, and laid in a heap; they shook hands with him heartily, the captain standing in the boat, and bidding them make haste. The sailors jumped in, and the boat was pushed off. Poor Selkirk! he had felt a bound, an exultation of spirit at the moment of stepping on shore; but now, as the boat was shoved off, and the men sat down to the oars with their faces toward him, pride, anger, resolution, all gave way; the horrors of his situation rose at once to his view, and rushing into the surf up to the middle, he stretched out his hands toward his comrades, and implored them to come back and take him on board again. With a jeering laugh, the brutal commander bade him stick to his resolution, and remain where he was, adding that it was a blessing for the crew to have got rid at last of so troublesome a fellow. The boat accordingly went off to the ship, and in a short time the Cinque Ports was out of sight. Selkirk remained on the beach beside his bundles, gazing after her till it grew dark; and then, with no sound in his ears but the melancholy moaning of the sea-waves, he waited for the light of day.

Juan Fernandez, the island on which our poor Scotchman was thus cast ashore, is situated in latitude 33 degrees 40 minutes south, and longitude 79 degrees west, about four hundred miles west of the coast of Chili. The name is properly applied to a group of islands, consisting of two larger and a few smaller; and the name now given to that inhabited by Selkirk, and which is the largest of the group, is Mas-a-tierra. The island was first discovered in 1572 by a Spanish navigator, who conferred on it his own name of Juan Fernandez.

The island is of an irregular form, from ten to twelve miles long, and about six broad, its area being about seventy square miles. "The south-west side is much the longest, and has a small island about a mile long lying near it, with a few visible rocks close under the shore. On this side begins a ridge of high mountains, that run across from the south-west to the north-west of the island; and the land that lies out in a narrow point to the westward appears to be the only level ground in it. On the north-east side it is very high land, and under it are the two bays, where ships always put in to recruit. The best bay is all deep water, and you may carry in ships close to the rocks, if occasion require. The wind blows always over the land, and at worst along shore, which makes no sea. Near the rocks there are very good fish of several sorts, particularly large crawfish, under the rocks, easy to be caught, also cavalloes, gropers, and other good fish, in so great plenty any where near the shore, that I never saw the like but at the best fishing season in Newfoundland. Pimento is the best timber, and most plentiful on this side of the island, but very apt to split, till a little dried. The cabbage-trees abound about three miles into the woods, and the cabbage is very good; most of them are on the top of the nearest and lowest mountains. The soil in these hills is of a loose black earth; the rocks are very rotten, so that, without great care, it is dangerous to climb the hills for cabbages; besides, there are abundance of holes dug in several places by a sort of fowls called puffins, which cause the earth to fall in at once, and endanger the breaking of a man's leg. Our summer months are winter here. In July snow and ice are sometimes seen; but the spring, which is in September, October, and November, is very pleasant. There is then abundance of good herbs, as parsley, purslain, etc." *

For many days after the departure of the Cinque Ports, Selkirk remained lingering about the spot where he was put ashore, unable to abandon the hope that Stradling would relent and come back for him. His constant occupation was gazing out into the sea. As soon as morning dawned he began his watch, sitting on his chest; and his deepest grief was when the evening came on, so that he could see no longer. Sleep came upon him by snatches, and against his exertions to remain awake. Food he did not think of, till extreme hunger obliged him; and then, rather than go in search of the fruits and game which the woods afforded, he contented himself with the shell-fish and seals' flesh, which he could obtain without removing from the beach. The sameness of the diet, the want of bread and salt, and the sinking sickness of his heart, caused him to loathe his food, so that he ate but at long intervals. Weary, and with aching eyes, he lay down at night, leaning his back against his bundles, listening to the crashing sound of rocks frequently falling among the woods, and to the discordant bleating of the shoals of seals along the shore. The

* Voyage by Captain Woodes Rogers in 1708-9.

horrors of his situation were augmented during the dark by superstitious alarms. Amid the murmur of the waves he could fancy he heard howlings and whistlings, as of spirits in the air: if he turned his head to the black and wooded masses behind him, they seemed peopled and in motion; and as he again turned it to the shore, phantoms stalked past. Often he cursed himself for the folly of the resolution which had brought him here; often, in the frenzy of fear, he would start up with the horrible determination of suicide; but a rush of softer feelings would come, and then he became calm. At length this gentler state of mind grew habitual; thoughts and impressions which had been familiar to him in childhood, again came up; and the years which he had spent with brawling and ferocious shipmates, in the lawless profession of a privateer, were swept out of his memory like a disagreeable dream.

The stores which Selkirk had brought ashore consisted, besides his clothing and bedding, of a firelock, a pound of gunpowder, a quantity of bullets, a flint and steel, a few pounds of tobacco, a hatchet, a knife, a kettle, a flip-can, a Bible, some books of devotion, and one or two concerning navigation, and his mathematical instruments. Such were the few implements and substances from the great civilized world which

Selkirk had to help him in the task of subduing to his own convenience seventy square miles of earth and wood. Yet, in the possession of that small package, what strength lay in his hands, and how superior was he to the savage children of nature! Within the small compass of his chest was wrapped up the condensed skill and wisdom of ages, the ingenuity and industry of hundreds of men who had long gone to their graves. The flint and steel, the firelock, the gunpowder, the knife and hatchet, what power over nature was there not compact in these articles!—the mathematical instruments, of what knowledge were they not the symbols!—and, above all, the Bible, and the books which accompanied it, what wealth of conversation, what health of spirit, did they not bring with them!

The first object that occupied his attention, besides the daily supply of such food as was necessary for his subsistence, was the construction of a dwelling to serve him as a shelter from the weather. Selecting a spot at some distance from the beach, he cut down pimento wood, and in a short time built a hut in which he could reside. To this he afterward added another. They were both constructed during the first eighteen months of his residence; but the task of improving them, and adding to their neatness, was a constant occupation to him during his stay on the island. The larger of his two huts, which "was situated near a spacious wood, he made his sleeping-room, spreading the bedclothes he had brought with him upon a frame of his own construction; and as these wore out, or were used for other purposes, he supplied their places with goat-skins. The smaller hut, which he had erected at some distance from the other, was used by him as a kitchen, in which he dressed his victuals. The furniture was very scanty, but consisted of every convenience the island could afford. His most valuable article was the pot or kettle he had brought from the ship to boil his meat in; the spit was his own handiwork, made of such wood as grew upon the island; the rest was suitable to his rudely-constructed habitation. The pimento wood, which burns very bright and clear, served him both for fuel and candle. It gives out an agreeable perfume when burning. He obtained fire after the Indian method, by rubbing two pieces of pimento wood together till they ignited. This he did, as he was ill able to spare any of his linen for tinder, time being of no value to him, and the labor rather an amusement."* The necessity of providing for his wants had the effect of diverting his

* Howell's Life of Selkirk

thoughts from the misery of his situation; yet every day, for the first eighteen months, he spent more or less time on the beach, watching for the appearance of a sail on the horizon. At the end of that time, partly through habit, partly through the influence of religion, which here awakened in full force upon his mind, he became reconciled to his situation. Every morning, after rising, he read a portion of Scripture, sang a psalm, and prayed, speaking aloud, in order to preserve the use of his voice; he afterward remarked that, during his residence on the island, he was a better Christian than he had ever been before, or would probably ever be again. He at first lived much upon turtles and crawfish, which abounded upon the shores—his powder, with which he could shoot the goats of the island, having soon been exhausted; but afterward he found himself able to run down the goats, whose flesh he either roasted or stewed, and of which he kept a small stock, tamed, around his dwelling, to be used in the event of his being disabled by sickness. One of the greatest inconveniences which afflicted him for the first few months was the want of salt; but he gradually became accustomed to this privation, and at last found so much relish in unsalted food, that, after being restored to society, it was with equal difficulty that he reconciled himself to take it in any other condition. As a substitute for bread, he had turnips, parsnips, and the cabbage-palm, all of excellent quality, and also radishes and water-cresses. When his clothes were worn out, he supplied their place with goat-skins, which gave him an appearance much more uncouth than any wild animal. He had a piece of linen from which he made new shirts by means of a nail and the thread of his stockings; and he never wanted this comfortable piece of attire during the whole period of his residence on the island. Every physical want being thus gratified, and his mind soothed by devotional feeling, he at length began positively to enjoy his existence—often lying for whole days in the delicious bowers which he had formed for himself, abandoned to the most pleasant sensations.

Among the quadruped inhabitants of the isle were multitudes of rats, which at the first annoyed him by gnawing his feet while asleep. Against this enemy he found it necessary to enter into a treaty, offensive and defensive, with the cats, which also abounded in his neighborhood. Having caught and tamed some of the latter animals, he was soon freed from the presence of the rats, but not without disagreeable consequences in the reflection that, should he die in his hut, his friendly auxiliaries would probably be obliged, for their subsistence, to devour his body. He was, in the mean time, able to turn them to some account for his amusement, by teaching them to dance and perform a number of antic feats, such as cats are not in general supposed capable of learning, but which they might probably acquire, if any individual in civilized life were able to take the necessary pains. Another of his amusements was hunting on foot, in which he at length, through healthy exercise and habit, became such a proficient, that he could run down the swiftest goat. Some of the young of these animals, he taught to dance in company with his kittens; and he often afterward declared that he never danced with a lighter heart or greater spirit than to the sound of his own voice in the midst of these dumb companions.

Selkirk was careful, during his stay on the island, to measure the lapse of time, and distinguish Sunday from the other days of the week. Anxious, in the midst of all his indifference to society, that, in the event of his dying in solitude, his having lived there might not be unknown to his fellow-creatures, he carved his name upon a number of trees, adding the date of his being left, and the space of time which had since elapsed. When his knife was worn out, he made new ones, and even a cleaver for his meat, out of some hoops which he found on the shore. He several times saw vessels passing the island, but only two cast anchor beside it. Afraid of being taken by the Spaniards, who would have consigned him to hopeless captivity, he endeavored to ascertain whether these strangers were so or not before making himself known. In both cases he found them enemies; and on one of the occasions, having approached too near, he was observed and chased, and only escaped by taking refuge in a tree.

As Selkirk was only about thirty years of age, and as he found his constitution, which was naturally good, improved and fortified in a wonderful degree by his mode of life, the only cause which he could fear as likely to cut short his days, and prevent him from reaching the old age which he might expect to attain to in his island, provided no ship appeared to carry him off, was the occurrence of some accident, such as might very possibly befall him in his expeditions through the woods. Only one such accident occurred during his stay on the island; it had nearly proved fatal, however. It has already been mentioned that in many parts of the island the soil was loose, and undermined by holes, and the rock weathered almost to rottenness. Pursuing a goat once in one of these dangerous places, the bushy brink of a precipice, to which he had followed it, crumbled beneath him, and he and the goat fell together from a great hight. He lay stunned and senseless at the foot of the rock for a great while—not less than twenty-four hours, he thought, from the change of position in the sun—but the precise length of time he had no means of ascertaining. When he recovered his senses, he found the goat lying dead beside him. With great pain and difficulty he made his way to his hut, which was nearly a mile distant from the spot; and for three days he lay on his bed, enduring much suffering. No permanent injury, however, had been done him, and he was soon able to go abroad again.

Four years and four months had elapsed since Selkirk was left by Stradling on the island of Juan Fernandez. It was now the month of January, 1709; his reckoning enabled him to know the lapse of time, at least within a week or two. Four times had the January summers of Juan Fernandez passed over his head, and already he was looking forward to the coming of the fifth autumn and winter. The whole island was now familiar to him, with its appearances and productions at various seasons. Custom had reconciled him to it; had almost brought him to regard it as his home; had almost made him cease to remember with regret the world from which he was an outcast. Occasionally, indeed, such thoughts as the poet has supposed must have occurred to him even now, after so long a period of acquaintance with solitude.

"I am monarch of all I survey,
  My right there is none to dispute;
From the center, all round to the sea,
  I am lord of the fowl and the brute.
O, solitude! where are the charms
  That sages have seen in thy face?
Better dwell in the midst of alarms,
  Than reign in this horrible place.

I am out of humanity's reach;
  I must finish my journey alone—
Never hear the sweet music of speech:
  I start at the sound of my own.
The beasts that roam over the plain,
  My form with indifference see;
They are so unacquainted with man,
  Their tameness is shocking to me.

Society, friendship, and love,
  Divinely bestowed upon man,
O, had I the wings of a dove,
  How soon would I taste you again!
My sorrows I then might assuage
  In the ways of religion and truth—
Might learn from the wisdom of age,
  And be cheered by the sallies of youth.

Religion! what treasure untold
  Resides in that heavenly word!
More precious than silver and gold,
  Or all that this earth can afford.
But the sound of the church-going bell
  These valleys and rocks never heard—

Never sighed at the sound of a knell,
  Or smiled when a Sabbath appeared.

Ye winds, that have made me your sport,
  Convey to this desolate shore
Some cordial, endearing report
  Of a land I shall visit no more.
My friends, do they now and then send
  A wish or a thought after me?
O, tell me I yet have a friend,
  Though a friend I am never to see!

How fleet is a glance of the mind,
  Compared with the speed of its flight,
The tempest itself lags behind,
  And the swift-winged arrows of light!
When I think of my own native land,
  In a moment I seem to be there;
But, alas! recollection at hand
  Soon hurries me back to despair.

But the sea-fowl has gone to her nest,
  The beast is laid down in his lair;
Even here is a season of rest,
  And I to my cabin repair.
There's mercy in every place;
  And mercy, encouraging thought!
Gives even affliction a grace,
  And reconciles man to his lot."

thoughts, however, were not habitual. the idea of dying alone, and leaving his stretched out, to be found some day, at istance of years, by those whom chance bring to his moldering hut in the woods, l to affect him sorrowfully. The religious ssions of his childhood had gained a supreme influence over him; and in communion with his Bible and with his own soul, the solitary man, clad in his goat-skins, became meek, thankful, and tender-hearted. How different from the rough young sailor who, not many years before, had been struggling in the grasps of his brother, his sister-in-law, and his old father, on the floor of the cottage in Largo! Whether the change of character was permanent, we shall now see, as we are about to relate the circumstances which led to his release from his solitude, and his final restoration to society.

One hope of relief for Selkirk, even if other chances had failed, consisted in the probability that intelligence of his situation would reach England through some of the crew of the Cinque Ports, and that some vessel might, in consequence, be induced to pay a passing visit to Juan Fernandez for the purpose of ascertaining his fate. If Selkirk, however, had relied strongly on this probability, he would have been disappointed. The Cinque Ports never reached England. Old, crank, and worm-eaten, she foundered off the coast of Barbacoa not long after setting sail from Juan Fernandez. Out of the whole crew, only Captain Stradling and six or seven of his men were saved; and these were long detained prisoners among the Spaniards at Lima. They were in captivity during the whole time of Selkirk's residence on his island; and long after he had returned to England, most of them were captives still. Stradling at length obtained his liberty, but his ultimate fate was never known.

Deliverance was to reach Selkirk from another quarter. Dampier, who, it will be remembered, had parted company with the Cinque Ports about five months before Selkirk had been abandoned by Stradling, had continued his voyage through the South Seas in search of Spanish vessels. Various success had attended him for several months; a considerable portion of his crew forsook him; and at length, crossing the Pacific to the East Indies, he and his companions fell into the hands of the Dutch, who seized his ship and all that he had. The expedition of the St. George and the Cinque Ports, planned by him, had therefore turned out a total failure. "Dampier returned naked to his owners, with a melancholy relation of his misfortunes, occasioned chiefly by his own strange temper, which was so self-sufficient and overbearing, that few or none of his officers could endure it. Even in this distress he was received as an eminent man, notwithstanding his failings; and was introduced to Queen Anne, having the honor to kiss her hand, and to give her Majesty some account of the dangers he had undergone. The merchants were so sensible of his want of conduct, that they resolved never to trust him any more with a command."*

The bad success of Dampier's expedition however, did not prevent the fitting out of another with similar designs against the Spaniards of the South Seas; and about the middle of the year 1708, two vessels, the *Duke* and the *Duchess*, the property of Bristol merchants, set sail for the Spanish main, having in all three hundred and thirty-three men on board. The Duke, a vessel of thirty guns, was commanded by Captain Woodes Rogers, a very able and prudent man; the Duchess, of twenty-six guns, by Captain Stephen Courtney. Poor Dampier, who could not be intrusted with the command, and whose poverty obliged him to accept some occupation of the same kind as that which he had all his life been accustomed to, was glad to sail in the Duke in the capacity of a pilot to the expedition. Great care had been taken in the manning of both vessels, and regulations had been drawn up before sailing, to prevent disputes.

Captain Rogers, whose proceedings during the voyage it is not necessary for us to detail,

---

* Kerr's Voyage—Funnel's Narrative.

pursued the same track as the former expedition; and after cruising along the Brazilian coast, rounded Cape Horn in the month of December, 1708, bearing for Juan Fernandez, to take in water. The crews came in sight of the island on the 31st of January, 1709, little anticipating the surprise which awaited them. What occurred as they approached is thus related by Captain Rogers himself in the account which he published of the voyage: "About two o'clock, P. M., on the 31st of January, we hoisted our pinnace out; Captain Dover—second captain of the Duke—with the boat's crew, went in her to go ashore, though we could not be less than four leagues off. As soon as the pinnace was gone, I went on board the Duchess, the crew of which were astonished at our boat attempting to go on shore at so great a distance from land: it was against my inclination, but, to oblige Captain Dover, I consented to let her go. As soon as it was dark, we saw a light ashore; our boat was then about a league from the island. She stopped, and bore away again for the ships as soon as she saw the light. We put out lights for the boat, though some were of the opinion that the light we saw was not on the island, but the boat's light; but as night came on, it appeared too large for that. We fired one quarterdeck gun and several muskets, showing lights in our mizzen and fore-shrouds, that our boat might find us, while we plied in the lee of the island. About two in the morning our boat came on board the Duchess: we were glad it got well off, because it began to blow. We were all convinced that the light was on the shore, and designed to make our ships ready to engage, as we believed it to come from French ships at anchor, and that we must either fight them or want water.

"The next day we stood along the south end of the island, in order to lay in with the first southerly wind, which Captain Dampier told us generally blows there all day along. In the morning, being past the island, we tacked, to lay it in close aboard the land; and about ten o'clock, ran close aboard the land that begins to make the north-east side. The flaws came heavy off the shore, and we were forced to reef our topsails when we opened the middle bay, where we expected to find the enemy, but saw all clear, and no ships in that or the other bay. We guessed there had been ships there, but that they had gone away on sight of us. We sent our yawl ashore about noon with Captain Dover, Mr. Fry, and six men all armed; meanwhile we and the Duchess kept turning to get in. Our boat did not return, so we sent out our pinnace with the men armed, to see what was the occasion of the yawl's stay; for we were afraid that the Spaniards had a garrison there, and might have seized it. We put out a signal for our boat, and the Duchess showed a French ensign. Immediately our pinnace returned from the shore, and brought abundance of crawfish, with a man clothed in goat-skins, who looked wilder than the first owners of them."

Selkirk, the man whose appearance caused such surprise, had seen the sails of the vessels at a distance, but had avoided making any signals which could indicate his presence till he ascertained them to be English. As soon as he had assured himself on this point, his joy was extreme. When night came on, he kindled a large fire on the beach, to inform the strangers that a human being was there. It was this signal which had alarmed the crews of the vessels, and deterred the pinnace from landing. During the night, hope having banished all desire of sleep, he employed himself in killing goats, and preparing a feast of fresh meat for those whom he expected to be his deliverers. In the morning he found that the vessels had removed to a greater distance, but erelong he saw the boat leave the side of one of them and approach the shore. Selkirk ran joyfully to meet his countrymen, waving a linen rag to attract their attention; and having pointed out to them a proper landing-place, soon had the satisfaction of clasping them in his arms. Joy at first deprived him of that imperfect power of utterance which solitude had left him, but in a little he was able to offer and receive explanations. Dover, the second captain, Fry, the lieutenant, and the rest of the boat party, after partaking of Selkirk's hospitality, invited him on board; but so little eager was he to leave his solitude, that he was not prevailed upon to do so till assured that Dampier had no situation of command in the expedition—his former experience of Dampier's mode of conducting a ship having given him no great confidence in him. When he was told that Dampier was only a pilot on board he made no further objection. He was then, as we have seen, brought on board the Duke, along with his principal effects; and on the same day by the recommendation of Dampier, he was engaged as a mate. "At his first coming on board us," says Captain Rogers, "he had so much forgot his language, for want of use, that we could scarcely understand him, for he seemed to speak his words by halves. He would touch no liquor, having drank nothing but water on the island; and it was some time before he could relish our victuals."

For a fortnight the two vessels remained at Juan Fernandez refitting, recruiting their sick, and taking in water and provisions. In this they were greatly assisted by Selkirk, or the "governor," as they used to call him; who, besides giving them all the information necessary respecting the island, made it a daily practice to catch several goats for the use of the sick. "He took them," says Rogers, "by speed of foot; for his way of living, and continual exercise of walking and running, cleared him of all gross humors, so that he ran with wonderful swiftness through the woods, and up the rocks and hills. We had a bull-dog, which we sent with several of our nimblest runners to help him in catching goats; but he distanced and tired both the dog and the men, caught the goats, and brought them to us on his back. Being forced to shift without shoes, his feet had become so hard, that he ran every-where without annoyance; and it was some time before he could wear shoes after we found him; for, not being used to any for so long, his feet swelled when he came first to use them again." Besides giving these particulars, Captain Rogers details, at some length, Selkirk's mode of life during the four years and four months he had spent on the island, concluding: "We may perceive, by this story, the truth of the maxim, that necessity is the mother of invention, since this man found means to supply his wants in a very natural manner, so as to maintain his life, though not so conveniently, yet as effectually as we are able to do with the help of our arts and society. It may likewise instruct us how much a plain and temperate way of living conduces to the health of the body and the vigor of the mind, both of which we are apt to destroy by excess and plenty, especially of strong liquor, and the variety as well as the nature of our meat and drink; for this man, when he came back to our ordinary method of diet and life, though he was sober enough, lost much of his strength and agility. But these reflections are more proper for a philosopher and divine than a mariner."

After a successful buccaneering expedition, with Rogers, Selkirk reached England in October, 1711. His singular history was soon made known to the public; and immediately he became an object of curiosity not only to the people at large, but to those elevated by rank and learning.

Defoe's romance of Robinson Crusoe was not published till the year 1719, when the original facts on which it was founded must have been nearly forgotten.

It was a fine Sunday morning in the spring of 1712; the kirk bells of Largo had for some time ceased ringing, and the parishioners were assembled in church, when a handsomely-dressed stranger knocked at the door of old John Selkirk's dwelling. No one was within, and the stranger bent his steps toward the parish church. He entered, and sat down in a pew near the door. His late entrance, the fact of his being a stranger, and his fine gold-laced clothes, attracted attention to him, and divided the interest of the congregation with the clergyman's sermon. The service proceeded: not far from the place where the stranger had stationed himself was the pew where old John Selkirk, his wife, and others of the family were sitting, and toward this pew the stranger continued to direct his eyes. The occupants of the pew returned the glance as discreetly as they could; old Mrs. Selkirk especially several times eyed the stranger with curiosity over her Bible. At length the glances became a fixed gaze; the old woman's face grew pale; and crying, "It's Sandie!—it's Sandie!" she tottered up to the stranger, and flung herself into his arms. The clergyman stopped, the congregation rose in a bustle of excitement, and quiet was not restored till the whole Selkirk family left the church in a body, to give full scope at home to their mutual congratulations and inquiries.

Alexander Selkirk subsequently entered the naval service, and became a lieutenant on board the Weymouth; on board of which vessel he died in 1723.

The island of Juan Fernandez has passed through the hands of a succession of owners since he quitted it. For upward of thirty years after his departure, it remained in the condition in which he had left it—an uninhabited island, where ships, sailing along the western coast of South America, occasionally put in for water and fresh victuals. Once or twice, indeed, the chances of shipwreck gave it one or two inhabitants, who did not remain long. In 1750 the Spaniards again formed a settlement on it, and built a fort. Both were destroyed by an earthquake in the following year; but another town was built at a greater distance from the shore. It continued to be inhabited for about twenty years, but was then abandoned, as the former Spanish settlement in the island had been. Early in the present century, the Chilian government began to use Juan Fernandez as a penal settlement, transporting their state criminals to it; but in consequence of the expense, it was soon given up; and when Lord Cochrane visited the island in 1823, there were but four men stationed on it, apparently in charge of some cattle. The following description is given of the island by a lady who accompanied Lord Cochrane and a party on shore: "The island is the most picturesque I ever saw, being composed of high perpendicular rocks, wooded nearly to the top, with beautiful valleys, exceedingly fertile, and watered by copious streams, which occasionally form small marshes. The little valley where the town is, or rather was, is exceedingly beautiful. It is full of fruit-trees and flowers, and sweet herbs, now grown wild; near the shore, it is covered with radish and sea-side oats. A small fort was situated on the sea-shore, of which there is nothing now visible but the ditches and part of one wall. Another, of considerable size for the place, is on a high and commanding spot. It contained barracks for soldiers, which, as well as the greater part of the fort, are ruined; but the flag-staff, front wall, and a turret, are standing; and at the foot of the flag-staff lies a very handsome brass gun, cast in Spain, A. D. 1614. A few houses and cottages are still in a tolerable condition, though most of the doors, windows, and roofs have been taken away, or used as fuel by whalers and other ships touching here. In the valleys we found numbers of European shrubs and herbs—'where once the garden smiled.' And in the half-ruined hedges, which denote the boundaries of former fields, we found apple, pear, and quince trees, with cherries almost ripe. The ascent is steep and rapid from the beach, even in the valleys, and the long grass was dry and slippery, so that it rendered the walk rather fatiguing; and we were glad to sit down under a large quince-tree on a carpet of balm, bordered with roses, now neglected, and feast our eyes with the lovely view before us. Lord Anson has not exaggerated the beauty of the place, or the delights of the climate. We were rather early for its fruits, but even at this time we have gathered delicious figs, cherries, and pears, that a few days more of sun would have perfected. The landing-place is also the watering-place. There a little jetty is thrown out, formed of the beach pebbles, making a little harbor for boats, which lie there close to the fresh water, which comes conducted by a pipe, so that, with a hose, the casks may be filled, without landing, with the most delicious water. Along the beach some old guns are sunk, to serve as moorings for vessels, which are all the safer the nearer in-shore they lie, as violent gusts of wind often blow from the mountain for a few minutes. The hight of the island is about three thousand feet."

With all its beauties and resources, the island seemed destined never to retain those who settled on it—whether from its isolated position at so great a distance from the continent, or from some other cause, is uncertain. Not long after

Lord Cochrane's visit, however, it received an accession of inhabitants, some of them English, who settled in it under the protection of the Chilian government. According to the latest accounts, it had undergone another change of proprietorship, having been taken in lease from Chili by an enterprising American, who had colonized it with a number of families from Tahiti, and intended to cultivate it, rear cattle on it for exportation, and so improve the bay and harbor, as to render it a habitual resort for whalers and trading vessels navigating the Pacific.

X.

Escape of Count Lavalette.

COUNT LAVALETTE, in early life, was an attached friend of the Bourbon dynasty, but the exciting events of the Revolution having opened to him the prospect of an ambitious career, he became one of the most intrepid soldiers and supporters of the French Republic. During the latter years of the reign of Napoleon, he held the chief place in the post establishment, from which he retired on the introduction of the Bourbons. He was now accused of having been an accomplice in the conspiracy which brought on the events which terminated in the battle of Waterloo, and, after two days' discussion, was condemned to death. Immured in prison, he endeavored to avert his fate by a writ of error, but this, along with a petition for pardon presented by Madame Lavalette, was refused. "The day of his execution approached," says the writer of his memoirs; "the unfortunate man had no hope left; the turnkeys themselves trembled. On the eve of that last day, the Countess Lavalette entered his prison. She had put on a pelisse of merino, richly lined with fur, which she was accustomed to wear when she left a ball-room; in her reticule she had a black silk gown. Coming up to her husband, she assured him, with a firm voice, that all was lost, and he had nothing more to hope than in a well-combined escape. She showed him the woman's attire, and proposed to him to disguise himself. Every precaution had been taken to secure his escape. A sedan chair would receive him on his coming out of prison; a cabriolet waited for him on the Quay des Orferres—a devoted friend, a safe retreat, would answer any further objections. M. Lavalette listened to her without approving of so hazardous a plan—he was resigned to his fate, and refused to fly from it. 'I know how to act my part in a tragedy,' he said, 'but spare me the burlesque farce. I shall be apprehended in this ridiculous disguise, and they will perhaps expose me to the mockery of the mob! On the other hand, if I escape, you will remain a prey to the insolence of prison valets, and to the persecution of my enemies.' 'If you die, I die; save your life to save mine!' The prisoner yielded to her urgent entreaties. 'Now, put on the disguise,' she added; 'it is time to go; no farewell—no tears—your hours are counted!' And when the toilet was finished, 'Adieu,' she said. 'Do not forget to stoop when you pass under the wickets, for fear the feathers in your bonnet should stick fast.'

"The jailer's step was now heard. Emilie sprung behind the screen—the door opened; I passed out first, next my daughter, then the old nurse. On coming to the door leading from the passage to the outer room, I had at the same time to lift my foot and stoop my head to prevent the catching of my feathers—no easy matter; but I succeeded, and had now to face in this large room a file of five seated jailers ranged along the wall. I held my handkerchief to my eyes, of course, and expected my daughter to come, as directed, on my left; but in her flurry the poor child took the right, thus leaving the jailer at liberty to hand me out as usual. He laid his hand on my arm, evidently much moved—for he concluded we had taken an eternal leave of each other—and said, 'You leave early to-night, madam?' It has been said that my child and I gave way to screams and sobs. So far from that, we durst not so much as indulge in a sigh. At length I got to the further end, where, night and day, sat a jailer in a huge arm-chair, in a space sufficiently contracted to allow him to place his two hands on the keys of two doors; one an iron grating, the other—the outer one—called the first wicket. This man looked at me, but did not open. I had to put my hand through the bars to hurry him. At length he turned his two keys, and we were out. And now, recollecting herself, my daughter took my right arm. We had twelve steps of a stair to go up to get at the court where the chair waited; and at the foot of them was the guard-house, where twenty soldiers, with an officer at their head, stood within three steps of me, to see Madame Lavalette pass! My foot was at length on the last step, and I got into the sedan, which was close by. But not a chairman was there—not a servant! only my daughter, and the old woman standing beside it, and a sentry not six feet off, immovable on his post, staring at me. My first surprise was giving way to violent agitation; I felt my eyes fixed like a basalisk's on that sentry's musket, which, at the smallest noise or difficulty, I should certainly have sprung on, and used it against any one who offered to take me. This dreadful suspense may have lasted some two minutes, which to me appeared the length of a night. At length I heard the voice of Bonneville, my valet, whispering to me, 'One of the bearers has failed me, but I have found another!'

"I then felt myself caught up, the chair

crossed the court, and we went down a street or two. When it was set down, the door opened, and my friend Baudus offering me his arm, said aloud: 'Madam, you know you have a visit to make to the president.' I got out, and he pointed to a cabriolet which stood a short way off down a little dark street. I sprang into it, and the driver said to me, 'Hand me my whip.' I sought it in vain; it had fallen. 'Never mind,' said my companion, giving the reins a shake, which set off the horses at a round trot. As I passed, I caught sight of my daughter, Josephine, standing on the quay, with her hands joined, praying for me with all her soul before getting into the chair; which, as I had predicted, was quickly overtaken, and finding her only in it, was allowed to proceed.

"Beginning to breathe at length, when we had driven a long way, I had time to look at my coachman, and what was my astonishment to recognize the Count de Chassenon, whom I little thought of seeing in that capacity. 'Is that you?' asked I, in unfeigned surprise. 'Yes; and you have at your back four well-loaded pistols, which I hope you will use in case of need.' 'Not I, indeed; I have no mind to involve you in ruin!' 'Well, then, I suppose I must show you the example, and woe to whoever attempts to stop us!' We drove on to the boulevard neuf, where we stopped, and I displayed my handkerchief, as agreed, on the apron of the cab; having, by the way, got rid of all my female paraphernalia, and slipped on a groom's frock, with a round laced, livery hat. Monsieur Baudus soon joined us: I took leave of the good Count, and modestly followed in the wake of my new master. It was now past eight; the rain fell in torrents; the night was dark; and nothing could be more lonely than this part of the town. It was with the greatest difficulty I could keep pace with Monsieur Baudus before I lost one of my shoes, which did not mend matters. We met several gendarmes at full gallop, little aware that he whom they were probably in pursuit of was so near them! At length, after an hour's march, worn out with fatigue, and with one foot bare, we came to a large mansion. 'I am going in here,' said Monsieur Baudus; 'and while I engage the porter in conversation, slip into the court-yard; you will find a staircase on the left; go up it to the highest story. At the end of a dark passage to the right is a pile of fire-wood; stand behind it, and wait.' I grew dizzy, and almost sunk on seeing Monsieur Baudus knock at the very door of the minister for foreign affairs, the Duke de Richelieu! But while the porter let him in, I passed on quickly. 'Where is that man going?' cried the porter. 'O, 'tis only my servant.' I found the staircase and every thing else as directed, and was no sooner on the appointed spot, than I heard the rustling of a gown; my arm was gently taken; I was pushed into a room, and the door closed upon me."

Lavalette was now concealed in what was in all probability the least suspected place in Paris—the house of the minister of foreign affairs. For an asylum under this roof he was indebted to the gratitude of Madame de Brisson, the wife of the cashier. M. de Brisson, it appears, had been proscribed at the first revolution for voting against the king's death, and was two years in hiding, along with his wife, among the Vosges, a cluster of mountains on the east of France. Here they received so much kindness from the inhabitants, that Madame de Brisson made a vow to save, if ever in her power, a person similarly circumstanced. She now had it in her power to afford a shelter to Lavalette, and nobly did she redeem her vow. Every comfort, down to the minutest luxuries of the toilet—so acceptable to a prisoner long deprived of them—had been provided by this lady's thoughtful kindness; even the felt slippers in which alone he was to dare to move about, and the profusion of books and wax lights, which were to compensate to a studious man for the necessity of keeping his windows carefully closed all day. When the shades of night permitted him to open them, it was often to hear street-criers bawling forth proclamations, of which he could sometimes catch little more than his own name, threatening with the utmost penalties of the law all landlords or lodgers who might be giving him a harbor; and truly, considering not only the dangers to which their generous conduct in his behalf was exposing his benefactors, but the fearful risk to all involved, in a nephew—who slept next room to him—and a couple of faithful servants being necessarily in the secret, it may be imagined that Lavalette's was not a bed of roses. His meals had to be literally purloined from their own table by Madame de Brisson, who, on some refreshment not habitually consumed by the family being requested by her prisoner, was obliged to remind him of the recapture and death on the scaffold of Monsieur de Montmorine, from the trifling circumstance of some chicken bones being found near the door of his landlady—a woman too poor to indulge in such dainties. She was, however, able to afford him the more substantial alleviation of hearing that, spite of proclamations, at which every one laughed, his escape was the subject of rejoicing all over Paris; that Madame Lavalette was extolled to the skies, and every possible allusion to her conduct at the theater received with rapturous applause.

It is now time to return to that interesting woman, whose agitating suspense after her husband's departure may be easily conceived. No sooner was Lavalette beyond the gates, than the jailer peeped as usual into the room, and hearing some one behind the screen, went out. He returned, however, in five minutes, and still seeing no one, bethought him of pushing aside a leaf of the screen, and at sight of Madame Lavalette, gave a loud cry, and ran toward the door. She flew to prevent him, and in her despair, kept such fast hold of his coat that he left part of it in her hands. "You have ruined me, madam!" he exclaimed in a rage, and extricating himself by a desperate effort, and calling out as he went along, "The prisoner has escaped!" he ran, tearing his hair like a madman, to the prefect of police.

The intelligence of Lavalette's escape, hastily communicated to the prefect, spread universal surprise. Indignant at the trick which had been played, the prefect, who was officially responsible for the safety of the prisoner, instantly ordered the widest and most minute search to be made to recover the lost captive. Gendarmes galloped about in all directions, and every suspicious-looking individual was seized. Cafes, hotels, and all places of public resort, were visited. Every supposed lurking-place was searched. The pursuit continued all night, and domiciliary visits of the strictest kind were made, not only at the house of every acquaintance of the Count, but of all who had ever held official connection with him. The effort was vain. Clever as the police of Paris unquestionably are, they were completely baffled on this memorable occasion. To intercept a possible flight to the country, the barriers were closed, and no one was permitted to pass without undergoing a personal scrutiny. All, however, would not do. Lavalette, safe in the house of the minister of foreign affairs, who little knew what guest he entertained, continued undiscovered; and all Paris chuckled to see the police fairly at fault.

Defeated in their attempts to recover the fugitive, the police and other authorities meanly revenged themselves on Madame Lavalette, who for some time remained in an agony of suspense with respect to the fate of her husband. From the brutal insults of the enraged jailers, she was rescued by the arrival of the attorney-general, but only to be exposed to a set of formal interrogatories and reproaches from that functionary. In the eye of the law, she had been guilty at most of a misdemeanor, for which a severe punishment could not properly be inflicted. By the orders of the attorney-general, however, she was treated with unbecoming disrespect and severity; and being at the time in a poor state of health, this treatment was not only a sore aggravation of her immediate distresses, bodily and mental, but laid the foundation of complaints which afterward unsettled her reason.

Instead of throwing open to this magnanimous woman the doors of the prison she had hallowed, her confinement was, for six weeks, as close and rigorous as that of the worst criminals. She was subjected to the nuisance of being within hearing of the reprobate of her own sex, while no female attendant was allowed her save a jailer; not a line was she permitted either to dispatch or receive, and therefore a continual prey to anxieties on her husband's account, which, at every change of sentries, made her start up, concluding they were bringing him back, and for twenty-five nights wholly deprived her of sleep. Fortunately for her husband, he was kept in ignorance of these distressing details, and taught to believe that, though subject to restraint, she was enjoying every comfort under the roof of the wife of the prefect of police.

To him we must now return. In consequence

of the unabated vigilance of the authorities, the friends of Lavalette were anxious to get him conveyed, if possible, beyond the barriers, and thence out of France. Several plans of escape from the country were suggested, without success. One, to escape in the suit of a Russian General, failed, from the dread inspired, by hearing the name of Lavalette, of himself being sent to Siberia. Another, more promising, to join a Bavarian battalion quitting Paris, whose commandant, a friend of Prince Eugene, would have earned praise instead of blame by conniving at it, was frustrated by the surveillance and keen scrutiny naturally enough exercised by the police over both men and officers of this suspected corps. At length, on the eighteenth day of his seclusion, Monsieur Baudus, in a transport of joy, announced to Lavalette his probable escape through the co-operation of Englishmen.

The political sentiments of some then in Paris had been too openly declared, against the execution of Marshal Ney, especially, to make sounding them a matter of difficulty; and the office being undertaken by some French ladies of rank and the most amiable character, had all the success anticipated with Mr. Michael Bruce, in the first instance, and through him, with yet more efficient coadjutors, General Sir

Robert Wilson, and Captain Hutchinson, of the Guards. It was humanely resolved by these gentlemen that Lavalette should, if possible, escape from France by wearing the uniform of a British officer. This plan, which was accordingly put in execution, is described as follows by Sir Robert in a letter to Earl Grey, which was intercepted on its way to England, and led to the subsequent trial and imprisonment of the parties engaged.

"It was agreed," says Sir Robert, "that the fugitive, wearing, as well as myself, the British uniform, should accompany me beyond the barriers in an English cab; that I should have a fresh horse stationed at La Chapelle, and from thence get on to Compiegne, where I was to be joined by my own carriage, in which Lavalette and I would proceed by Mons to Cambray. At my request, and on my responsibility, I easily procured passports from Lord Stewart for General Wallis and Colonel Losack; names which we made choice of, because their initials corresponded with the real ones. On their being taken to be signed at the foreign office, one of the secretaries took it in his head to ask who Colonel Losack was? when Hutchinson coolly answered, 'O, the son of the admiral.' Bruce now found out that the brigade of his cousin, General Brisbane, was at Compiegne, and that his aiddecamp was to leave Paris next day with his horses and baggage. With this young man, reluctantly as we involved him in the affair, it was agreed that he should provide for us a place where an individual, desirous of avoiding publicity, might remain *perdu* a few hours at Compiegne—a precaution which proved of the greatest use.

"Bruce next procured Lavalette's measure, and a uniform was ordered as if for a quartermaster of the Guards; but the regimental tailor happening to observe that it was for a very stout gentleman, and, moreover, that it had not been taken by a professional *snip*, the parties got alarmed, and fell on the plan of borrowing for the expedition the coat of a strapping brother guardsman—a very young man, whom they persuaded it was wanted to assist in an elopement."

It is not the least curious of the many odd features of this remarkable escape, that on Lavalette proceeding under cloud of night, the previous evening, to Captain Hutchinson's lodgings in the Rue de Hilder, he only exchanged one lion's den for another, having for a neighbor, under the same roof, the very judge who had presided at his trial! He was there met by Mr. Bruce—whom he had once or twice seen at the queen of Holland's—and Sir Robert

Wilson, who, after partaking of a bowl of punch—the ostensible pretext for the meeting—left him to take on the sofa such slumbers as, on the eve of such an expedition, he could hope to enjoy. These were rudely broken in upon about one in the morning by a prodigious noise and loud colloquy at the outer door, the object of which was plainly to effect a forcible entry. Lavalette, never doubting he was discovered, and firmly grasping his pistols, woke his companion, who, he tells us, went out very quietly, and after five minutes—which to Lavalette seemed ages—came back and said, "It is only a dispute between the porteress and a French officer, who lodges on the third floor, about letting him in at so late an hour; so we may go to sleep again."

There was no more sleep, however, for his guest, who got up at six and dressed himself, and at half-past seven was called for by Sir Robert in a general's full uniform, in Bruce's cabriolet, while Captain Hutchinson rode along side, both to give it the air of a pleasure party, and that Lavalette, if hard pressed, might exchange the carriage for a swifter conveyance. "The weather," says our hero in his memoirs, "was splendid, all the shops open, every body in the streets; and, by a singular coincidence, as we passed the Greve—the place of execution in Paris—they were setting up the gallows customarily used for the execution in effigy of outlawed criminals."

Numerous were the occasions on which the party were threatened with discovery; indeed, that one with such marked features as Lavalette—personally known, from his office, to half the postmasters in France, and, moreover, minutely described in placards in almost every body's hands—should have escaped detection, seems little short of a miracle. Before they were out of Paris, they met an English officer, all surprise at seeing a British general with whose person he was unacquainted. The gendarmes at the gate took a hearty stare at him; but the ceremony of presenting arms screened at once his profile and his life. When they met people or carriages, Sir Robert took care to talk very loud in English, and Colonel Losack to sit well back in the carriage, the white feather in his regimental hat serving to divert attention from the wearer. Another object of the same color had, however, nearly served to betray him; namely, a few white hairs straggling from beneath his wig, which Sir Robert observed ere entering Compiegne, and being fortunately provided with scissors, was enabled to act the barber's part.

Their chief peril was at the previous village

of La Chapelle, where their relay horse had been stationed at a bustling inn, about the door of which four gendarmes were lounging, and were only got rid of by the presence of mind of Captain Hutchinson, who, by pretending to be on the look-out for cantonments for a corps of English troops, diverted their attention, and kept them drinking till the others had got clear off. Their stay of some hours at Compiegne, to await the arrival from Paris of Sir Robert's carriage, passed off equally well, and under cloud of night it arrived safe. With post-horses the rest of the journey could now be more expeditiously, and, thanks to the words English carriage and English general, passed on from postillion to postillion, was at length safely performed.

At Cambray three hours were lost at the gates by the supineness of the English guard, who, having no orders to call up the porter, refused to do so, and might have ruined all. At Valenciennes, the party were three times examined, nay, their passports carried to the commandant. A long time elapsed, and Lavalette felt as if on the brink of shipwreck when almost in port. Luckily, it was very cold weather—early in January—and day had scarcely dawned; and the officers, instead of coming to inspect the travelers, signed their passports in bed. "On the *glacis* of the same town," says Lavalette, "an officious douanier chose to examine if all was right. His curiosity, however, was satisfied, and we were erelong bowling joyously along the firm road to Mons. Now I would peep out of the little back window, to see if we were pursued; and then I would fix my longing eyes on a large building pointed out to me as the first Belgian custom-house, which, drive as we would, never seemed to me to get any nearer. At length we gained it: I was out of the French territory, and saved! Seizing hold of the General's hand, I poured forth, deeply moved, the whole extent of my gratitude, while he only answered me by a quiet smile." "Having made at Mons every arrangement for facilitating Monsieur Lavalette's ulterior proceedings, I returned," says his generous deliverer, "to Paris, from whence I had been absent only about sixty hours."

Lavalette was now safely sheltered in a foreign country. From the Netherlands he proceeded to Germany, and there found a refuge in the dominions of the king of Bavaria, though scarcely with the willing consent of that monarch. In a remote country retreat Lavalette lived for years, almost forgotten by the world. The only matter for serious regret was the absence of his affectionate wife, the state of whose mind rendered seclusion from the world indispensably necessary. The manner in which the Count spent the greater part of his time may be gathered from a touching letter which he wrote to the Duchess of Ragusa, the wife of General Marmont.

"You ask me where I live, and how. I dwell on the banks of a lake not unworthy of Switzerland, for it is five leagues long by one broad. I have a room and a closet at the lodge of the keeper of a forsaken chateau. My view consists of a fine sheet of water, pretty low hills, and high mountains beyond, covered with snow. For walks, I have wild woodlands, abounding with game, which remain unmolested for me. My hosts are honest peasants, whose Spartan broth and black bread I partake of with tolerable relish. I dare not have in a servant a possible spy, so my sole companion is a poor artist unknown to fame, who smokes all day long, and does not know one word of my language; but I am learning his, and we get on very well. He wakes me every morning at six, and we labor together till nine. After the most frugal of breakfasts, we set to work again till noon, and after dinner from two till five. I then read a couple of hours; and at seven we go to walk till supper. I have taught him chess, and we play till ten, when I go to my room, but seldom to bed till one o'clock. These hours of night are for the heart's anguish, and a host of bitter reminiscences. I pray and weep over all those I love, and in thinking of my poor humbled, subjugated country.

"But I do not at all times give way to such sad thoughts. I should be unworthy of my glorious misfortune did I not draw from it the sweetest consolations. I often feel less thankful at having escaped the scaffold, than for being saved from it by such generous hearts. Wife, child, friends, domestics, nay, those noble strangers, all combined to suffer, to sacrifice themselves; but, thank Heaven, ultimately to triumph in my cause. I of all mankind have no right to complain of my fellows. Never was unfortunate being honored by so much devotedness and courage!

"I am so happy that you are within reach of my poor wife. You love and appreciate her. She is not understood in a world of base wretches, who little thought that that weak, dejected, unhappy woman would prove too strong and bold for them all! O, take care of her, I beseech you; watch over her, and shield her from every sorrow! And my poor little Josephine; good God! what will become of her? How fondly had I looked forward to perfecting her education! When I think of all this, I could beat my head against the very walls, and dread what I may be tempted to do! Above all, my wife!—see her often, console, and protect her, if necessary."

It is consolatory to know that Lavalette outlived the vengeance of his enemies. After an exile of six years, the crime of which he stood guilty was remitted, and he was allowed to return to France a free man. He now had the additional happiness of being permitted to see his wife, and to repay, by the most devoted attentions, her exertions in his behalf. The acute mental malady brought on by anxiety and terror, under which she had for some years labored, seems to have gradually yielded to a deep melancholy and frequent abstraction; "but she remained," says Lavalette, "as she had ever been, good, gentle, and amiable, and able to find enjoyment in the country;" where, for her sake, he chiefly resided, pretty much forgotten by the world, till his death, in 1830. Whether Madame Lavalette ultimately recovered from her alienated mental condition, we have not heard: it is, however, gratifying to learn that her daughter Josephine, who was married to a man of worth and talent, lived to contribute to her comfort and happiness, in that scene of rural quiet to which she had been removed by an affectionate and grateful husband.